The Gospel Offer *is* Free

A reply to George M.Ella's
The Free Offer and The Call of the Gospel

David H.J.Gay

BRACHUS

First published by BRACHUS 2004
Second edition 2012

davidhjgay@googlemail.com

Scripture quotations, unless otherwise stated,
are from the New King James Version

OTHER BOOKS BY THE SAME AUTHOR
UNDER DAVID GAY
Voyage to Freedom
Dutch: Reis naar de vrijheid
Christians Grow Old
Italian: I credenti invecchiano
Battle for the Church (First Edition)

UNDER DAVID H.J.GAY
Particular Redemption and the Free Offer
Infant Baptism Tested
Septimus Sears: A Victorian Injustice and Its Aftermath
Baptist Sacramentalism: A Warning to Baptists
Battle for the Church (Second Edition)
The Priesthood of All Believers
John Colet: A Preacher to be Reckoned With
The Pastor: Does He Exist?
Christ is All: No Sanctification by the Law

Comments and Reviews

Gordon Murray: *The argument is based solidly on Scripture and is supported by innumerable quotations from a wide group of preachers and writers. As a demolition job you are hardly likely to find anything more thorough. Yet the book is far more than that. It is even more than an excellent biblical justification for preaching the gospel call freely to all. There is a passion about it that should move all of us who are called to minister the word to others. We know that the work that makes an unbeliever a Christian can only be done through the Holy Spirit, but are our hearts really moved with compassion and the desire that others should come to the Lord? It would be worth reading this book simply to have that impressed on our minds and hearts, but there is far more as well.*

Paul Bevan: *It is certainly a much needed message. First, among those who have developed a 'theology' that is unbiblically restrictive. And, secondly, it is most necessary in the present day Reformed preaching which often tends to 'labour' the gospel and not stress the urgency and the 'now' to repent, believe and trust in Christ. Thank you again for your very relevant book. I trust it will be greatly used by God to encourage preachers in their gospel work.*

Robert Oliver: *It did me good to read it. The subject is so important and you have written so well. The cause of Christ in England has been grievously damaged by the denial of the free offer of the gospel... I pray that God will... make your book useful and home and abroad.*

Aubrey Ridge: *Using economy of expression and abundant sweet reasoning from Scripture, this experienced author pleads for an acceptance of God's word against man's interpretation, to place before us the irrefutable truth: The Gospel Offer* **is** *Free... The book is a treasure that cannot be bettered for value. Do buy it.*

Percival Tanierla: *I am truly encouraged by your clear and scriptural stand. I like your style of writing and the simple English constructions of your sentences. I like your discussions about duty faith, etc. I gave a copy to some friends who are sympathetic to the gospel offer. This is to make them more firm and to be encouraged to continue in defending the real faith once delivered to the saints.*

Joe Sheetz: *Your book is being well received... Robert Briggs is very excited about it – says it is the best he has ever read regarding the gospel offer.*

Hugh Collier: *The book... finding it very helpful.*

B.A.Ramsbottom: *This is a book with which we do not agree!... [But] we appreciate the courteous way in which Mr Gay has written, and also that he never tries to set up some monster of his own devising – an exaggerated position which no one has ever held or even thought – and then hurl stones at it. Sadly, many have spoiled their arguments by doing this.*

William Macleod: *Your excellent book. I very much enjoyed reading it and found it gave an excellent readable presentation of the subject.*

Ted Chubb: *Delighted... such a useful volume on such an important and apposite matter... I feel this will be a valuable contribution to the subject – especially in Reformed circles where, sadly, men still look over their shoulders – metaphorically speaking – when preaching the gospel, in case they are accused of too much freedom in the offer of Christ. That is obviously why you wrote this book (among other higher reasons), I am sure, so thank you for a timely publication.*

Iain Murray: *Just a line to thank you heartily for your new book* The Gospel Offer **is** Free. *It is splendid – I have read it all with much appreciation and thankfulness. May it have a wide circulation.*

Bob Gilbert: *I have found it both helpful and challenging 'Who is sufficient?'... I think your book would be valuable as part of [The Preachers' Seminary] as part of their book reading list.*

Trevor Knight: *I have delayed sending my 'thank you'... until I had actually read your book. This I have now done – so herewith my hearty thanks... Those of us who believe 'the gospel offer is free' and endeavour to preach it as such (though I feel personally I fall far short of the 'compassion' element you refer to), are too frequently 'written off' as being of simplistic (if not 'unscriptural') views... It has been refreshing to be reminded of Spurgeon's attitude in particular. Thank you for all your valiant work. May the Lord make your little volume a blessing to others, encouraging many more to 'preach for a verdict'.*

First Edition Note to the Reader

Although my book is a reply to George M.Ella's *The Free Offer and The Call of the Gospel*, it stands on its own; you do not need Ella's book in order to understand what I say about the free offer of the gospel. Furthermore, my book is not merely negative, but sets out what I see as the biblical basis of this very important issue.

Second Edition Note to the Reader

I am delighted that this volume has proved a blessing, and I wish to make it available to a wider public through the internet. In preparing this second edition for printing on-line, I have taken the opportunity to correct some typos, and to make a few additional remarks. Further, since the first edition in 2004, I have published *Particular Redemption and The Free Offer*. References to *The Gospel Offer **is** Free* which occur in the *Particular* are, of course, to pages in the first edition of the *Offer*, but it should not be difficult to find them in this second edition.

Contents

Introduction

George M.Ella, to put it mildly, does not agree with what is known as the 'free offer', and he makes no bones about it. Indeed, he has written a book on the subject: *The Free Offer and The Call of the Gospel*, in which, we are told, he has set out 'sound reasons for rejecting the "free offer" method of evangelising', and given 'solid scriptural principles by which our commission to preach the gospel of sovereign grace to every creature can properly be met'.[1]

Very well.

Let me declare an interest. I am an advocate of the 'free offer' and I, too, have written about it. For this reason, Ella has had me, as one among many, in his sights. But I welcome his attention; I am delighted to think my words have provoked thought. And if my arguments are wrong, I need to be told, and put back on the straight and narrow. What we all want, surely, is to be biblical, and in furthering this aim, reasoned, loving argument with those who do not see eye-to-eye with us can do no harm at all. No harm? Quite the opposite; informed and constructive criticism can do nothing but good. Let's have a bit more 'iron sharpening iron'! We can't have too much of 'sound reasons' and 'solid scriptural principles'.

Ella, I freely acknowledge, wrote his book out of deep concern for the glory of God, for the defence of the preaching of the gospel, and for the advance of the salvation of sinners. I am convinced he desired to further these aims by dealing with what he sees as an erroneous practice based upon a defective theology. I admire his intention. It is mine in publishing this reply.

Having said that about Ella's book, in my opinion it falls far short of its claims, does not represent a serious attempt at coming to grips with a vital question, and fails to set out a reasoned account of his own position. For a start, he never even defined what he was supposed to be criticising! Just to assume what he was attacking is cavalier. Furthermore, Ella made sweeping allegations without justification, sometimes using excessive language. More

---

[1] Ella: *The Free Offer* p7.

9

Introduction

than once he dismissed the views of those he was censuring, but
did so – wrongly – by association.[2] Speaking for myself, he has not
dealt fairly with what I have said, and has attributed beliefs to me
which I do not hold and have never expressed. He used caricature.
He repeatedly dragged red-herrings across the track, taking his
readers into areas of no relevance to the question in hand.[3] Above
all, when it came to expounding Scripture, the time and care which
Ella showed was abysmally small.[4]

All this is grievous, a sad distraction, and leaves a crucial issue
cloaked in fog. Nor is it the first time. Consequently, I have
decided to reply; the free offer is too important to be left as it is in
Ella's book.

But I will deal with only a part of what Ella said. Whilst I am
not the only person whose views he has attacked – I use the word
advisedly – I cannot speak for others. There are sections in Ella's
work which have no connection with me, sections in which he has
criticised views I do not hold. I will not concern myself with such.
What I will do is come to the crux of the matter. There is only one
question to be answered. Is the free offer biblical?

Let us begin at the beginning. What are we talking about? What
was Ella supposed to be refuting?

What is the free offer?

As I have said, Ella did not define what he was writing against.
Now to misuse terms leads only to confusion. So, even though it is
not entirely satisfactory, since Ella has attacked me for holding to
the free offer, the best I can do is to state what I think he meant by
it. I do so by taking Peter L.Meney's words in his Introduction to
Ella's book, and sticking as close as I can to them. This, therefore,
is what I think Ella meant by 'the free-offer preacher':

---

[2] For instance, see Ella's juxtaposition of Grotius, Wesley, Fuller, Gay
and (John) Murray, and his 'link' between false sects and 'the free offer
enthusiasts' (Ella: *The Free Offer* pp39,49).
[3] Reader, if you wish to see the sort of remarks I am talking about, please
glance at Appendix 1.
[4] For his 'exposition' of Isa. 45:22, see Ella: *The Free Offer* pp26-27; for
Isa. 55:1ff and John 6:29, see the same volume pp49-55.

The 'free-offer' preacher [is compelled][5] to invite all sinners to believe on the Lord Jesus Christ, promising them salvation if they do. This he does [while holding][6] that Christ's atonement was neither made for all, nor intended for all who hear the gospel message... It is not the preacher [only] with his limited knowledge, but the all-knowing, eternal God who freely, sincerely and genuinely offers salvation to all mankind. This is in spite of the Father's eternal purpose to save only the elect, the substitutionary nature of Christ's atoning work and the distinguishing, effectual call of the Holy Spirit.[7]

This is as close as I can get to Ella's view of the free offer. I do wish, however, he had defined it for himself, and then we all would have known precisely what it was he was trying to refute. I am truly sorry he at least implied that 'definitions of the "free offer" are... of little importance'.[8] In order to make some progress, however, as far as I can judge, this is what Ella was challenging:

The free offer is the invitation to all sinners to believe on the Lord Jesus Christ, promising them salvation if they do, even though Christ's atonement was neither intended for all, nor accomplished for all.

It is certainly what I understand by the free offer.

Of course, there is much more to gospel preaching than this. In content, the whole of Scripture must be preached, centring on Christ and him crucified (Acts 20:17-32; 1 Cor. 2:2; Gal. 6:14). No element of truth can be omitted. And preaching involves declaring the gospel to sinners, calling them, trying to persuade them, commanding them, reasoning and pleading with them, warning them, and so on, in addition to inviting them. So I agree with Ella: 'Sinners must be called, commanded, even beseeched to repent and turn from their evil ways'.[9] Indeed, I would apply his words to

---

[5] Meney had 'presumes', thus begging the question right at the outset.

[6] Meney had 'even if he holds'. But this is not the point. We are discussing Calvinistic preachers, surely, not Arminian. See note below.

[7] Ella: *The Free Offer* pp5-6.

[8] Ella: *The Free Offer* p66. Since Ella was saying 'their' (the free-offer preachers') 'definitions of the "free offer" are... of little importance', why did he himself not define what he was trying to refute?

[9] Ella: *The Free Offer* p71.

more than calling and commanding sinners to *repent*.[10] But more of this later.

What was Ella's task?

In writing against the free offer, the task Ella needed to address was this: Is the above statement scriptural? If not, he needed to show where it diverges from Scripture. In Meney's words, we ought to have had his 'sound reasons... and solid scriptural principles' argued out for us. The issue is not whether the free offer is Grotianism, Fullerism, or any other 'ism', but is it scriptural? Coming from the other direction, Ella gained nothing by proving the free offer is a contradiction of John Gill or William Huntingdon. He had no need to spill ink on such matters. By aiming at Fuller, he was aiming at the wrong target; the views of Gill and Huntingdon are not the standard. It is 'to the law and to the testimony' (Isa. 8:20) we must turn; it is God's word we must 'tremble at' (Isa. 66:5).[11]

Nor was Ella's task, again using Meney's words, to prove that we cannot 'reconcile God's purpose to save only some, redeem only some, freely and unconditionally bestow the gift of faith on only some', on the one hand, 'with a genuine free offer to all to believe and be saved', on the other.[12] There are many things in Scripture which we cannot reconcile. God calls us to believe and obey his word, to preach it, not to reconcile it. In my writing about the free offer, I have stated my position explicitly; we cannot and should not try to reconcile God's unknowable decree with his revealed desire as expressed in Scripture. I stand by it. I will

---

[10] I agree with John Elias: 'I cannot understand how those that are against calling, inviting, persuading, and compelling sinners to come to Christ, can be said to preach the gospel' (Morgan p317).

[11] I do not say the views of men are irrelevant, but while principles may be *supported* from the works of men, they must be *established* from Scripture. Just to say, in all my extracts from other authors, if need-be I modernise spelling and grammar without altering the sense. As for Gill, I quote him extensively, partly because Ella has spoken so highly of his written works. See, for instance, Ella: *Gill* pp22-26.

[12] Ella: *The Free Offer* p5.

develop the point as I go on. 'The secret things belong to the LORD our God, but those things which are revealed belong to us and to our children' (Deut. 29:29). 'Oh, the depth of the riches both of the wisdom and knowledge of God! How unsearchable are his judgements and his ways past finding out!' (Rom. 11:33). So let us not waste time in tackling the impossible by probing into the unknowable.

Nor did Ella have to concern himself with preachers who do not believe and preach the gospel in line with what are commonly known as the doctrines of grace, the five points of Calvinism.[13] Ella gained nothing, for example, by drawing attention to preachers who believe in a universal atonement and thus address sinners in an unbiblical way. It may well be the case. But it has nothing to do with what he was supposed to be refuting.

Nor was Ella required to establish the doctrines of grace. This is not at issue. Obviously, I can speak only for myself – but I am sure all free-offer preachers (as defined above) can say the same – I am in full accord with Ella's statement on 'a particular atonement, on the invincible work of the Spirit in turning man from damnation to salvation, and on the fact that Christ's atonement was not in vain, and those whom he aimed to save are saved'.[14] I believe it and preach it. I do not believe in 'a gospel of

---

[13] I use the term 'Calvinism' merely as a convenient historical catch-word to denote 'the gospel, God's system of salvation by grace'. Calvin, great as he was, did not found this system, nor is he its standard. See Spurgeon: *New* Vol.4 p341; *New and Metropolitan* Vol.7 pp298,302; Murray: *Spurgeon* p40. Calvinism does not clash in any way whatsoever with the full free-offer of the gospel; in fact, such an offer can be made only within the structure of the doctrines of grace. See Kelly pp49-50,78. Spurgeon: 'Calvinism... gives you ten thousand times more reason for hope than the Arminian preacher'. 'Someone asks me, "Why talk of Calvinism?" Why I talk of it [is] because you dislike it. I use that very word because it happens to displease you... Calvinism... is really Bible-ism. But as you have given it a nickname, I will label the article as you have done. You may reject it if you like, but... if you read the Bible, you will find it to be according to the oracles of God' (Spurgeon: *The Pulpit Library* pp25,127-128).

[14] Ella: *The Free Offer* p31.

universal redemption, nor even of universal atonement'.[15] I never preach such a thing. Yes, 'belief comes solely through God's sovereign will... [it] is the [gift] of God'.[16] I preach it to sinners. Yes, in becoming a believer a man is 'granted repentance, faith, justification...'.[17] I am persuaded of it. I have no quarrel with Ella when he said the free-offer preacher 'teaches that God genuinely offers forgiveness of sin and salvation to sinners, irrespective of the eternal decree of election, despite the particular, substitutionary atonement of the Lord Jesus Christ, and regardless of the distinguishing effectual call of the Holy Spirit'.[18] No quarrel with it? It is meat and drink to me, and describes my position as well as I could. The doctrines of grace are not at issue. I believe them and preach them to sinners. I believe and preach total depravity, unconditional election, particular redemption, effectual calling and the perseverance of the saints, but none of this restricts the invitation to all sinners to come to Christ. The issue, I repeat, is not the doctrines of grace, *but the way these doctrines are preached to sinners.*

I go further. Preaching doctrine, *as such*, is not the way to bring sinners to salvation. As I said earlier, the biblical way is to preach Christ (2 Cor. 4:5; Phil. 1:18; Col. 1:28), and to woo men to him. I am one with Spurgeon when he declared:

I believe, most firmly, in the doctrines commonly called Calvinistic... but if any man shall say that the preaching of these is the whole preaching of the gospel, I am at issue with him. Brethren, you may preach those doctrines as long as you like, and yet fail to preach the gospel... Preach Christ, young man, if you want to win souls... Facts about Christ Jesus, and the promise of life through him, these are the faith of the gospel.[19]

---

[15] Ella: *The Free Offer* p64, whatever the difference may be.
[16] Ella: *The Free Offer* p61. Ella had 'the work of God'. Faith is never called this – see chapter 3.
[17] Ella: *The Free Offer* p61.
[18] Ella: *The Free Offer* back cover.
[19] Spurgeon: *Metropolitan* Vol.13 pp706-707; see also *Soul Winner* pp18-21,108-109,188-189. What is more, God's decrees ought not to be preached in such a way as to stifle the invitation of the gospel. See Murray: *Spurgeon* pp114-117.

Two issues to be faced: duty faith and God's desire to see sinners saved

What was Ella's task? He needed to show that the free offer is unbiblical, and then set out the truth. In my opinion, he failed to do it. Now the question of the free offer is very serious, and has large implications. Since, therefore, Ella challenged the doctrine behind the free offer, I want to look at his assertions, and try to set out what I consider to be the biblical position. I restrict myself to two matters which Ella raised and denied. There is far more to preaching the gospel than these two points, I hasten to add, but since this is where he directed his attack on me, I confine myself to them.

First, are sinners to be commanded to believe? that is, does the Bible teach what is commonly known as duty faith?

Secondly, has God shown us in his word that while he has decreed the salvation of his elect, he has also shown a general desire for the salvation of all men – which desire has to be expressed in the preaching of the gospel to sinners?

These two principles are fundamental to the free offer. To the first of them I now turn.

Part One

Duty Faith

In chapter 1, I explain what I mean by duty faith. In chapters 2 and 3, I show from Isaiah 45:22 and John 6:28-29 that duty faith is biblical. In chapter 4, I give some examples of Calvinists who have argued for duty faith.

1

What is Duty Faith?

I said there are two questions arising out of Ella's book. The first is what is known as duty faith. Let me define my terms:

Duty faith is the duty, the obligation, the responsibility, of all sinners to trust Christ. The gospel preacher must command all sinners to believe.[1]

Let us start at the beginning – where Ella and I agree.

A command implies a duty

Ella: 'One can only have a duty towards the law when the law is given... the command to exercise duty applies to the law'.[2] I agree. But the principle is general. Any law – not only the law of God – inevitably imposes a duty on all who are under it. Their duty is to obey, to carry out, to fulfil what is commanded.

In particular, since all men are God's created subjects, he has the right to impose upon them any law or command he wishes, which command they are duty-bound to obey. Above all, when God in the gospel issues a command, then those he addresses – whether believers or unbelievers – are obliged to obey that command. And God in the gospel does issue commands, scores of them.[3] Here are two: 'Look to me, and be saved, all you ends of

---

[1] Please note, reader, it is not the duty of an unconverted sinner to believe that Christ died for him in particular; his duty is to trust Christ. In any case, the sinner cannot know the former until he has done the latter; and even if he could, he would be exercising historical faith, accepting a fact, when what is required is saving faith, reliance upon Christ. See chapter 3; Owen: *Death* in *Works* Vol.10 pp404-410.

[2] Ella: *The Free Offer* pp57-58.

[3] Contrary to Gill: 'The gospel... is a pure declaration of grace and salvation by Christ; it has no commands, but all promises' (Gill: *Sermons* Vol.4 p183). As Gill himself said on Acts 17:30: 'Repentance being

the earth! For I am God, and there is no other' (Isaiah 45:22). 'God... commands all men everywhere to repent' (Acts 17:30).

So this is the principle: When God issues a command, then those to whom he issues that command are duty-bound to comply.

But, it is vital to note, when God commands men, it does *not* imply they have the ability to perform. God commands his created subjects because he has the right, whether or not they can comply. The command implies their duty, their responsibility, their obligation, *not* their ability. As Gill said: 'The commands of God show his authority, and man's duty'. He drove the point home by saying that although 'the promises of God... are a relief to man's weakness... [they] no way lessen his obligation to duty... Nor does... prayer... excuse men from obligation...[4] or any duty'; God's 'will of command... signifies [that] what is the pleasure of God should be the duty of man, or what he should do'. Referring to specific biblical texts in which sinners are commanded, he said these 'declare God's will of command, or what he has made man's

---

represented as a command... a command to all'. I agree with Gill, of course, repentance is a gift of God's free grace, and not in man's power, but this does not alter the fact that God in the gospel commands all men to repent. Gill was wrong to try to water down Acts 17:30 by introducing the notion of 'natural repentance'. The fact is, in the gospel, God commands all sinners to repent; to repent, full stop! And what did Gill mean when, speaking of 'the gospel ministry', he said: 'Though in the gospel, strictly taken, there is no command, yet being largely taken for the whole ministry of the word, it includes this [the grace of evangelical repentance], and everything else which Christ has commanded, and was taught by him and his apostles'? Gill had earlier (on Luke 24:47) called 'repentance and remission of sins' 'the sum of the gospel ministry', saying 'the doctrine of repentance is not of the law, which neither requires, nor admits of it, but [it is] of the gospel' (Gill: *Commentary* Vol.5 pp589,939). Gill, it seems to me, was saying, quite rightly, that the gospel requires repentance; in other words, it is a duty under the gospel because it is commanded.

[4] Gill's words, in light of what is to come below, are most interesting: 'God's requiring [internal conversion] does not suppose man's ability to perform it, but his need of it; and is done with a view to bring him to a sense of his state, and that he may apply to God for it... *Nor does such a prayer for conversion excuse men from obligation to turn to the Lord*' (emphasis mine). This is duty faith!

duty'.[5] I couldn't agree more. As John Berridge put it: 'It is not in man to direct his steps. Then, it may be asked, of what use are commands, exhortations, promises and threatenings? I answer, they do not respect [concern] our native ability, but our *duty*; and are not designed to show us what we *can* do, but what we *ought* to do. The command directs our *duty*'.[6]

But we do not need Gill's or Berridge's support for the principle. Christ taught a parable in which a servant 'did the things that were commanded him'. Christ drew the lesson: 'When you have done all those things which you are commanded, say, "We... have done what was our duty to do"' (Luke 17:9-10). The principle is clear: A command implies a duty.

In this book I am concerned with the commands of the gospel. Let's get down to brass tacks.

The gospel commands all sinners to repent; therefore it is their duty to repent

Sinners, asserted Ella, are commanded in the gospel to repent: 'In Scripture, all sinners are called to repentance'. I agree. It is their duty to repent, said Ella: 'Scripture teaches man's duty to repent'. I agree.

I am also of the same mind as Ella when he said the command does not imply ability. Ella, on the command to repentance: 'Scripture also teaches that man has no natural abilities to do so'. I agree. God commands all sinners to repent but no sinner by nature has the power to comply. On this, I agree with Ella.

I am one with Ella when he said: 'The Christian's calling and

---

[5] Gill: *Cause* pp114-115,159.

[6] Berridge pp165-166, first emphasis mine, the others his. Berridge continued: 'The command directs our *duty*, and the promise, or [the] grace in the promise, gives strength to perform it. Besides, God is pleased to make these exhortations and promises the means of conveying spiritual life and strength. Hence these effects are ascribed to the word, which are really and only wrought by the grace conveyed with the word. God may therefore order commands and exhortations to be used towards us, notwithstanding our inability to comply with them, since he can and does make them effectual to the end aimed at' (emphasis his).

duty in evangelisation is to follow Christ's example, and call and command sinners to repentance'. Indeed, I go further. It is the duty of believers to command sinners to repent, not merely because Christ himself did it, but because he *commanded* them to do it in preaching the gospel to every creature (Luke 24:47).

So I am in complete agreement with Ella when he said: 'Sinners must be called, commanded, even beseeched to repent and turn from their evil ways. God commands all to repent, and grants repentance to some who would not otherwise repent'.[7] Christ did it; he commanded his disciples to do it; the apostles did it; we must do it.

So Ella and I are agreed: Sinners are unable to repent, but in the gospel God commands them to repent. In other words, he commands them to do what they cannot do. Just as Christ commanded the man to stretch out his withered hand (Mark 3:5) – the very thing the man could not do, but by Christ's power was enabled to do – so must dead sinners,[8] unrepentant sinners, be commanded to repent. And this must be done even though God grants the gift of repentance only to his elect; God still commands *all* sinners to repent, and *all* sinners have a duty to repent. This surely is the teaching of Acts 17:30: 'God... commands all men everywhere to repent'.

But what about faith?

The gospel commands all sinners to believe; therefore it is their duty to believe

Repentance does not exist in isolation from faith. No man can truly repent without exercising saving faith. Nor can he savingly believe without truly repenting. He must turn from sin in turning to God. 'Repent, and believe', said Christ (Mark 1:15). 'A great number believed and turned to the Lord' (Acts 11:21). 'Whatever is not from faith is sin' (Rom. 14:23); repentance must, therefore, be from faith. And both faith and repentance are the gift of God to his

---

[7] Ella: *The Free Offer* pp58,71. Indeed, unless Christ grants repentance, no sinner can or will repent.

[8] By 'dead sinners', I mean, of course, unregenerate sinners, the spiritually dead (Eph. 2:1).

elect (Acts 5:31; Eph. 2:8). What is more, the same benefits are promised to both repentance and faith, unitedly called 'turning to God' (Luke 24:47; Acts 2:38; 3:19; 8:22; 10:43; 11:17-18,21; 13:38-39; 16:31; 26:18-20; Rom. 3:22; 4:24; 10:10; 1 Cor. 1:21; Gal. 2:16; 1 Thess. 1:3-6,9-10 *etc.*) To try to drive a wedge between faith and repentance is futile.

Now this is where I part company with Ella. On repentance, we are of one mind; *on faith, we are not.* On repentance, Ella and I are agreed: Sinners must be commanded to repent, and it is their duty so to do. In other words, we both hold to duty repentance. But whereas I say the same for faith, Ella does not.

Does it matter? Very much so! R.J.Baldwin asked: 'Is saving faith a duty?... Does God command all men to believe?' As he said: 'These are extremely important questions, because if God commands all men to believe, and we... preach it not, then we are not preaching all the counsel of God, and therefore our preaching is not consistent with our divine commission'.[9]

What was Ella's position? 'Does the Bible invite [command] all men indiscriminately and everywhere to believe?' he asked. Here is his unequivocal answer: 'No, says the Bible. Repentance must come first... When God grants repentance we may talk of belief, but not before'.[10] In other words, only repentant sinners may be commanded to believe. Consequently, according to Ella, the unrepentant must be commanded to repent – even though they cannot – but the unbelieving must not be commanded to believe. Certainly the unrepentant must not be commanded to believe, even though they must be commanded to repent. It is only the repentant who are to be commanded to believe.

I strongly disagree with Ella. Calvin was clear:

Those who think that repentance precedes faith instead of flowing from, or being produced by it, as the fruit of the tree, have never understood its nature.[11]

---

[9] Baldwin p1, my numbering, the paper being unnumbered. Baldwin's question was rhetorical. He did not believe saving faith is a duty for all men.

[10] Ella: *The Free Offer* p61.

[11] Calvin: *Institutes* Vol.1 p510.

I go further. Not only is Ella's logic baffling, it is not possible biblically to discriminate between faith and repentance as he did. John Colquhoun:

In the moment of regeneration the Holy Spirit implants... at the same instant the root or principle of saving faith and true repentance. He gives these two graces together and at once in respect of time; and therefore, though in our conception of them, they are to be distinguished, yet they are never to be separated from each other. The principle of faith in the regenerate soul... is not in point of time before that of repentance, nor is the principle of repentance before that of faith.[12]

C.H.Spurgeon made the same point in his usual pithy way: Faith and repentance, he said, 'are like the Siamese twins; they are born together, and they could not live asunder, but must die if you attempt to separate them.[13] Faith always walks side by side with his weeping sister, true repentance. They are born in the same house at the same hour, and they will live in the same heart every day... They are so united, so married and allied together, that they never can be parted'.[14]

What is more, by saying only the repentant may be commanded to believe, Ella has opened a Pandora's box.[15] Let me explain. How can a preacher tell who is repentant? But he has to know, otherwise he cannot command his hearers to believe. And the

---

[12] Colquhoun p105. Indeed, Colquhoun, entitling his chapter, 'The priority of the acting of saving faith to the exercise of true repentance' (Colquhoun pp105-118), argued faith comes before repentance. As did Gill: Repentance and faith – 'where the one is, there the other is; they are wrought in the soul at one and the same time... the one is not before the other in order of time... repentance is mentioned before faith, not that it precedes it... faith as to its inward exercise on Christ is full as early [as repentance], *if not earlier*; souls *first* look to Christ by faith, and *then* they mourn in tears of evangelical repentance' (Gill: *Commentary* Vol.5 p961, emphasis mine). I myself would not try to dissect the operation of the Spirit too precisely (John 3:8).

[13] I am quoting the Spurgeon of 1860, needless to say, not a surgeon of the twenty-first century.

[14] Spurgeon: *New* Vol.6 p346; see also *Soul Winner* pp31-32.

[15] 'A process that once activated will generate many unmanageable problems' (*Concise*).

sinner has to know he is repentant – truly repentant – before he can believe. I will not digress to develop the point,[16] but when this notion has gripped preaching, it has had a dire effect. It has its own vocabulary. Only those sinners who are 'fit for Christ', or 'prepared' or 'sensible'[17] sinners, may be commanded to believe. But the truth is, there is no biblical way a sinner can know he is warranted to believe because he is repentant or 'sensible'. The Spirit convicts sinners of sin because they do not believe in Christ (John 16:8-9). We are never told he will convict repentant sinners that they are truly repentant so that they might then believe. Nor are we told the Spirit will inform a preacher when his hearers are repentant, so that he may call them to faith. Such promises do not exist in Scripture. In other words, there is no biblical way a sinner can know he is repentant and so may believe, and there is no way a preacher can know his hearers are repentant and so can command them to believe.

Spurgeon put it like this:

We have a new legalism to fight with in our... churches. There are men and women who think they must not believe on Christ till they feel their sins up to a most agonising point. They think they must feel a certain degree of sorrow, a high degree of sense of need before they may come to Christ at all... Man... come and take Christ just as he is, and come to him just as you are. 'But, sir, *may* I come? I am not invited to come'. Yes you are: 'Whosoever will, let him come'. Don't believe that the invitations of the gospel are given only to characters [that is, those who meet certain conditions];[18] they are, some of them,

---

[16] I intend to publish on preparationism, the notion of being 'fit for Christ', in a forthcoming book on the law. But see, for instance, Spurgeon: *Metropolitan* Vol.9 pp529-540. Spurgeon frequently denied preparationism. See also Appendix 2.

[17] 'Sensible' sinners are the regenerate who, conscious of their sin and need of salvation, repent, and desire Christ. They are, therefore, demonstrating that they must be elect. Lest I should be misunderstood, although I speak against preparationism, I am convinced a sinner must be convicted of his sin, and will be convicted of his sin, before he comes to Christ, but his conviction is not the warrant for his being invited to come. He is invited because he is a sinner, and he must come as a sinner; but he will only come when he is a sensible sinner.

[18] See Appendix 2.

unlimited invitations. It is the duty of every man to believe on the Lord Jesus Christ. It is every man's solemn duty to trust Christ, not because of anything that man is, or is not, but because he is commanded to do it... Trust now in his precious blood [and] you are saved.[19]

'Many minds... make repentance a preparation for Christ',[20] said Spurgeon, and consequently argue: 'Sir, I must repent before I come to Christ'. To all such, Spurgeon issued this challenge: 'Find such a passage in the word if you can'.[21]

As I say, it is at this point that I part company with Ella. On repentance, we are of one mind; on faith, we are not.

For example, as I have shown, on repentance, Ella felt able to write:

Scripture teaches man's duty to *repent*... The Christian's calling and duty in evangelisation is to follow Christ's example, and call and command sinners to *repentance*... Sinners must be called, commanded, even beseeched to *repent* and turn from their evil ways. God commands all to *repent*, and grants *repentance* to some who would not otherwise *repent*.[22]

But not:

Scripture teaches man's duty to *believe*... The Christian's calling and duty in evangelisation is to follow Christ's example, and call and command sinners to *believe*... Sinners must be called, commanded, even beseeched to *believe* and turn from their evil ways. God commands all to *believe*, and grants *saving faith* to some who would not otherwise *believe*.[23]

Ella was right, of course, to say: 'The Christian's calling and duty in evangelisation is to follow Christ's example and call and

---

[19] Spurgeon: *New* Vol.6 p107, emphasis his. And in the same volume (not to mention the rest of the books of his sermons), see pp59-64,171-172, 218-219,397-399,403-406.
[20] Spurgeon: *New and Metropolitan* Vol.7 p204; see also same volume pp108-109.
[21] Spurgeon: *New* Vol.6 p60.
[22] Ella: *The Free Offer* pp58,71.
[23] As I noted above on repentance, unless Christ grants faith, no sinner can or will believe.

command sinners to repentance'.[24] But why did Ella stop short? Why did he tell only half the story? We are in no doubt as to what Christ did. We have his example. And, as Ella said, we must 'follow Christ's example'. Let us do as Christ did, therefore, when he went to Galilee, preaching the gospel of the kingdom of God. How did he preach? What did he say? He commanded all his hearers to 'repent, and believe' (Mark 1:14-15). Christ did not divide faith from repentance. He preached both at the same time, to the same sinners, and in the same breath. Christ knew nothing of Ella's division between repentance and faith. So why did Ella not say we should 'follow Christ's example', and command sinners to repent *and believe*? Notice Christ did not command sinners to repent, and, *when they had repented, then* command them to believe. Oh no! He commanded all his hearers to repent and believe at the same time. Repentance and faith go hand in hand. The gospel commands all sinners to repent *and* believe, and all sinners are duty-bound to repent *and* believe.

Paul certainly followed Christ, 'testifying to Jews, and also to Greeks, repentance toward God and faith toward our Lord Jesus Christ' (Acts 20:21). It would be the merest quibble to say the word 'command' is not in the verse. No. It is not. But whatever Paul did as regards repentance – and, as Ella agreed, we know Paul commanded his hearers to repent – he did the same for faith, and did it at the same time. There is no suggestion he divided or distinguished the two in any way.[25] As he explained to Agrippa, he 'declared... that [Jews]... and... Gentiles... should repent, turn to God, and do works befitting repentance' (Acts 26:20). Note the 'should'; sinners '*should* repent', they '*should*... turn to God'. This is the language of command, of duty. And if 'turning to God' does not include trusting Christ, what does it include? Should sinners 'turn to God' *in unbelief*? Thomas Goodwin: 'As Christ did... so did the apostles also; they did still put men upon believing as well as upon repenting... They always held it forth clearly and nakedly

---

[24] Ella: *The Free Offer* p58.
[25] See Gill: *Commentary* Vol.5 pp960-961. Note how Gill said Paul was 'urging and insisting upon' both repentance and faith, and that both were spiritual.

to them'.[26]

John Owen connected repentance with the notion of 'duty'. As it is the duty to believe, so it is the duty to repent:

After the angels had sinned, God never once called them to repentance... He has no forgiveness for them, and therefore would require no repentance of them. It is not, nor ever was, a duty incumbent upon them to repent. Nor is it so unto the damned in hell. God requires it not of them, nor is it their duty... Assignation then, of repentance, is a revelation of forgiveness. God would not call upon a sinful creature to humble itself and bewail its sin if there were no way of recovery or relief... What, then does God aim at in and by [various scriptures]?... It is to bring [the sinner] to repentance... [And] no repentance is acceptable with God but what is built or leans on the faith of forgiveness... [For God] to prescribe repentance as a duty unto sinners, without a foundation of pardon and forgiveness in himself, is inconsistent with... all [the] glorious excellencies and perfections of the nature of God... Repenting is for sinners only... It is for them, and them only. It was no duty for Adam in Eden, it is none for the angels in heaven, nor for the damned in hell... [In] Isa. 55:7, [God] speaks... to men perversely wicked, and such as make a trade of sinning. What does he call them unto? Plainly, to repentance, to the duty we have insisted on.[27]

Of course faith is the gift of God; but so is repentance.[28] This is not at issue. Repentance, according to Ella,[29] is commanded – and therefore must be a duty – so why not faith? If Ella was right to dismiss duty faith by saying: 'The command to exercise duty faith[30] can only be given to those who have a faith to exercise dutifully', why did he not apply the same argument to repentance – which he listed with faith – and which he said sinners are commanded to do, and which he joined with faith as the gift of God?[31] If the command to believe implies the ability to comply –

---

[26] Goodwin p584.

[27] Owen: *Psalm 130* in *Works* Vol.6 pp437-440.

[28] As Ella stated (Ella: *The Free Offer* pp58-59).

[29] And Scripture, of course.

[30] Does any free-offer preacher tell his hearers to 'exercise duty faith'? I don't. The same goes for duty repentance – see below. I tell sinners to repent and believe, that it is their duty so to do, or words to that effect.

[31] Ella: *The Free Offer* pp58-59,62.

as Ella alleged – why does the same not apply to repentance? But neither command implies any ability. When Ella cited Gill, who 'could not believe [that it] was... the duty of the evangelist... to preach that sinners were duty-bound to exercise a faith savingly of which they knew nothing, and of which they had nothing', what now of commanding the unrepentant to repent?[32] How could Ella continue to argue it *is* the duty of the unrepentant to repent? If the argument destroys duty faith, it destroys duty repentance.

The truth is, the gospel never restricts God's commands to what sinners are able to do by nature.[33] It pays not the slightest attention

---

[32] Ella: *The Free Offer* pp62,67. And what of Gill, who, when speaking of the one who 'with his heart, or heartily... believes in Christ for righteousness; which righteousness... is imputed to him for justification', declared: 'Faith, as an act of ours, is a duty; for whatsoever we do, in a religious way, we do but what is our duty to do'? Gill, I realise, was here arguing for eternal justification, tortuously defending the truth that righteousness, not faith, is imputed for justification, and, as a consequence, he dismissed duty faith as belonging to the law. I do not want to digress into tackling eternal justification, so I will say no more about it here – except that I heartily agree with Gill when he said 'it is God, and not faith, that justifies', and 'faith is not the cause... of justification', but I disagree with him when he said 'faith is... the fruit and effect of justification' (Gill: *Sermons* Vol.4 pp185-187,197). No! Faith is the *means* of justification, and is the fruit and effect of *election*. See my note in chapter 5. To return to the main point: Gill's words – that 'faith, as an act of ours, is a duty' – are right. Even so, I admit that Gill limited this requirement to the sensible: If God reveals his gospel inwardly to sinners, 'by the spirit of wisdom, in the knowledge of Christ; or God by his word calls men effectually by his grace, and reveals his Son in them, as well as to them; this sort of revelation comes with such power and influence upon the mind, as certainly to produce a true and living faith in the soul, which infallibly issues in eternal life and happiness; and of such persons, and of such only, acts of special [that is, spiritual or saving] faith in Christ are required' (Gill: *Sermons* Vol.1 pp122,135). Gill, however, was clearly arguing in a circle; he required saving faith only of those who had already exercised it! Indeed, in the same sentence he actually called them 'believers'; as they were, since God had already produced 'a true and living faith' in them. But it is *un*believers who have to believe! And one thing unbelievers do not have is a living faith!

[33] Whoever and whatever Ella was speaking of when he said 'Fullerite' preaching 'combines the free offer of salvation with the notion that

to it; rather, it commands them to do what they cannot do. The basis of the command is God's authority, and not, I repeat, the sinner's ability. God demands repentance, nothing less, even though sinners cannot repent. And God also demands saving faith, nothing less, even though sinners cannot believe savingly. I have already mentioned Christ's miraculous cure of the man with the withered hand, by which he aptly illustrated the principle. Let me glance at it again. He told the man to 'step forward'; then he told the man to stretch out his hand. It was an impossibility, but 'he stretched it out' (Mark 3:3-5)! Observe the difference in the two commands. In the first, Christ told the man to step forward – something he could do; this does not illustrate the gospel. In the second, Christ told the man to do what was impossible for him to do; and he did it! This *does* illustrate the gospel! Likewise, the dead Lazarus came out of the grave, the widow's dead son got out of his coffin at Nain, Jairus' dead daughter got up, the paralytic walked with his bed, the deaf man heard, the dumb spoke, the blind saw, the lame leaped, and so on – all miracles, impossible by human power, but all accomplished by Christ's command. Furthermore, it was Lazarus' duty to come out of the grave, Jairus' daughter's duty to get up, the paralytic's duty to walk with his bed, and so on.

It is exactly the same with the gospel. God commands the sinner to believe, and the sinner's duty is to obey. Ella, however, stoutly disagreed. He thought sinners may not be commanded to believe, because they have no power to believe, and have no faith to believe with.[34] Only awakened, sensible, regenerate, repentant – even believing – sinners may be commanded to believe. But this is wrong, utterly wrong. Christ did not command a man who had a

---

believing in Christ is the natural duty of all men according to natural abilities', and teaching 'two routes for salvation' (Ella: *The Free Offer* p19), I hope he exempted me and my preaching. I suspect, however, from what he said immediately after these words, he had me in his sights. If so, let me state my position loud and clear: I believe and preach nothing of the sort; nothing of the sort, I say! I do not 'preach to persuade men according to their natural abilities to repent and believe on... purely rational grounds' (Ella: *The Free Offer* p22).

[34] See above for Ella's citation from Gill.

healthy hand to stretch it out; he commanded a man with a withered hand. Christ did not command a man with excellent sight to see. Christ did not tell an able-bodied man to walk. In its call for salvation, the gospel does not command believers to believe, the repentant to repent, the awakened to live, the looking to look, the seeing to see. The preacher's task is not to command living sinners to believe; he is to command dead sinners! The gospel commands sinners to do what they cannot do, and although these commands do not inform them of their ability, they do tell them their duty. What is more, God gives grace with his command so that the withered hand can be stretched out. In the same way, the unbelieving are enabled to believe, and the unrepentant are enabled to repent of their sins.[35]

Spurgeon raised the objection of one who 'wants to know how it is that men are bidden to come – and yet we are taught in Scripture that no man can come – and he must have that cleared up; just as if the poor man who had a withered arm, when Christ said, "Stretch out your arm", had replied, "Lord, I have got a difficulty in my mind; I want to know how you can tell me to stretch out my arm when it is withered". Suppose when Christ had said to Lazarus, "Come forth", Lazarus could have said, "I have a difficulty in my mind; how can a dead man come forth?"'

Spurgeon replied:

Why, know this, vain man! When Christ says, 'Stretch out your arm', he gives you power to stretch out your arm with the command, and the difficulty is solved in practice; though I believe it never will be solved in theory. If men want to have theology mapped out to them, as they would have a map of England; if they want to have every little village

---

[35] See Spurgeon: *Soul Winner* pp174-177. Compare God's command to Ezekiel to prophesy to the dry bones (Ezek. 37:1-14). Take the raising of Lazarus as an illustration of the principle. We have the sinner's state: 'Lazarus is dead'. We have the gospel call to the dead sinner: 'Lazarus, come forth!' (As above, the command to take away the stone (John 11:39) does not illustrate the gospel). We see the result: 'He who had died came out' (John 11:14,43,44). I admit, of course, that in the miracles, specific individuals were commanded and the 'success rate' was 100%. The preacher of the gospel, however, issues the gospel command promiscuously; it is God who, by his secret working, makes it effectual in the case of the elect. See Appendix 2.

and every hedgerow in the gospel kingdom mapped out to them, they will not find it anywhere but in the Bible; and they will find it so mapped out there that the years of a Methuselah would not suffice to find out every little thing in it. We must come to Christ and learn, not learn and then come to Christ.[36]

Berridge, commenting on Acts 16:31, said: 'Believe on the Lord Jesus Christ. Faith, as wrought in us by the Holy Ghost, is a grace of the Spirit; but as commanded in the word, it is a duty – a duty of high rank; and help may be had for its performance'.[37]

I agree with Ella when he said 'no true Christian would deny that man is responsible for not believing'.[38] But this raises an important question: How then can it not be man's obligation to believe? As John Elias put it: 'If [since] unbelief of the gospel is a sin, is not believing it a duty?' Indeed, it is! But this in itself leads to an inevitable conclusion; in light of the fact that sinners have a duty to believe, ministers therefore must have a duty to preach it. Otherwise, as Elias asked: 'How can it be a duty of some to believe what is not the duty of ministers to preach?'[39]

But as for preaching duty faith, and the sinner's duty to believe, some common misunderstandings cloud the subject. Elias swept them away:

No one ever saw before he believed in Christ that he was elected or redeemed. So there is no need of preaching general redemption as a ground to call lost sinners to Christ; and there is no need of preaching that man can of himself believe the gospel, as a ground to encourage ruined sinners to believe in Christ.[40] Not the ability of fallen man is the rule or measure of his duty, or the ground for the justice of God to require it. [Conversely,] the inability of man is no excuse for his

---

[36] Spurgeon: *New* Vol.4 p439, emphasis his.

[37] Berridge p175.

[38] Ella: *The Free Offer* p55.

[39] Elias was not saying that only some have the duty to believe; clearly, he held that it is the duty of all men. Rather, as I say, Elias was making the obvious point; namely, since sinners have the duty to believe, preachers have the duty to preach it.

[40] Elias was not saying that it is acceptable to preach general redemption and creature power; both are false. He was rightly arguing that neither is the basis of duty faith or the free offer – mistaken allegations which are often made.

disobedience. His sin, his enmity, are his inability. He ought to be ashamed on the account of them... [Of course,] faith is the gift of God. But notwithstanding this, faith is the duty of man.[41]

Ella thought 'the New Testament method of preaching is to... preach the need for repentance and the need for faith in the Saviour'.[42] But this, reader, falls a long way short of 'the New Testament method of preaching'. The New Testament preacher does not preach merely the *need* for repentance and faith; he calls for it, he commands it, he demands it. Ella himself said so concerning repentance, but stopped short of saying it about faith. Why?

'The main weakness of the free offer dogma', Ella argued, 'is that in warranting and offering salvation to all, sinners are being offered the gospel who have no ability of their own to accept it'.[43] This is not its weakness,[44] but allowing it for the moment, if Ella is right, what now of commanding all sinners to repent? All sinners must be called and commanded to repent even though no sinner has any power to comply. Ella, as I have shown, agreed with this. Why not, therefore, the same for faith?

Of course it is not right to appeal to the sinner's 'sense of duty' to repent or believe.[45] I don't know of any free-offer preacher who does it. Sinners are dead in sin, totally depraved, without any sense of the duty to repent or believe. There is nothing to 'appeal to'. But this is not the issue.

* * *

Enough of this skirmishing. It is high time we got to grips with the question. The facts are simple. The sinner must be commanded to repent; it is his duty. Ella and I agree. The sinner must be commanded to believe; it is his duty. So I say, but Ella disagrees.

---

[41] Morgan pp317-318; see also pp368-372.

[42] Ella: *The Free Offer* p58.

[43] Ella: *The Free Offer* p56. The free-offer preacher, of course, can only warrant (guarantee) salvation to sinners on condition that they believe: 'Believe on the Lord Jesus Christ, and you will be saved' (Acts 16:31).

[44] It is foolishness in the eyes of men, but it is God's ordained way of calling sinners (1 Cor. 1:17-21).

[45] Ella: *The Free Offer* p58.

But what I say or Ella says is of little importance. What does Scripture say? What does Ella make of those places in Scripture where sinners – as sinners – are commanded to believe? For lack of space, I take just two, both of which Ella raised;[46] namely, Isaiah 45:22 and John 6:28-29.

I begin with Isaiah 45:22.

---

[46] Unfortunately, Ella spent little time on his 'exposition' of the first, most of it attacking John Murray's view. And although he said he was going to 'look closely' at the second, he devoted only two small paragraphs to his 'exposition' of it, mostly attacking Robert Oliver concerning Fuller (Ella: *The Free Offer* pp26-28,54-55).

2

Isaiah 45:22

'Look to me, and be saved, all you ends of the earth! For I am God, and there is no other' (Isa. 45:22)

As Ella rightly pointed out, the verse 'has to do with salvation and that on a world-wide scale'. So far so good. He went on: 'Two things must be noted, however. Rather than salvation being offered here, God is commanding. The people are ordered to assemble (verse 20), tell, bring (verse 21) and look (verse 22). They are told what will happen if they obey and what will happen if they do not obey. Those that disobey will be ashamed and confounded (verses 16,24), and those that obey will be saved (verses 17,22). Here we have a clear testimony to the fact that God's call to the world is a discriminating call'.[1]

Ella was right to draw attention to the commanding aspect of the verse and its context. But, reader, he was wrong to say Isaiah 45:22 is a *discriminating* call. This is precisely what it is not! It is a *universal* call; it is totally *in*discriminate. It is addressed to 'all you ends of the earth'. The gospel, I hasten to add, *is* discriminating. Most definitely it is! The Spirit effectually works in the elect as he applies the benefits of the particular redemption accomplished by Christ according to God's decree. But this is not the issue in Isaiah 45:22. God through the prophet was giving the universal call and command of the gospel to all sinners. God is highly discriminate in whom he works, but totally indiscriminate as to whom he commands to look to him and be saved.

Notice, reader, the verse includes a promise, while the context (Isa. 45:24) includes a warning. As Ella noted, sinners 'are told what will happen if they obey and what will happen if they do not obey'. They are promised salvation if they look. This is nothing less than what I understand by the free offer.

---

[1] Ella: *The Free Offer* pp26-27.

Let me take a closer look at it.

Who is speaking? It is God. What is the call? It is a command to sinners to look to God, to look spiritually, to look expectantly to him, to come to him, to trust him; in short, to believe. What is promised to sinners? It is salvation. God promises everlasting salvation from all sin, not a mere temporal or general welfare or deliverance. The context makes it clear: 'Israel shall be saved by the LORD with an everlasting salvation; you shall not be ashamed or disgraced for ever and ever' (Isa. 45:17).[2] To whom is the call made? It is to all the ends of the earth.

Isaiah 45:22 shows us that every sinner in the world is commanded to look to God for salvation, to look in faith and be saved. If not, words have lost all meaning. Here we have nothing less than God's own call to sinners, his command to all sinners to believe. And because God commands every sinner to look to him and be saved, every sinner has the right or warrant to call upon the name of the Lord. What is more, every sinner is obliged to believe. This, in short, is duty faith. If it is not the duty of sinners to obey God and look, they do not sin by not looking. Yet, as Ella said, 'they are told what will happen... if they do not obey'. Quite! They will face judgement and condemnation (Isa. 45:24). As Christ said: 'He who believes in [the Son] is not condemned; but he who does not believe is condemned already, because he has not believed in the name of the only begotten Son of God' (John 3:18). 'He who believes in the Son has everlasting life; and he who does not believe the Son shall not see life, but the wrath of God abides on him' (John 3:36).

And this, I repeat, is what I understand by the free offer of the gospel. Here God promises salvation – he offers it – to all who look. 'Look to me, and be saved, all you ends of the earth!' But what is it to look? It is to believe: 'The LORD said to Moses, "Make a fiery serpent, and set it on a pole; and it shall be that everyone who is bitten, when he *looks* at it, shall live". So Moses made a bronze serpent, and put it on a pole; and so it was, if a

---

[2] As to the question of 'Israel', in my forthcoming book on the law I will look at the way the New Testament interprets and applies such prophecies. But the issue does not arise here since Ella and I agree that Isa. 45:22 is the gospel call.

serpent had bitten anyone, when he *looked* at the bronze serpent, he lived' (Num. 21:8-9). Now this *looking*, Christ calls *believing*: 'As Moses lifted up the serpent in the wilderness, even so must the Son of Man be lifted up, that whoever *believes* in him should not perish but have eternal life. For God so loved the world that he gave his only begotten Son, that whoever *believes* in him should not perish but have everlasting life... He who *believes* in him is not condemned' (John 3:14-18). 'Whoever calls on the name of the LORD shall be saved' (Joel 2:32; Acts 2:21; Rom. 10:13); but the sinner can only call on Christ, will only call on him, if he savingly believes: 'How then shall they call on him in whom they have not believed?' (Rom. 10:14). 'The gospel' has to be 'mixed with faith' in those who hear it (Heb. 4:2). This is a vital element of duty faith. The sinner who believes has 'obeyed the gospel' (Rom. 10:16), while the sinner who refuses to believe is disobedient (Heb. 3:18-19 with 4:6,11). (See also Rom. 1:5; 6:17; 10:21; 11:20,23,30-32; 15:18; 16:26; 2 Thess. 1:8; Heb. 5:9; 1 Pet. 1:2,21-22; 2:7-8; 3:1; 4:17).

In addressing 'all you ends of the earth', God indiscriminately calls out to all men without distinction, to all men everywhere. The invitation or command is addressed to men merely as created human beings (Isa. 45:12). God, as Creator, invites and commands all his created subjects. Furthermore, the universal scope of the command is made very clear by Isaiah 45:23: 'Every knee shall bow, every tongue shall take an oath'. There is no exception to this. Since every sinner will bow the knee (Isa. 45:23; Rom. 14:11-12; Phil. 2:9-11), every sinner is commanded to look (Isa. 45:22). Both are universal in extent; there is no exception. It will not do to interpret 'all the ends of the earth' as meaning 'all nations without distinction'; it means all *men* without distinction. It is not merely the nations who will bow the knee; men, as individuals, will bow the knee. Likewise, God does not call nations to look to him; he calls men as individuals. Both salvation and judgement are personal and individual, and thus God commands all men to believe, men simply as men, sinners as sinners. God created all men, and all men will have to bow the knee to him; therefore all men, all sinners without exception, are invited, called and commanded by God to look to him and be saved.

37

What is more, God issues this call to sinners without any qualification. He does not address awakened sinners; he does not address repentant sinners; he does not address the elect. He addresses all sinners everywhere. God does not say: 'Look to me, and be saved, all you *sensible* sinners on the earth', 'all you *repentant* sinners', 'all you *elect* sinners'.[3]

Nor does the fact that he has not decreed the salvation of all men stop him commanding *all* sinners to look, nor does it remove their obligation to believe. This is not at issue. Speaking of the gospel call, David J.Engelsma was right to say: 'The call makes known [even] to [the reprobate] what they ought to do, not what God wills to do with them'. 'The reprobate... have an obligation to believe on Jesus Christ, even though they are unable to do so'.[4]

Moreover, God does not content himself with merely *commanding* or *inviting* sinners; he condescends to *argue* with them. He gives reasons to persuade and encourage them to believe and be saved, including his sovereignty and uniqueness (Isa. 45:5,18,21). And since it is God who issues this command or invitation, obviously it must express his pleasure and revealed will.[5] In other words, it is God's will that all sinners should be freely called to come to him for salvation, and it pleases him when they do come.

Notice, God gives this command to sinners through the lips of a man; in this instance, the prophet. Thus it is the duty of gospel preachers to give this free invitation to sinners in the name of God, to issue such an indiscriminate call to sinners in the preaching of the gospel. The preacher has to command all sinners to look. What is more, he does not have to ask himself if his hearers are elect or awakened or sensible or repentant before he can invite them. He does not have to worry himself as to whether or not God has decreed to save them. He does not have to ask himself if Christ has

---

[3] See Appendix 2.

[4] Engelsma pp87,121. Engelsma was here speaking of the call in general; he was not referring to Isa. 45:22, which he did not mention in his book. Although I agree with Engelsma on the point in question, his book was against the free offer.

[5] Here is the link between the two parts of my book – duty faith and God's desire. This will come up repeatedly.

died for them. In any case, he can ask as much as he likes; he will get no answer! In fact, these are questions he has no right to ask. God will not tell him! All the preacher has to worry about is to be sure his hearers are human beings! As long as they are, they are sinners, and God is pleased to command and invite all of them to salvation in the gospel. Therefore it is the preacher's duty and privilege to address his hearers as such, and call them to saving faith. Those who say it is wrong to invite all sinners indiscriminately, condemn both God and his prophet. When J.H.Gosden, for instance, dismissed the giving of indiscriminate calls to sinners, saying it is 'misleading for ministers indiscriminately to scatter invitations among a mixed congregation',[6] he was in effect castigating God. For God went much further than he to scatter an indiscriminate invitation among a mere congregation; he himself did it to the entire world, to every man, woman and child on the planet! As Stanley Delves said:

We [here] get a call to all the ends of the earth without any restriction or definition. It extends everywhere and to all people. For as sin extends to the ends of the earth, and there are no parts and no people exempt from the common evil of sin and ruin, so the power of the gospel extends equally to the ends of the earth. There are no parts and there are no people exempt from that gracious word – 'Look to me and be saved'.[7]

Edward J.Young:

It might seem... that for the heathen there remained nothing but destruction. Such is not the case, for an invitation of mercy is extended to them. They are not to continue in their former ways but are to turn from them. The verb suggests a turning away from something and a turning to something; a true conversion. Conversion is similarly presented in the New Testament (*cf.* 1 Thess. 1:9; Acts 14:15; 15:19)... The reference is to men individually. If the ends of the earth turn unto God, it is only because the individual men who make up the ends of the earth have themselves turned. There is a stress upon individual conversion. The invitation to turn... is couched in the imperative, and thus the responsibility of the individual is set forth... [But,] although God here commands men to turn to him, it does not

---

[6] Gosden p122.
[7] Delves p65.

follow that he gives to all who hear the command the power and ability to obey... It is God who commands; and man, the creature, has the responsibility of obeying. The phrase 'the ends of the earth'... includes all who dwell upon the earth... [There is a] close relationship between true conversion and the universality of the gospel message. The two imperatives belong together; the first, as has often been pointed out, is hortatory [urging an action], and the second promising. The thought is, 'turn to me and you will surely be saved'.[8]

God, Calvin observed, 'invites the whole world to the hope of salvation... He therefore commands all "to look to him", and to the precept adds a promise... The Lord... invites all without exception to come to him... The Lord therefore stretches out his hand, in order to rescue all and point out the method of obtaining salvation'.[9]

Gill properly maintained that God calls sinners to look to Christ, to believe on him, assuring them that all who look will be saved. So said Gill. Excellent! But he ruined all by introducing a qualifying adjective and a mood change to the verb: 'And therefore *sensible* sinners *may* safely look to him, and venture their souls on him'.[10]

This falls short of the facts. For a start, sensible sinners not only *may* look to Christ – they can and they do! Coming to the verse itself, Isaiah 45:22 is not addressed to sensible sinners; it is addressed to sinners. And it does not stop at saying that sinners *may* look to Christ and be saved. There is no *may* about it! It says that all sinners *ought* to look and be saved. God commands them to do it. This is what the text says. Where did Gill find the notion of sensibility in the verse? A new twist, indeed, to 'seeing the invisible'! Sadly, by his talk of sensibility, Gill cut out the encouraging aspect of the verse for all men. He did more; he killed off its insistence on universal responsibility. All sinners ought to look to God, since God commands them to! Most seriously of all, Gill effectively silenced the note of urgency. God commands all men to look to him, but Gill made men look at themselves to see if they are sensible. And when God commands all men to look to

---

[8] Young pp215-216.
[9] Calvin: *Commentaries* Vol.8 Part 1 p425.
[10] Gill: *Commentary* Vol.3 pp943-944, emphasis mine.

him, obviously he means they should look at once (Isa. 55:6; 2
Cor. 6:2). Look now! Gill, driving men to test themselves to see if
they are sensible, makes them embark on what can often be a long
drawn-out process of self-examination.[11] When Gill said God calls
sinners to look to Christ to be saved, 'that men may be saved by
him; and it is the will of God, not only that men should look to
him, but that whosoever sees him, and believes in him, should not
perish, but have everlasting life',[12] he was right. Why did he ruin it
by introducing the idea of sensibility? Of course, only sensible
sinners will come, but the passage deals with God's command, not
his secret working within the soul of the elect sinner. There is not
an atom of sensibility or fitness in the text. Nothing of the sort is
required for the gospel invitation or command.[13]

Goodwin:

Christ, under the simple and absolute consideration of being a
Saviour, is represented to us in the promises as the object of our faith:
'Look unto me, and be saved, all the ends of the earth; for I am God,
and there is none else' (Isa. 45:22). Christ is there spoken of, as
appears from what follows in verse 23. He is set forth as the only
Saviour... and we see him as such nakedly proposed to our faith, as
these words show, 'Look unto me...'. We have a place parallel to this

---

[11] See my note, in the previous chapter, on preparationism.

[12] Gill: *Commentary* Vol.3 p943.

[13] If Gill's view of Isa. 45:22 was inadequate, Gosden's was frankly
ridiculous: 'Perhaps ["the ends of the earth"] intends the realisation in the
experience of each individual child of God of the end of all his natural
resources with respect to his religion. God brings his people there, brings
them to realise that there is nothing for them but destruction, ruin, despair,
and eternal woe, except God saves them' (Paul pp172,175). I suspect he
got the idea from Philpot pp177-178. B.A.Ramsbottom, disagreeing with
what I had written, took the same line as Gosden when he reviewed the
first edition of this present book: '"The ends of the earth" can be spoken
of as sinners who feel left out or far off – not necessarily "every person
without exception"' (Ramsbottom p95). Might I ask how Gosden's and
Ramsbottom's suggestions would apply to Deut. 33:17; 1 Sam. 2:10; Job
28:24; 37:3; 38:13; Ps. 2:8; 22:27; 48:10; 59:13; 65:5; 67:7; 72:8; 98:3;
135:7; Prov. 17:24; 30:4; Isa. 24:16; 40:28; 41;5,9; 42:10; 43:6; 48:20;
49:6; 52:10; Jer. 10:13; 16:19; 25:31; 31:8; 50:41; 51:16; Dan. 4:11; Mic.
5:4; Zech. 9:10; Matt. 12:42; Luke 11:31; Acts 13:47; Rom. 10:18? Note,
particularly, the nine references in the context of Isa. 45:22.

in the New Testament: 'And this is the will of him that sent me, that everyone who sees the Son, and believes on him, may have everlasting life...' (John 6:40). He that sees the Son, *i.e.* with a spiritual light, so as to believe on him. These are acts purely acting upon him as he is the Christ and a Saviour. And the believing on that object requires no conditions first to be looked at by him who is to believe. And Christ had proposed himself... in like manner [in] John 3:14-15... We have another instance of his being declared and set forth as a Saviour [in] 1 Timothy 1:15... The words are a bare proposal of him, wherein he is set forth as the immediate object to a sinner's faith. His being a Saviour, and his intent to save sinners of this world... is nakedly declared... The apostle... means that it deserves hearty welcome and receiving by faith. And of this faith on Christ the apostle had proposed himself an example in the preceding verse [1 Tim. 1:14], so that this faithful saying had been the ground of his own faith.[14]

In short, Isaiah 45:22 is God's command to all sinners to trust Christ. It teaches duty faith.

Now for the second passage.

---

[14] Goodwin pp216-217.

3

John 6:28-29

'What shall we do, that we may work the works of God?' Jesus answered and said to them, 'This is the work of God, that you believe in him whom he sent' (John 6:28-29)

There are three questions:

1. What did Jesus mean by 'the work of God'?
2. What did Jesus mean when he told the people to believe?
3. Were they sensible sinners who were told to believe?

1. 'The work of God' – what is it?

There are two alternatives. Either it is the work which God himself does, or else it is the work God requires men to do. If the former, then since the Jews asked Christ what they had to do (John 6:28), they must have been asking how they could do what only God can do, and Christ told them how to do it. A most remarkable suggestion! Did they want to create? Did they want to rule all nations? Or what? The notion is absurd. We can dismiss it. What is more, Christ's answer, to 'believe in him whom he sent', can hardly be described as God's own work. Sinners have to believe, not God![1]

But before I move on, let me deal with a refinement of the idea. Were the Jews thinking in a much more subtle way – were they

---

[1] I acknowledge, of course, the obvious; 'the works of God' *can* mean God's own works. When Jesus told his disciples that the blind man had been born blind so 'that the works of God should be revealed in him' (John 9:3), this is precisely what he was talking about. God was going to display *his* works – his compassion, his power, and so on – in giving the man sight. Yes, of course. But Jesus made this very clear by saying the works of God were to be *revealed in* the man; God was about to demonstrate his compassion and his power. But this is very different to John 6:28-29.

thinking of saving faith as the work of God in his elect? In other words, were they asking how God would work in them, enabling them to believe? This too we can dismiss. The suggestion that they had reached this level of spiritual understanding, and reached it *before* believing,[2] and were sincerely asking how God would work faith in them, is too much to swallow. Saving faith came into the conversation only *after* the Jews had asked their question about the work of God, and it arose only because Christ raised it. It had not entered the minds of the Jews. Above all, the idea introduces a dreadful confusion. The Jews were asking about what *they* had to do, not what God would do. The confusion is this: When a sinner believes, who does the believing? Is it the sinner or God? It is the sinner. While faith is the *gift* of God (Eph. 2:8), it is never called the *work* of God. Although God gives faith to the elect sinner, working in him, it is the sinner who believes (Eph. 2:8-10; Phil. 2:12-13). The Holy Spirit does not believe for the sinner; God does not do the believing. Gill had it right when he said 'it is the convinced sinner, and not God or Christ, or the Spirit, who repents and believes'.[3] 'Faith... as a principle, is purely God's work; [but] as it is an act, or as it is exercised under the influence of divine grace, it is man's act'.[4] Yes, indeed, 'it is man's act'. The upshot is, even if the Jews were asking about saving faith – which they were not – they were asking about what God required of them, not what he would do in them.

Let me stress this. The fact is, the Jews were not talking about God's *own* work at all! They wanted to know what *they* had to do. They wanted to know how *they* could please God, what did he require of *them*, what was *their* duty.[5] Indeed, they had asked their question only because Christ had spoken of what they ought to 'labour' for (John 6:27). This is what they wanted to know, and

---

[2] They were not spiritual men; see below for proof of their carnality.
[3] Gill: *Cause* p112.
[4] Gill: *Commentary* Vol.5 p654. 'Faith, as it is our act, is our own; hence we read of *his* faith, and *my* faith, and *your* faith, in Scripture' (Gill: *Sermons* Vol.4 p185, emphasis his). 'Whilst faith is unquestionably God's gift, it must be your act' (White p39).
[5] Once again, note the link between duty faith – that which God requires – and God's desire – that which would please him.

this is what Christ told them. The work under discussion was not
the work which God *does*, but the work which *pleases* him, the
work God *requires*. As Goodwin put it: 'By works of God they
mean works acceptable to God'.[6] Lexicons tell us it is 'the works
required and approved by God, the deeds that God desires'.[7] Henry
Alford: '"The works of God" must not be taken to mean "the
works which God works", but... "the works well pleasing to
God"'.[8] As the NIV translates it: 'What must we do to do the
works God requires?' And Jesus, by his answer, was telling them:
'This is your responsibility, this is what you must do to please
God, this is what God requires of you, this is the work of God, this
is your duty'. 'Do not labour for the food which perishes, but for
the food which endures to everlasting life, which the Son of Man
will give you,[9] because God the Father has set his seal on him...
This is the work of God, that you believe in him whom he sent'
(John 6:27,28). Alford again: 'The meaning is not that faith is
wrought in us by God... but... working the work of God is to
believe on him whom he has sent'.[10] Believing in Christ is that
which pleases God, it is what God requires, it is what he demands,
it is the sinner's duty.[11]

Consider Christ himself. He did 'the works of God'. What did

[6] Goodwin p584.

[7] Thayer; Arndt and Gingrich.

[8] Alford p518.

[9] Of course, salvation, and all the things which accompany it – repentance,
faith, and so on – are gifts and graces which only God can give and
produce. This is not at issue!

[10] Alford p518.

[11] 'The work of God is to believe. Faith includes all the works which God
requires' (Vincent Vol.1 p441). Compare 'the work of the LORD' (Jer.
48:10), the work God requires, 'which is said with respect to the
Chaldeans, who were enjoined to destroy the Moabites, which is called
the work of the Lord, because he had given them a commission to do it;
and which was to be done by them... This is a general rule... every man
has work to do for God' (Gill: *Commentary* Vol.4 p209). Compare also
'my [Christ's] works' (Rev. 2:26): 'By his works are meant [here], not the
works which were done by him... but the works which are commanded,
and required by Christ to be done by his people... [such] as the work of
faith... and every act of obedience' (Gill: *Commentary* Vol.6 p949).

this entail? Take the curing of the blind man which I noted a moment ago. Yes, God was about to reveal his works in making the blind man see (John 9:3), but as Jesus immediately went on to say: 'I must work the works of [God] while it is day; the night is coming when no one can work' (John 9:4). Clearly, Christ was speaking of the work *he himself* would do. Yes, it was 'the work of God' in that it would be done by God's power (John 14:10), and would please God; yet, in making the blind man see, whilst it was God's work which Christ did, *it was Christ who did the work*. It was one of *his* works (John 15:24).

Christ's curing the blind man is not an isolated example of the way he pleased his Father by his works. Christ's entire life and death was a constant demonstration of it. Coming into the world, he set out his manifesto: 'I have come... to do your will, O God' (Heb. 10:5-7,9). Addressing his disciples, he elaborated the point: 'My food is to do the will of him who sent me, and to finish his work' (John 4:34). In other words, Christ was saying he delighted to obey God his Father, to carry out his commands, to complete the work, the duty, the Father had given him to do. In this way Christ was at work. 'My Father has been working until now, and I have been working' (John 5:17), he told the Jews. True, as he explained, 'I can of myself do nothing' (John 5:19,30), but even so his works were *his* own works; *he* did them. In all this, he could say, 'I do not seek my own will but the will of the Father who sent me' (John 5:30); in other words, I do my works in order to please the Father; indeed, 'I always do those things that please him' (John 8:29); 'the works which the Father has given me to finish – the very works that I do – bear witness of me' (John 5:36), 'for I have come down from heaven, not to do my own will, but the will of him who sent me' (John 6:38). Of 'the works that I do in my Father's name' (John 10:25), one – which he called 'the will of the Father' – was not to lose any who had been given him by the Father (John 6:39); this work he did (John 17:12). Further, we hear him praying in the garden: 'O my Father, if it is possible, let this cup pass from me; nevertheless, not as I will, but as you will' (Matt. 26:39). It was just as he had said: 'I have come... to do your will, O God' (Heb. 10:5-7,9). And he completely fulfilled and accomplished all the work the Father had given him to do: 'I have glorified you on the earth. I have finished the work which you have given me to do' (John 17:4), 'I have accomplished it'. We hear it loud and clear in his triumphant cry on the cross, 'It is finished' (John 19:30), 'it is accomplished'.

In short, Christ did the works of God; that is, he did those works (John 14:31; 15:10) and said those words (John 12:49; 14:10,24) which God commanded him, which God required of him, and which pleased the Father (John 10:37). But it was Christ himself who did the works. While they were 'the works of God', they were *Christ's own* works.[12]

In John 6:28-29, therefore, the Jews were asking, as William Gurnall put it, about 'that part of his will which above all he desires should be done – called therefore with emphasis "the work of God" (John 6:29)'.[13] And this is what Christ meant when he told them to believe. God requires you to believe, he told them. In short, Christ preached duty faith.

The principle is established: God requires sinners to believe; it is their duty; it is what pleases him.

Ella, however, did not agree. The people, he thought, were asking Christ 'what is to be done so that they might be sealed and be given everlasting food'. No! The people were not asking *what needed to be done*, but *what they needed to do*. 'What shall *we* do, that *we* may work the works of God?'[14] As Ella said: '"You must believe in me", Christ tells them'. At which point, Ella dragged a red-herring across the track: 'Christ's hearers do not ask him how they can work to obtain this belief'. I agree. There is not the slightest suggestion of it in the passage. What is more, in the free

---

[12] To cap it all, Christ promised his disciples, 'He who believes in me, the works that I do he will do also; and greater works than these he will do' (John 14:12). And when we come to sanctification, believers – who are God's 'workmanship' – produce 'good works, which God prepared beforehand'. But, I emphasise, believers do the good works. God doesn't. 'We are his workmanship, created in Christ Jesus for good works, which God prepared beforehand that *we* should walk in them' (Eph. 2:10). See also Phil. 2:12-13. Of course, believers can only do the works by God's grace, but the point stands; believers do the works.

[13] Gurnall Vol.2 pp49-50. The Jews said 'works' (τα εργα). Jesus replied 'work' (το εργον).

[14] They were using the active voice, not the passive.

offer, in duty faith, there is not a hint that any sinner can work to obtain faith. But this is irrelevant. As Ella said, this is what they did *not* ask. So what *did* they ask? That is the question. Ella again: They ask 'how Jesus will work to give them that belief', the work God will do. No! I have already answered this. Are we to understand they sincerely wanted to believe, and knew Christ would have to give them faith, but they did not know how he would work to give them that faith? The notion is so far removed from reality, words fail.[15] The fact is, they were asking what works *they* had to do, not what works *Christ* would do. Ella, however, cited John 6:30 as proof of his point.[16] Yet, once again, this is irrelevant. The Jews opening question came in John 6:28: What do we have to do? Christ's answer came in John 6:29: You must believe. In John 6:30, the Jews were trying to side-step Jesus' doctrine – by demanding a sign from Christ – *after* he had told them what they must do. They were trying to divert his attention; they were on the defensive. And the best form of defence? Attack! The Jews took this route.[17] 'You talk about what we have to do. What will *you* do?' they snapped. 'What work will you do?' (John 6:30). 'You're quick enough to tell us about what we have to do, to tell us our work; what's yours?' All this is a far cry from asking

---

[15] Note how hyper-Calvinists are obsessed with a sinner's doctrinal understanding before conversion. Their demand for 'sensibility', for instance, means the sinner has to be persuaded of his regeneration, repentance and desire for Christ, before believing. Quite a list! Here, it is claimed, unbelievers are curious about how God will give them faith! But none of this is the unbeliever's concern; he has to trust Christ! See Murray: *Spurgeon* p72. By a 'hyper-Calvinist', I mean one who does not hold with the free offer, who does not hold with duty faith. Some hyper-Calvinists are knowingly so, but many are what I call 'incipient' or *de facto* hypers; that is, while they accept the principles of the free offer, in practice they fail to preach it. See chapter 9. Unfortunately, the word 'hyper' makes it sound as though it is a 'superior', 'stronger' sort of Calvinism; it would be better thought of as 'exaggerated', 'false' or 'defective' Calvinism. See Spurgeon: *New* Vol.4 p341; *New and Metropolitan* Vol.7 p302; Murray: *Spurgeon* pp39-40.

[16] Ella: *The Free Offer* pp55,61.

[17] Just like the woman at Jacob's well who struggled hard, in as many ways as she could think of, to attack Jesus or divert him (John 4:9,12,20,25).

sincere questions about how Christ would work saving faith in them, or how 'they might be sealed and be given everlasting food'.

Ella was wrong. The Jews were asking what works they had to do in order to please God. John Brine conceded as much. He said the work was not something which God did in them but it was 'an act acceptable and pleasing to God'. And Gill agreed. It is something which is enjoined by God's 'will and commandment', he said.[18] Calvin rightly said the men in John 6 'ask what they ought to do', and 'by "the works of God" we must understand those [works] which God demands, and of which he approves'. Calvin went on to explain 'that faith alone is sufficient, because this alone does God require of us, that we believe'. He then dealt with that misunderstanding I raised a few moments ago: 'Those who infer from this passage that faith is the gift of God are mistaken; for Christ does not [here] show what God produces in us, but what he wishes and requires from us'.[19]

Ella missed the point. The work in question is that which God requires of sinners; it is their duty. And Christ told them that God requires faith.

2. But what is the faith which pleases God?

As Ella said, Christ told the people: 'You must believe in me'.[20] I agree. But what sort of faith was he demanding? There are different kinds of faith.[21] Was Christ calling for saving faith, or what? If it was saving faith, since he told the people God requires faith, the principle of duty faith is established. But did Christ demand saving faith?

Ella had no doubt about it; Christ meant saving faith.[22] Once again, I agree. In the context, Christ was speaking of 'everlasting life' (John 6:27,40,47,51,54,58); of the one 'who comes to me'

---

[18] Both quoted by Fuller: *Defence* in *Works* p197.

[19] Calvin: *Commentaries* Vol.17 Part 2 pp243-244. Faith *is* the gift of God, of course, but it is not what Christ was saying in John 6:29.

[20] Ella: *The Free Offer* p55.

[21] In particular, historical faith is an acceptance of the facts of the gospel (Mark 1:24; Acts 26:27; Jas. 2:19); saving faith is trusting Christ.

[22] Ella: *The Free Offer* pp54-55,61.

(John 6:35,37,44,45); of the elect (John 6:39); of irresistible and essential grace (John 6:44); of being 'taught by God' (John 6:45); of the atonement (John 6:51); of 'eating [Christ's] flesh and drinking his blood' (John 6:53-58); of 'believing' (John 6:29,35,36,47,64); of regeneration (John 6:63); and so on. Christ could be speaking of nothing but saving faith.

Calvin was of this opinion.[23] Matthew Poole likewise: 'Our Lord calls them to a work they never thought of, the owning and acknowledgement of him to be the true Messiah; the embracing and receiving him as such, and trusting him with all the concerns of their souls... This our Saviour calls "the work of God", in answer to what they had said'.[24] Matthew Henry: 'That faith is the work of God which closes with Christ, and relies upon him'.[25] Owen also saw it as saving faith, calling it the 'fundamental act of faith, whereby we close with Christ, whereby we receive him'. He referred to John 6:29, saying, 'the act, work, or duty of faith, in the receiving of Christ... is not to be reckoned unto... common duties... but the soul must find out wherein it has in a singular manner closed with Christ upon the command of God'.[26] To please God, sinners must believe savingly in Christ. Indeed, as Fuller said, not only is believing a duty which will please God, but 'this is the first and greatest of all duties'.[27]

Gill did not agree with this; saving faith was not the issue, he said. Christ, he alleged, was replying to a request by the Jews as to whether he had any other laws to give them in addition to the laws of Moses, in order that they might do them to please God. Gill thought 'believing in Christ, is believing in God that sent him'.[28] But Christ was saying nothing of the sort. Whereas Gill claimed Christ demands that sinners believe in the one who did the sending, Christ said God commands sinners to believe in the one who was

---

[23] Calvin: *Commentaries* Vol.17 Part 2 pp244-245.

[24] Poole pp308-309.

[25] Matthew Henry.

[26] Owen: *Meditations* in *Works* Vol.1 pp427-428.

[27] Fuller: *Worthy* in *Works* p158. Quoted and dismissed by Ella (Ella: *The Free Offer* pp54-55).

[28] Gill: *Commentary* Vol.5 p654.

sent![29]

Goodwin, even though he made the same point as Gill about Moses' law, unlike Gill, was in no doubt about the real issue. Christ was teaching, said Goodwin, 'that which is acceptable to God, which God delights in... [Christ] puts them upon believing alone... [and] immediately... he puts them upon believing'.[30] And Goodwin meant saving faith.

But Gill did not give up easily. On John 6:37 – the same context – he wrote: 'The Jews might be reasonably accused for not believing on [Christ] as the Messiah'; this, Gill defined as 'a bare assent to him as such'.[31] In saying this, he avoided the crux of Christ's demand by taking the escape route of historical faith,[32] rejecting the claim that Christ was speaking of saving faith – the very thing Christ *was* insisting on.

What is more, Gill contradicted himself, for when writing on Acts 16:31 he described the faith Paul spoke of as being 'much the same' as the faith in John 6:29.[33] He further said the faith which Paul commanded the jailer to exercise was not 'a bare historical faith, as only to believe that [Christ] was the Son of God, and the Messiah... but so as to look unto him alone for life and salvation, to rely upon him, and trust in him; to commit himself, and the care of his immortal soul unto him, and to expect peace, pardon, righteousness, and eternal life from him'.[34] Gill was right on Acts 16 and wrong on John 6. So which kind of faith did he think it was – historical or saving? Did Christ tell these sinners that God

---

[29] They asked what sign Jesus would perform that they might believe *him* (John 6:30). He told them it was *he himself*, 'the bread from heaven... the bread of God', they had to be concerned about, telling them again and again they had to come to *him*, believe in *him*, see (that is, look to) *him*, eat *his* flesh and drink *his* blood (John 6:32-33,35-40,44-58).

[30] Goodwin p584.

[31] Gill: *Cause* p87.

[32] See note above.

[33] If so, and I agree with Gill, then Paul made the same demand of the jailer (a sensible sinner, I presume), as Christ did of the Jews (non-sensible sinners – see below); namely, saving faith. In other words, God requires saving faith of sinners whether or not they are sensible. My point exactly!

[34] Gill: *Commentary* Vol.5 p930.

demanded faith, but not saving faith, only historical faith? that God was looking for a bare mental assent? Is this what Christ meant? Is God satisfied when men get as far as agreeing that Jesus is the Messiah? Is this the faith which God demands? To ask such questions is to answer them.

Brine, unlike Gill, did not try to deny the obvious. He agreed it is saving faith which Christ referred to. But he had another way of trying to side-step the inevitable. He said all Christ was doing was *telling* sinners what it is that God requires; he was not *commanding* sinners to do anything. How lame, how desperate, an argument! If Christ tells men what God requires of them, then God in Christ is actually commanding those men. Will hyper-Calvinists not face up to it? In the following, note Brine's use of the word 'declaration' in his attempt to get round the idea of 'command' and 'duty'.[35] Brine alleged:

The words contain a declaration that believing in Christ for salvation is necessary to the enjoyment of eternal life, and that faith in him is an act acceptable and pleasing to God; but afford no proof that it is required of men in a state of unregeneracy. To declare to unregenerate persons the necessity of faith in order to salvation, which is what our blessed Lord here does, falls very far short of asserting it to be their present duty.[36]

Now by this, as Fuller pointed out, Brine shot himself in the foot. *First*, Brine agreed that Christ was speaking to the unregenerate; he was not addressing sensible sinners. This is most important; I will come back to it in a moment. *Secondly*, Brine acknowledged that Christ was talking about saving faith; this is the point we are looking at now. *Thirdly*, Brine agreed that the work was not God's own work but the work he requires of sinners, that which pleases him; in other words, the first point above. In this way, Brine here destroyed the hyper-Calvinistic case he tried so hard to build. He allowed that unregenerate sinners were addressed on the subject of saving faith, and that unregenerate sinners were told saving faith is

---

[35] A preacher must 'declare', of course, but he must also 'command', 'beseech', 'urge', 'invite', and so on. Sinners need to be told the facts of the gospel, yes, but they also need to be commanded to believe, and urged to come to Christ. See chapter 9.

[36] See Fuller: *Worthy* in *Works* p158.

what God requires, that saving faith is necessary for salvation. The only way Brine could evade the consequence of his correct analysis was to say that Christ was simply making a factual statement about faith; he was not demanding it of his hearers.

But it will not wash. The sinners who spoke to Christ wanted to know how they could please God – how *they* could please God, mark you – 'that *we* may work the works of God', they said. They were not looking for an abstract declaration of how certain sorts of sinners under various specified conditions might work the works of God. They were asking for *themselves*: Tell us what *we* have to do. I do not say their motives were pure,[37] but I do say they were not speaking in theoretical terms. They were asking a practical question: What is our God-ward duty? What does God require of us? This is it, said Christ, believe on me! And Christ did not merely *describe* their duty; he told them what they must do to please God. In other words, he told them their duty. This is what they had to do!

It is impossible to avoid the conclusion that Christ was preaching duty faith here. Just because Jesus did not use the word 'command' it does not mean he was not commanding his hearers. What else was he doing? They asked what their duty was; Christ told them. And their duty was savingly to believe. Some who deny duty faith seem to think that Christ was prepared to deal in generalities and abstract theories, when we know he came into the world to seek and to save sinners. He addressed men in the second person, and did so in the imperative, the commanding mood. This is the essence of John 6:28-29. Christ did not say merely that God is pleased when men believe. What he said was: This is what *you* must do!

Thus the passage teaches that to exercise saving faith in Christ is the sinner's duty.

3. Were they sensible sinners who asked the question and who were told their duty?

As I have hinted, those who asked Christ about 'the works of God'

---

[37] See my comments above on the way they wanted to divert Christ.

were far from sensible sinners who were sincerely interested in salvation. Indeed, as I have said, they were attacking Christ in order to ward off his penetrating demand. A few moments ago, I showed how Brine admitted they were unregenerate, and Poole considered the believing in question was 'a work they never thought of'. Indeed, it is utterly self evident.[38] The men who asked the question, the men to whom Christ directed his reply, were carnal men who were interested in Christ only because he could give them bread (John 6:26). They certainly did not believe, no, not even after Christ had commanded them (John 6:36). Having been told in no uncertain terms that they ought to believe, they did not like it, and immediately tried to side-track Jesus, and get him on to Moses and the manna – anything but face up to Christ's call for faith (John 6:30-31).[39] They either showed a preoccupation with a full stomach or mocked Christ by demanding bread (John 6:34). When Christ rebuked them for their lack of faith (John 6:36), they 'murmured [grumbled] against him', 'complained about him' (John 6:41,43), and belittled him (John 6:42). And when they found out what was involved in trusting Christ, it was the last straw; the sheer spirituality of the commitment he was demanding of them totally exposed them as carnal and rebellious, men who had no more time for him (John 6:66). Alford: 'The seeking [of Christ]... was merely a low desire to profit by his wonderful works, not a reasonable consequence of deduction from his miracles that he was the Saviour of the world'. Alford called it 'this low desire of mere satisfaction of their carnal appetite'.[40]

Were they sensible sinners? Were they repentant? They were not!

Yet these were the very sinners whom Christ addressed concerning their spiritual duty. He commanded these very men to believe savingly, men who had their minds set on earthly, carnal

---

[38] 'They do not understand what they say, and talk without any definite object' (Calvin: *Commentaries* Vol.17 Part 2 p243). I do not agree with Matthew Henry when he said: 'I... take it as a humble serious question, showing them to be... willing to know and do their duty'. Christ was telling them their duty, but they didn't want to hear it!

[39] See above for more on the way they tried to divert Christ.

[40] Alford p517.

satisfaction (John 6:26-27). Indeed, their question about wanting to know the work which would please God was an attacking reply to Christ's rebuke of their carnality. 'You only sought me because you wanted bread. Get your priorities right; set your minds and hearts on everlasting life, not mere bread', Christ told them. 'What do you want us to do?' they retorted. 'Your first and greatest duty is to believe in me', said Christ. To claim these were sensible sinners is ludicrous. To deduce that only sensible sinners may be commanded in the gospel, is to miss the target by a mile.[41]

The evasions will not stand up. Christ did not say God commands sinners to exercise natural faith[42] and repentance. Nor can it be said God merely encourages sinners by his commands. Nor is it enough to say we must merely declare and describe the way of salvation to sinners. Nor is it sufficient to tell sinners God alone can give them repentance and faith. Of course this last is true, and of course we must let sinners know it. But this is not enough. Far from it. God, in the gospel, commands all sinners to believe savingly. To use Ella's words – which he limited to repentance: 'Sinners must be... commanded'.[43] So they must! And they must be commanded to believe, to trust Christ for salvation. Preachers must command sinners in no uncertain tones. Faith is what God requires of all sinners. Faith, therefore, must be the duty of all sinners. Since all men are created by God, it is the duty of all men – not just sensible, repentant sinners – to please him. Consequently, since it pleases God when men believe in the one whom he sent, it must be the duty of all sinners to trust Christ. All men are *obliged* to please God, for it cannot be indifferent as to whether or not men please him. Thus all men are obliged to trust Christ.

In short, faith is every sinner's duty because God commands every sinner to believe.

There is a further point to be made. Not only is it the duty of sinners to believe, it is the duty of preachers to command them to believe. Now if preachers fail in this, but rather keep telling their

---

[41] See Appendix 2.

[42] For instance, a man exercises 'natural' faith when he sits on a chair, believing it will bear his weight.

[43] Ella: *The Free Offer* p71.

hearers they have no power to believe, it is little wonder if such an unbalanced presentation of the truth leads sinners to lose all sense of urgency and, even worse, feel somewhat excused for their unbelief and lack of repentance. Indeed, instead of being awakened to seek for mercy and so escape the wrath to come, they might well be encouraged to stay where they are, feel justified in their lack of response, and think themselves, not so much objects of wrath, but objects of pity. The harm to such sinners, and the accountability of such preachers, will be great.

* * *

There are many other passages of Scripture which ought to be looked at in detail, but for lack of space I must move on to glance at what others have said on the subject of duty faith. As I have already made clear, I do not do this to establish principles – I have tried to do this from Scripture – but I think it is important to know that many undisputed Calvinists have held – and still hold – to duty faith.

4

Some Testimonies Concerning Duty Faith

What have other Calvinists[1] said about duty faith?
    Arthur Pink:

It is the binding obligation of those claiming to be called of God to preach, to exhort unbelievers and believers, realising that it rests entirely in the hands of a sovereign God to make [it] effectual... [The preacher] has no right whatever to pick and choose: his business is to 'declare *all* the counsel of God', and as Luke 24:47 and Acts 20:21 show, part of that 'counsel' is to call upon men to repent. If the ungodly are not pointedly and authoritatively called unto repentance of their sins and belief of the gospel, and if on the contrary they are only told that they are unable so to do, then they are encouraged in their impenitency and unbelief. If the gospel [preacher] gives such a disproportionate presentation of the truth that the unconverted are made to feel they are more to be pitied than blamed for their spiritual impotency, then their responsibility is undermined and their conscience is lulled to sleep. To the objection that to call upon the unregenerate to turn from the world and come to Christ is to inculcate creature-ability and to feed self-righteousness, we ask, Were Christ and his Spirit-taught apostles ignorant of this danger? Was it left for the 18th and 19th centuries to make such a discovery? Were men so mightily used of God as Jonathan Edwards, George Whitefield, and C.H.Spurgeon wrong, when, in promiscuously exhorting all their hearers to flee from the wrath to come, they followed the example of John the Baptist and the Son of God?[2]

Matthew Henry, commenting on Psalm 2, said: 'To welcome Jesus Christ and to submit to him... is the great *duty* of the Christian religion; it is that which is required of all... Our *duty* to Christ is

---

[1] Some may dispute the Calvinism of some of the following – but surely not all of them?

[2] Murray: *Pink* pp232-233, emphasis Pink's. Unless otherwise specified, in this series of extracts the emphasis is mine.

here expressed'.

Fuller concluded his comments on Psalm 2:11-12 thus: 'The result is, unconverted sinners are commanded to believe in Christ for salvation; therefore believing in Christ for salvation is their *duty*'. Moving immediately on to Isaiah 55:1-7, linking it with 'repentance toward God and faith toward our Lord Jesus Christ' (Acts 20:21), he said:

The encouragements held up to induce a compliance with this *duty* are the freeness, the substantial nature, the durableness, the certainty, and the rich abundance of those blessings which as many as repent and believe the gospel shall receive. The whole passage is exceedingly explicit, as to the *duty* of the unconverted; neither is it possible to evade the force of it by any just or fair method of interpretation.[3]

Robert S.Candlish directed men to 'take a right view of the *duty* of believing. It is not using a great liberty to believe on the name of Jesus'.[4]

Spurgeon spoke of 'a certain body of Ultra-Calvinists' who 'caricature the word of God', by preaching sovereign grace, but 'who are doing ten thousand times more harm than good, because they don't preach' human responsibility. Such men, he said, vilify 'those of us who teach that it is the *duty* of man to repent and believe'. As to his own position, Spurgeon certainly made good his claim that he preached duty faith:

It is mine... to exhort the sinner to come to Christ; it is the Holy Spirit's work to enforce the exhortation, and draw the sinner to Christ... Fly to Christ, and find mercy... I believe some of our hearers expect to feel an electric shock, or something of that kind, before they are saved. The gospel says simply: 'Believe'. That they will not understand. They think there is to be something so mysterious about it. They can't make out what it is; but they are going to wait for it and then believe. Well, you will wait till doomsday... Your position is this – you are a sinner, lost, ruined; you cannot help yourself. Scripture says: 'Jesus Christ came into the world to save sinners'. Your immediate business, your instantaneous *duty* is to cast yourself on that simple promise, and believe on the Lord Jesus Christ.

---

[3] Fuller: *Worthy* in *Works* p157.
[4] Candlish Vol.2 p59.

Again:

It is the *duty* of every man to believe on the Lord Jesus Christ. It is every man's solemn *duty* to trust Christ, not because of anything that man is, or is not, but because he is commanded to do it.

Yet again:

The only reason why you do not believe in Christ is because you will not... It is a gross lie to say that God is responsible for your damnation. If [you persist in unbelief and thus] your soul shall perish, it shall perish as a suicide; for you will have ruined yourself... You will see written in lines of fire: 'You knew your *duty*, but you did it not!' and when you cry for mercy this shall be God's answer: 'I called and you refused, I stretched out my hand and no man regarded it; I also will laugh at your calamity; I will mock when your fear comes'.

And once more:

The faith here intended [1 John 5:1] is the *duty* of all men... It can never be less than man's *duty* to believe the truth; that Jesus is the Christ is the truth, and it is the *duty* of every man to believe it. I understand here by 'believing', confidence in Christ, and it is surely the *duty* of men to confide in that which is worthy of confidence, and that Jesus Christ is worthy of the confidence of all men is certain, it is therefore the *duty* of men to confide in him. Inasmuch as the gospel command, 'Believe in the Lord Jesus Christ and you shall be saved', is addressed by divine authority to every creature, it is the *duty* of every man so to do... I know there are some who will deny this, and deny it upon the ground that man has not the spiritual ability to believe in Jesus, to which I reply that it is altogether an error to imagine that the measure of the sinner's moral ability is the measure of his *duty*... The command of Christ stands... and when he commands all men everywhere to repent, they are bound to repent... In every case it is man's *duty* to do what God bids him.[5]

Indeed, Spurgeon, far from apologising for duty faith, extolled God's mercy to sinners in establishing the principle: 'Faith in Christ... is a commanded *duty* as well as a blessed privilege, and what a mercy it is that it is a *duty*'. Why?

---

[5] Spurgeon: *New* Vol.4 p341; see also p344; Vol.5 p79; see also p247; Vol.6 p107; *Metropolitan* Vol.9 pp357-358; Vol.17 pp136-137; see also Vol.15 p626; Vol.20 pp125-127.

Because there never can be any question but that a man has a right to do his *duty*. Now on the ground that God commands me to believe, I have a right to believe, be I who I may. The gospel is sent to every creature. Well, I belong to that tribe; I am one of the every creatures, and that gospel commands me to believe, and I do it. I cannot have done wrong in doing it for I was commanded to do so. I cannot be wrong in obeying a command of God. Now it is a command of God given to every creature that he should believe on Jesus Christ whom God has sent. This is your warrant, sinner, and a blessed warrant it is, for it is one which hell cannot gainsay, and which heaven cannot withdraw. You need not be looking within to look for the misty warrants of your experience... to get some dull and insufficient warrants for your confidence in Christ. You may believe Christ because he tells you to do so. That is a sure ground to stand on, and one which admits of no doubt.[6]

J.L.Dagg:

Reason teaches that it is the *duty* of men, as sinners, to repent of their sins... But the *duty* of repentance is not left to be inferred from the common sense of mankind... When the gospel began to be preached, its first proclamation was, 'Repent, for the kingdom of heaven is at hand'. In all the ministry of the gospel, this is the first *duty* required of men. Without it, not a step can be taken in the way of return to God; and, without it, there is no possibility of obtaining the divine favour...
In close connection with repentance for sin, the word of God enjoins the *duty* of believing in Christ... Both the *duties* relate to men as sinners, and without the performance of them, escape from the penalty of sin is impossible.[7]

William B.Sprague: 'All will admit that it is the *duty* of a sinner to repent without delay'.[8]

Alvan Hyde: 'Christ and his apostles... in their preaching... inculcated repentance and submission to God, as the immediate *duty* of sinners'.[9]

The Sum of Saving Knowledge: 'Everyone who hears the gospel

---

[6] Spurgeon: *New and Metropolitan* Vol.7 p110.

[7] Dagg pp139-140,175.

[8] Sprague p179. I wish Sprague had been right; not all do admit the truth of what he said.

[9] Sprague p55 in the Appendix to Sprague's book. Hyde also emphasised 'duty'.

must make conscience of the *duty* of lively faith in Christ; the weak believer must not think it presumption to do what is commanded... Indeed, the most impenitent, profane, and wicked person must not thrust out himself, or be thrust out by others, from orderly aiming at this *duty*, how desperate soever his condition seems to be'.[10]

Simon Ash, James Nalton and Joseph Church: 'Seeking of Christ is the soul's *duty*'.[11]

The Helvetic Canons number XIX:

Likewise the external call itself, which is made by the preaching of the gospel, is on the part of God also, who calls, earnest and sincere. For in his word he unfolds earnestly and most truly, not, indeed, his secret intention respecting the salvation or destruction of each individual, but what belongs to our *duty*, and what remains for us if we do or neglect this *duty*... God always attains that which he intends in his will, even the demonstration of *duty*, and following this, either the salvation of the elect who do their *duty*, or the inexcusableness of the rest who neglect the *duty* set before them.[12]

William Gouge:

The *duty* which the [writer of Heb. 2:1] presses upon himself and others, as a matter of necessity, is to 'give earnest heed to the things which they had heard'. Hereby he means the gospel... He calls upon them to give heed thereto... and [he] intends more than a bare hearing... This being applied to God's word, is opposed to all manner of slighting it, whether by contempt or neglect of it. He that despises the word of the Lord... and they that turn away their ears from the truth... and they that make light of the offer of grace (Matt. 22:4-5)... do all of them that which is contrary to this *duty*; they do not give such heed to the word as is here required. The *duty* here intended is a serious, firm, and fixed setting of the mind upon that which we hear; a bowing and bending of the will to yield unto it; an applying of the heart to it; a placing of the affections upon it; and bringing the whole man into a holy conformity to it. Thus it comprises knowledge of the word, faith therein, obedience thereto, and all other due respect that may [in] any way concern it.[13]

---

[10] *The Sum* p336.

[11] Preface to Sibbes: *Heavenly* in *Works* Vol.6 p416.

[12] Hodge p661.

[13] Gouge p91.

Later, Gouge spoke about 'coming to God', which, as he explained, is the seeking of salvation by faith in Christ. Of this he said: 'This *duty* is enjoined to raise up in us a desire of salvation, and an expectation thereof'.[14]

Giles Firmin: 'It is the *duty* of all the sons and daughters of Adam, who hear the gospel preached, and Christ offered to them, to believe in [or, on], or receive Christ, whether they be prepared or not prepared'.[15]

James Durham, on Isaiah 53:1: 'The *duty* that lies on people to whom the Lord sends the gospel, or this report concerning Christ... that it lies on all who hear the gospel, to believe the report that it brings concerning Christ, and by faith to receive him... The complaint [of the prophet] is for the neglect of the *duty* they were called to... They, to whom Christ is offered in the gospel, are called to believe; it is their *duty* to do it; thus, believing, in all that hear this gospel, is necessary, by necessity of command'.[16]

William Kiffin: Although it is 'certain no man can, without the assistance of the Holy Spirit, either repent or believe, yet it will not therefore follow, that lack of repentance and unbelief are no sins; if these be sins, then the contrary must be their *duty*'.[17]

Thomas Boston:

Before a sinner will come to Christ by believing, he must be an awakened, convinced, sensible sinner; pricked in his heart with a sense of sin and misery; made to groan under his burden, to despair of relief from the law, himself, or any other creature, and to desire and thirst after Christ and his righteousness... These things also are required of the sinner in point of *duty*.[18]

---

[14] Gouge p527.

[15] Hulse p16.

[16] Durham p11.

[17] Naylor pp149-150.

[18] Boston: *Marrow* pp141-142. Yes, Boston spoke of the 'sensible sinner': 'Before a sinner will come to Christ by believing, he must be... an awakened, convinced, sensible sinner', and so on. Yes, only sensible sinners will come to Christ. But as Boston said, 'these things also are required of the sinner' – the sinner, not only the sensible sinner – 'in point of duty'. A sinner must be sensible before he comes to Christ, *but not before he is commanded or required to come*. Even those who opposed the Marrow men in Scotland still 'held to an obligation to believe in

David Clarkson: 'It is the great concern of sinners, and their *duty* too, to come unto Christ, to seek him'.[19]

Owen declared that God's ministers must:

Command and invite all to repent and believe... And when they make proffers and tenders in the name of God to all, they do not say to all, 'It is the purpose and intention of God that you should believe', (who gave them any such power [or right]?) but, that it is his command, which makes it their *duty* to do what is required of them... The external offer is such as from which every man may conclude his own *duty*; [but from which] none [may conclude] God's purpose, which yet may be known upon performance of his *duty*... This offer is neither vain nor fruitless, being declarative of their *duty*, and of what is acceptable to God if it be performed as it ought to be, even as it is required.[20]

Owen also asked:

When the apostle beseeches us to be "reconciled unto God", I would know whether it be not a part of our *duty* to yield obedience to the apostle's exhortation? If not, his exhortation is frivolous and vain; [but] if [we do have to yield obedience to it], then to be reconciled unto God is a part of our *duty*.[21]

What is more, Owen was not interested in proving merely that God will forgive sinners if they believe. Of course he will, but that was not the point Owen was making here. Far from it! Rather, as he bluntly stated:

[Christ is] by the command of God laid upon all men to whom the word comes' (Macleod p166).

[19] Clarkson: *Invitation* in *Works* Vol.2 p37. I have, with great reluctance, omitted Clarkson: *Faith* in *Works* Vol.1 pp89-91,96-97,132. Although in this work he said some excellent things on the duty of faith, I would have to digress too far into preparationism to deal with Clarkson's references to 'the sensible sinner', and his going beyond Scripture in the matter, where he was not as guarded as Boston above. Even so, Clarkson was clear; there is 'the general command to believe'. Having spoken of 'the misery of unbelievers', Clarkson spoke of 'exhortation. This should excite sinners' – not only sensible sinners – ' to mind this duty... Believing [is] the duty... To believe is... a duty'.

[20] Owen: *Death* in *Works* Vol.10 pp300-301; see also pp404-410.

[21] Owen: *Display* in *Works* Vol.10 p102. See also Fuller: *Worthy* in *Works* p161.

We ought to believe; it is our *duty* so to do... but we scarce think it our *duty* to believe the forgiveness of our sins. It is well, it may be, we think, with them that can do it; but we think it [is] not their fault who do not. Such persons may be pitied, but, as we suppose, not justly blamed.

Obviously, argued Owen, this is wrong, for:

What can be required to make anything a *duty* unto us that is wanting in this matter? for... what [God] declares, it is our *duty* to believe, or we frustrate the end of his revelation... We are expressly commanded to believe, and that upon the highest promises and under the greatest penalties. This command is that which makes believing... a *duty*. Faith is a grace, as it is freely wrought in us by the Holy Ghost... but as it is commanded, it is a *duty*. And these commands... are several ways expressed, by invitations, exhortations, propositions; which all have in them the nature of commands, which take up a great part of the books of the New Testament.[22]

Owen again:

The terms of the gospel are of two sorts: (1) Such as are proposed unto us; (2) Such as thereon are required of us. Those proposed unto us include the whole mystery of the salvation of sinners by Jesus Christ, unto the praise and glory of God. Those of the latter sort are faith, repentance, and new obedience.[23]

---

[22] Owen: *Psalm 130* in *Works* Vol.6 p504. When Owen wrote: Saving faith '*is not required of us*, cannot be acted by us, but on a supposition of the work and effect of the law in the conviction of sin, by giving the knowledge of it, a sense of its guilt, and the state of the sinner on the account thereof', he was answering the question: 'What is necessary to be found in us before our believing?' 'Conviction of sin is a necessary antecedent unto justifying faith... [It] is required unto believing', he said, and spoke of 'the necessity of this conviction previous unto believing' (Owen: *Justification* in *Works* Vol.5 pp74-76, emphasis mine). In my forthcoming book on the law, I will examine the idea of conviction by the law, but, leaving that aside, Owen was saying a sinner must be convicted before he believes. In this he was right. A sinner must be convicted before he *will* or *can* believe, but not before he is *commanded* to believe. Owen freely offered Christ to all sorts of sinners (see, for instance, Owen: *Psalm 130* in *Works* Vol.6 pp521-523): 'We invite... all men as sinners'; as sinners, please note, not as *convicted* sinners.
[23] Owen: *Hebrews* Vol.4 Part 2 p359, commenting on Heb. 12:25-27.

In short: 'To believe in [Christ], to believe on his name, is that signal especial *duty* which is now required of us'.[24]

Owen thought highly of William Guthrie's *The Christian's Great Interest*: Though 'I have written several folios', he said, 'there is more divinity in [Guthrie's small volume] than in them all'.[25] High praise indeed! In the light of this, it is most interesting to discover what Guthrie wrote on *The Duty of Closing with God's Plan of Saving Sinners by Christ Jesus*. If men would secure their state, Guthrie declared, they must immediately 'with all diligence, personally and heartily... accept of and close with God's device of saving sinners by Christ Jesus, held out in the gospel... [because] it is the necessary *duty* of those who would be in favour with God and secure their souls'. Guthrie explained 'what is... required of those who perform this *duty*, [and] what are the qualifications and properties of this *duty*, if rightly managed, [and] what are the... consequences of it, if it is performed aright'. He observed that sin has cut man off from 'God's favour', put him under God's 'curse and wrath', and made him powerless 'to regain the Lord's friendship', but the Lord has sent his Son to die 'for the sins of the elect, and to restore in them his image', and to bring them to glory.

Furthermore:

He has made open proclamation... that whosoever will lay aside all thoughts of saving themselves... and will agree heartily to be saved by Christ Jesus, they... shall be saved. So then, to close with God's device of saving sinners by Christ Jesus, is to quit and renounce all thoughts of help or salvation by our own righteousness, and to agree to this way which God has found out [that is, planned and revealed]; it is to value and highly esteem Christ Jesus as the treasure... to enrich poor sinners; and with the heart to believe this record... It is to approve this plan and acquiesce in it, as the only way to true happiness; it is to point towards this Mediator, as God holds him out in the gospel, with a desire to lay the stress of our whole state upon him. This is that which is called faith or believing, the 'receiving of Christ', or 'believing on his name' (John 1:12). This is that 'believing on the Lord Jesus Christ', commanded to the jailer... (Acts 16:31)... This is supposed in all those ordinary actings of faith to which promises are annexed in the Scripture...

---

[24] Owen: *Declaration* in *Works* Vol.1 p126.
[25] W.Grant in the Preface to Guthrie.

This is the *duty* of those who would be saved... this is the necessary *duty* of all such as would be in favour with God and secure their souls... This closing with God's device, or believing in Christ, is commanded everywhere in Scripture by the Lord as the condition of the new covenant, giving right and title to all the spiritual blessings of the same... This is commanded... (Isa. 55:1... Matt. 11:28... 1 John 3:23). This is enough to prove it a *duty* incumbent. But further, it is such a *duty* as only gives right and title to a sonship; for only they who receive him are privileged to be sons... (John 1:12)... It [is seen] to be the necessary *duty* of all... it is a necessary *duty* lying upon us... it is a most necessary *duty* thus to close with Christ Jesus, as the blessed relief appointed for sinners.

Further:

It appears of how great consequence this *duty* of believing is, by which a man closes with Christ Jesus, whom the Father has sealed and given for a covenant to the people... God [has]... sovereignly commanded men so to close with him in and through Christ... and has commanded me, as I shall be answerable at the great day, to close with him in Christ, [with the consequence that] I dare not disobey, nor inquire into the reasons of his contrivance and commands, but must comply with the command... [and] not... 'frustrate the grace of God' (Gal. 2:21), and in a manner disappoint the gospel, and falsify the record which God has borne of his Son... (1 John 5:10-11), and so 'make God a liar', and add that rebellion to all my former transgressions.[26]

* * *

Reader, this is but a thimbleful dipped from an ocean of such material. Countless Calvinists down the years have commanded unregenerate sinners to repent and believe, telling them it is their immediate duty so to do. And how! Even though it seems foolish to exhort dead sinners to do anything, these preachers have commanded such to trust Christ. If our preaching is not marked by a sense of foolishness, it cannot be the gospel we preach (1 Cor. 1:18,21), nor are we preaching. The truth is, we are to tell sinners that though the gospel command does not imply their power, it most definitely spells out their responsibility. In other words, the sinners to whom we preach must be told that they are obliged to

---

[26] Guthrie pp132-137,162,164-165.

believe, even though they cannot believe by their own ability. And what is this but obliged faith? In other words, duty faith! Saving faith in Christ is the duty of all men. This is what so many Calvinists have asserted, and still do assert, because it is a vital part of preaching the gospel.

Thus, by denying duty faith, Ella is out-of-step with a great many Calvinists. This in itself does not mean he is wrong, but it needs to be recognised. The testimony of so many Calvinistic preachers asserting that all sinners have a duty to come to Christ, to repent of their sins and believe in him, and who certainly let their hearers know it, cannot be ignored. And it shows the wrongness of the claim that duty faith cannot be a part of a Calvinistic preacher's armoury. Look again at the insistence upon the duty of all sinners to trust Christ, as seen in the above. And, I assure you reader, it is but a tiny fraction of the material which could be cited.

Far more important, by denying duty faith, Ella is out-of-step with Scripture. And this is fatal to his case.

Sadly, with the rise of hyper-Calvinism in the early 1700s,[27] the seed of the denial of duty faith was sown, and we are reaping yet. But under preaching which stresses duty faith, sinners are confronted with their immediate, urgent duty to trust Christ, their duty to welcome him, to believe in him for salvation, to turn to him, to seek, desire and thirst after him and his righteousness, to have a living faith in him. Duty faith is a mighty sword in the preacher's hand, put there by God himself. As the preacher wields the blade, he cuts away the sinner's excuses, pressing him, forcing him to the clinching point: The Lord demands saving faith of me,

---

[27] In fact, some of the statements of some of the preachers pre-1700 smacked of hyper-Calvinism; they were answered. Determined to keep my book in bounds, take just one example – Goodwin's reply to the denial of duty faith. Teaching that 'though faith be... above all our abilities, yet God commands us to use our utmost endeavours to believe, and it is our duty so to do', Goodwin answered those who misuse Eph. 2:8 to avoid duty faith. He had in mind, not only those who tell sinners 'as good [as] sit still', or 'do nothing else but... stand and wait' because 'God must do all', but also the sinners themselves who are hindered from believing because 'they are discouraged and disheartened from all endeavours' by such teaching (Goodwin pp546-563).

and demands it now.

And there is something else. By the preaching of duty faith, not only is the sinner *driven* to Christ, he is *drawn* to him; that is, not only does the preacher *confront* the hardened sinner with his unbelief, but he also *encourages* the hesitant sinner to come to faith: Not only do I have the *duty* to trust Christ, I have the *right* to trust him; the fact that God commands me to believe, constitutes my warrant for believing; I need not be afraid to come, for God has commanded me to come. Those who deny duty faith stifle this encouragement, leaving the anxious sinner to flounder in a slough of uncertainty. Instead of looking to God's command and promise, and thus looking directly to Christ, he is left looking at himself to see if he is sensible.

Preachers who are not hampered by hyper-Calvinistic views can – or ought to – make earnest and urgent appeals,[28] calls, invitations and commands to sinners. On the basis of duty faith it can be done; it has been done. Sadly, it is done too little these days. So many preachers – mistakenly thinking they must safeguard their Reformed credentials, or else not seeing that a full-blooded Calvinism includes the free offer – stop short of preaching the gospel as it should be preached; the curse of *unwitting* or unconscious hyper-Calvinism is plaguing churches and preachers in this generation. When it comes to it, I fear that many a Reformed preacher is not preaching in such a way that his hearers are made to feel it is their immediate duty to trust Christ, though the preacher would profess vehemently he holds to the doctrine. In principle, he is persuaded of duty faith; in practice, he does not preach it. Oh! he informs his hearers of the necessity of faith, describes for them the benefits of faith, tells them it is faith alone which saves, warns them that they will perish if they do not believe, and so on. *But this is not preaching the gospel.* The preacher has to confront sinners with their immediate responsibility of trusting Christ, directly encourage them to trust him, and appeal to them to do so now! The sinner must not be allowed to feel he is just one in a crowd listening to a lecture on

---

[28] Such as 2 Cor. 5:20. We must not allow Arminians to high-jack and distort the biblical practice.

the gospel, that he can take it or leave it.[29] He needs eye-contact from a Nathan in the pulpit: 'You are the man!' (2 Sam. 12:7). Dying sinners lie as a heavy burden upon us, my brothers. If we do not preach the gospel properly, we shall have to answer to God for it.[30]

* * *

I wish I had more space to set out the biblical details and proofs of what I have been saying, but I have to forbear. May I just indicate what I would have liked to develop? The Bible reveals the principles of duty faith and requires us to preach it. What are the scriptural arguments for it? Why is it the duty of all sinners savingly to trust Christ and spiritually repent of their sins? I suggest five reasons. They are:

First, and foremost, it is the duty of sinners to believe savingly, because God has commanded sinners to do so. The same goes for repentance. What is more, God commands all sinners as sinners to believe and repent; he does not command sensible sinners only.

Second, it is the duty of sinners to believe savingly, because unbelief is scripturally defined as a sin. What is the connection between the two? Just this: Unbelief cannot be a sin unless faith is a duty.

Third, the immediate cause of damnation is unbelief; therefore belief must be a duty. The sinner must be responsible for not believing, having failed to meet his obligation to believe, otherwise he could not be condemned for not believing in Christ.

Fourth, saving faith is a duty because faith is defined in terms of obedience. Since obedience implies a command, to believe must be the sinner's duty.

Fifth, faith is a duty because faith is essential for salvation. God requires men to believe before they are saved. Hence it is their duty.

* * *

---

[29] Or wait until he knows he is sensible.

[30] Reader, I assure you, I do not exclude myself from the above. I will return to the point in chapter 9.

The alternative to duty faith, of course, is appalling; it must be faced. If God does not require sinners to believe, he must be indifferent to their unbelief; it cannot be of any consequence to him whether or not men believe. If God does not demand faith of sinners, faith must be optional. Is it? Certainly not! It is obligatory. Men are held responsible and counted guilty before God if they do not believe; it is sin (John 16:8-9), and they are condemned for it: 'He who does not believe is condemned already'. Why? 'Because he has not believed in the name of the only begotten Son of God' (John 3:18). 'Go into all the world and preach the gospel to every creature. He who believes and is baptised will be saved; but he who does not believe will be condemned' (Mark 16:15-16). See also 2 Thessalonians 2:10-12.[31]

Unbelief is laid at the sinner's door: '*You* do not believe... *You* are not willing to come to me that you may have life... *You* do not have the love of God in you... *You* do not receive me... But if [since] *you* do not believe [Moses'] writings, how will *you* believe my words?' (John 5:38-47). So said Christ.[32] God, as I have explained, does not do the believing for the sinner; the sinner has to believe. And when the sinner refuses to believe, it is *he* who is the unbeliever. He will never be able to lay the charge anywhere

---

[31] I have already quoted Berridge, commenting on Acts 16:31. Here is a fuller extract: 'Believe on the Lord Jesus Christ. Faith, as wrought in us by the Holy Ghost, is a grace of the Spirit; but as commanded in the word, it is a duty – a duty of high rank; and help may be had for its performance; and an utter failure in this duty is certain damnation. Yet men look upon unbelief as a misfortune, rather than a crime; as a sad disease, rather than a damning sin. Thus the conscience is not duly affected with its guilt; and men do not labour, as they ought, to be rid of unbelief. They complain of it, as a burden; but do not feel and lament it as the top sin that seals [their] damnation' (Berridge pp175-176). On Mark 5:36: 'Only believe. Faith, as wrought in us by the Holy Ghost, is a grace; but, as commanded, is a duty. Yet few consider it as a duty; and hence their conscience is not burdened with guilt for the non-performance of it; but consider unbelief, though the only damning sin, as their misfortune, rather than their crime... Believing is commanded' (Berridge p170). See also Owen: *Discourse* in *Works* Vol.3 pp289-291.
[32] How often Christ made the charge (John 3:12; 6:36,64; 8:45-46; 10:25-26,38, for example).

else but on himself alone. Certainly he will never be able to blame God's sovereignty.[33]

As White put it:

When a man pleads, 'I would believe, if I could', he is deceiving himself. It would be nearer the truth to say, 'I could believe if I would'. The fact is he does not want to believe, is not willing to accept salvation on such terms as it is offered in the Bible. He does not believe there is a God who so freely receives sinners; thus he makes God a liar, 'because he believes not the record that God has given of his Son' (1 John 5:10). What the sinner calls his inability to believe, God calls his guilt (John 3:18). Unbelief is wilful wickedness, a deliberate refusal to receive the testimony of God himself. It counts the ever-blessed God unworthy of credence. The man who says, 'I cannot believe!' must be met by the Lord's own words, 'You *will* not'.[34] He has not yet reached the *can*not; the *will* not is the real and present barrier. Depend upon it, what Christ said to Jerusalem of old, he will say to every one to whom the offer of salvation has been made [and who refuses it] – 'I would, but *you* would not'.[35]

I recall a cartoon, many years ago. A schoolmaster, cane in hand, was towering above a truculent youth. 'Wilberforce', the master

---

[33] Gill: 'Not coming to Christ, and believing in him, in [a] spiritual [that is, saving] manner, when he is revealed in the external ministry of the word, as God's way of salvation, is criminal and blameworthy, notwithstanding men's want of both will and power, since this does not arise from any decree of God, but from the corruption of nature through sin' (Gill: *Cause* p87). Robert Murray M'Cheyne: 'Think of the causes in yourselves, O unconverted souls! Be sure of this, that you will only have yourselves to blame if you awake in hell. You will not be able to plead God's secret decrees... you will be speechless. If you die, it is because you *will* die; and if you *will* die, then you must die' (Bonar: *M'Cheyne* p248, emphasis his).

[34] The point is elegantly illustrated in Matt. 21:27. When Christ asked the chief priests and elders about John the Baptist's authority, they said: 'We do not know', 'we *cannot* tell', when they really meant: 'We *will not* say', 'we *don't want* to say'. Christ, knowing this, replied: '*Neither will* I tell you [the answer to your question]'.

[35] White pp39-40, emphasis his. None of this goes against Christ's words: 'No one can come to me unless the Father who sent me draws him... No one can come to me unless it has been granted to him by my Father' (John 6:44,65).

was saying, 'some blame your genes; some blame your upbringing; some blame your environment; but I blame *you*!'

Faith is not optional; hence it must be every sinner's duty. A preacher must never let his hearers think it is anything else. If sinners try to excuse themselves by pleading unbelief or inability, he must bluntly tell them they condemn themselves out of their own mouth, and add to their condemnation. And this is made infinitely worse because they are refusing the most gracious invitation, the most generous offer, they will ever receive.[36]

So much for duty faith. Now for the second question.

---

[36] Take, for example, Clarkson. When dealing with this matter, he patiently answered the sinner's objections, but did not leave it there. He went on to what he called 'uses'. He had two: Reproof and exhortation (Clarkson: *Invitation* in *Works* Vol.2 pp79ff).

Part Two

God's Desire to Save Sinners

In chapter 5, I explain what I mean by a scriptural paradox, and show there are many such. In chapter 6, I address the particular paradox which concerns the free offer of the gospel; namely, the seeming conflict between God's desire to save all sinners and his decree to save his elect only. Chapters 7 and 8 set out the reasons for this and other biblical paradoxes – in chapter 7, I show that God often speaks as a man, and this leads to the concept of the twofold will of God, the theme of chapter 8. Whilst I do not intend to be patronising, reader, if you find these two chapters difficult on a first reading, it is possible to skip them and go straight to chapter 9, where I show what we should do with the free-offer paradox between God's decree and his desire. Chapter 10 is devoted to Spurgeon's testimony on the subject.

5

Paradoxes in Scripture

The paradox in question

I said there were two topics I wished to raise with Ella. The first was duty faith. I now turn to the second; that is, the scriptural paradox between God's decree to save his elect and his desire to save all sinners. By a paradox I mean 'a *seemingly* contradictory statement'.[1] There is nothing contradictory in Scripture, of course, but there are many things which *seem* so.

What, precisely, is the paradox between God's decree to save his elect and his desire to save all? It is this: If God desires the salvation of all sinners, why are they not all saved? We know the will of God is irresistible; he can do whatever he pleases (Ps. 115:3; 135:6; Isa. 46:10). So, I ask again, why are all sinners not saved – since God desires it? Here we have the nub of the question. As Calvin said: This is a 'knot for you to untie. Since no one but he who is drawn by the secret influence of the Spirit can approach unto God, how is it that God does not draw all men indiscriminately to himself, if he really "wills all men to be saved" (in the common meaning of the expression)?' The answer, according to Calvin, is to say 'there is with [God] a secret reason why he shuts so many out from salvation'.[2] In other words,

---

[1] See *Concise*, emphasis mine. A nice point of semantics arises here. According to J.I.Packer, I should be using the word 'antinomy' instead of 'paradox' (Packer pp18-21), but I have not adopted his suggestion. Although a paradox is merely a figure of speech – 2 Cor. 6:10; 12:10, for instance – in which the seeming contradiction arises out of the words and not the facts, and an antinomy is a contradiction in the facts themselves, I still prefer 'paradox'. The reason is, I am speaking of a *seeming* contradiction, whereas an antinomy *is* a contradiction. Packer himself had to introduce the idea of 'seeming' or 'apparent' in his definition of 'antinomy'.

[2] Calvin: *Calvin's Calvinism* pp277-278; see also same volume p117. See chapter 9 for more of Calvin's 'untying the knot'. When all is said and

although God openly reveals his desire to save all sinners, secretly he has determined not to satisfy this desire. This is the paradox with which we must grapple.

Thomas Manton spoke of 'the will and pleasure of God' in contrast to his intending decree, saying: 'God may be said to like the salvation of all men, yet not to intend it with an efficacious will'. This is true, for, as Manton said, even though God has not decreed to save all sinners, yet 'he is unfeignedly pleased with the salvation of men'.[3] This is the paradox.

But before I look at it in detail, let me show that this paradox is far from unique; the Bible records many such.

Biblical paradoxes in general

For instance: God has absolute control over kings; he can make them do whatever he pleases (Prov. 21:1). Scripture affords many examples of the fact (Ezra 6:22; 7:27; 9:9; Neh. 1:11; 2:4-9; Ps. 105:14-15; 106:46; Isa. 49:23 *etc.*), including ungodly kings (Gen. 20:6; 41:37-45; Ezra 1:1; Isa. 44:28; 45:1; Dan. 1:19; 2:48; 3:30; 6:1-3,28; John 19:10-11; Acts 4:25-28; Rev. 17:16-17 *etc.*) Yet in Psalm 2, God calls upon kings to trust Christ. God must be sincere in this call and command; it must represent his desire. Nevertheless, not all kings obey him. Indeed, according to Acts 4:25-27, 'Herod and Pontius Pilate' were included in the call, yet they were, as far as we can tell, reprobate, and never did 'serve the LORD with fear, and rejoice with trembling', they never did 'kiss the Son' (Ps. 2:11-12). The same may be said of kings in general. Clearly God could ensure their trust in Christ by decreeing it, but he does not. Thus, although he has commanded all kings to trust Christ, and in this he is utterly sincere – it would please him – he has not purposed it. This is a paradox.

Again: It was a sin for Israel to ask for a king (1 Sam. 12:17), but God must have purposed that they should have a king, for he gave them one (1 Sam. 15:1). It did not please him, nevertheless he decreed it. This is a paradox.

---

done, however, we are still left with a paradox to which, as he himself declared, we have to submit.

[3] Manton: *Complete* p465.

God moved David to number Israel but in so doing David acted foolishly under Satan's influence and sinned. God judged the people because of it, staying his hand only after David's prayer (2 Sam. 24:1,10,25; 1 Chron. 21:1). The episode is full of paradoxes.

God had appointed Ben-Hadad to utter destruction, but Ahab let him slip out of his hand, and God held him accountable for it (1 Kings 20:42). This is a paradox.

Jehu did the will of God, fulfilling the LORD's pleasure (2 Kings 9:7ff; 10:30), but he did it by means of half-truths, evasion, lies and deceit (2 Kings 9:11-12; 10:18-19); he engaged in false worship in order to deceive (2 Kings 10:19,25); he was guilty of conspiracy, treason and murder (2 Kings 9:14,23-27,33; 10:6-17). In this way, God carried out his will through him (2 Kings 9:25-26,36-37; 10:10,17), and commended Jehu for it (2 Kings 10:30) even though he was a hardened sinner who did not keep God's law (2 Kings 10:29,31). In all this, God was not tainted with Jehu's sin; nevertheless the paradox remains.

And what of the seeming conflict between human responsibility and God's decree? Christ was crucified by the sin of wicked men, yet it was in the purpose of God (Luke 22:22; John 19:11; Acts 2:23; 4:27-28). Joseph was sold into Egypt by his wicked brothers, but God had decreed it (Gen. 45:5-8; 50:20). What of the division of Israel into two kingdoms? It was of God, even though it was sinful. Jeroboam was responsible, he rebelled against Solomon (1 Kings 11:26-27), he wanted power (1 Kings 11:37), but it was God's decree he should do so (1 Kings 11:11-13,29-40). See also 1 Kings 11:14. Likewise, Esau sinned over his birthright. He was responsible (Heb. 12:16-17), but God's sovereign purpose was thus fulfilled (Rom. 9:11-13). These are paradoxes.

As Basil Manley Sr said:

The captivity and bondage of the Israelites in Egypt were fixed, to a day (Gen. 15:13; Ex. 12:41). Yet Pharaoh was exhorted to release them earlier, and that by divine direction. He ought to have obeyed; and, in that case, it would have been better for him. Moses and Aaron were told that he would not let the people go, at the time they were sent with a message from God to demand it. [Similarly] Ezekiel was told that the people would not hear him, yet [he was] commanded to go and exhort them (Ezek. 3:4-7). [And] the crucifixion of our Lord... was by 'the determinate counsel and foreknowledge of God' (Acts

3:23), yet the hands that slew him were 'wicked hands'... Salvation... was suspended on the fact that the Son of God should die. This fact was foreseen – predetermined. Yet, will any man say that the parties concerned were not both free and guilty in their course, acting as they did from evil motives and the prompting of their own bad hearts?[4]

Take the following three biblical facts concerning justification: the elect were justified in Christ from all eternity; Christ was raised for their justification; and they are justified by faith in Christ. How can these be reconciled? 'The question may be put, "How could they be said to be justified before, both from eternity and in Christ, if they may be truly said even in God's judgement to be justified but now [that is, when they believe], and that they were till now [that is, until they believe] unjustified?"' Having proposed the question, Goodwin answered it: 'These seeming contradictions, in various respects, are both true'. Goodwin explained: 'Before God, according to the rules of his word, which are the rules of his proceedings before men, being God's revealed will, they [the elect before coming to faith] are as yet unjustified; but according to those secret passages of his secret will transacted with Christ, and to which he is privy, they are justified persons before him'.[5] This explanation is right but, even so, the seeming contradiction remains.[6]

Take God's providence. John Flavel was right to draw attention to its *mysterious* nature.[7] God's providences can seem chaotic; they can seem even to run counter to his promises, when all the time he is serenely and consistently working out his sovereign and eternal purpose. Such things are a paradox to our mind.

Take God's command to Abraham to sacrifice Isaac (Gen. 22:2), even though human sacrifice is a pagan practice which God hates (Ps. 106:34-39; Jer. 19:5; Ezek. 16:20), and in this case seemed to contradict his promise (Gen. 17:16,19). This is a

---

[4] *Southern Baptist Sermons* p27ff.
[5] Goodwin p138.
[6] There is a parallel with the free offer; just as hyper-Calvinists, not willing to let the biblical paradox stand, apply their logic to the free offer, so some of them do to the above question – and thus end up with their doctrine of eternal justification. See my note in chapter 1.
[7] Flavel: *Mystery*.

paradox.

Consider the question of faith. Only the elect can believe (John 6:44; 10:26), but all of them will believe (John 6:37), for faith is God's gift to them (Eph. 2:8). Even so, all unbelievers are condemned for not believing (John 3:18; 5:40); it is a sin (John 16:9). This is a paradox.

I leave it there. Having made the point that there are scores of paradoxes in Scripture, let me now move on to consider the one in question; namely, the seeming contradiction between God's desire to save all sinners and his decree to save only his elect.

6

The Paradox in Question

God desires to save all sinners but he has decreed to save only his elect. This is the paradox in question.

What is not at stake

Let me clear the ground and set out what is *not* at stake. God has decreed to save his elect, all his elect, and no others. Christ died for them, and no others. The Spirit works effectively in them, and no others. Ella and I are at one on these vital doctrines. I believe them and preach them. So whatever I think about the two aspects of God's will – the secret and the revealed (Deut. 29:29) – *these* doctrines are not in question.

But has God spoken in Scripture of his desire to save all sinners? This is where Ella and I part company. I say, Yes; Ella says, No.

Fair enough. Here we have something to get our teeth into. Let's discuss the matter. Let's examine the Scriptures. I would like to say I welcome Ella's contribution to this debate, but sadly I have found it very difficult to take him seriously. What was wanted was soft words and strong arguments. Intemperate language does not make a compelling case. If I may echo Job's complaint, and say to my brother: 'How forceful are right words! But what does your arguing prove?' (Job 6:25).

What am I talking about? Just this. Instead of getting to grips with the issue, Ella issued a crescendo of caricature, and indulged in silly – I speak advisedly – silly throw-aways. Let me illustrate. I do not think 'God the Father and God the Son quarrel over the salvation of sinners'; that they 'contend over the souls of sinners'; that 'there is an eternal tension in the Godhead concerning who should be saved';[1] that 'God... is at logger-heads with himself';[2]

---

[1] Ella: *The Free Offer* p20.

that there are two gospels;[3] 'two routes for salvation'.[4] Nor do I set out 'a moving Father-Son soap opera relationship [in which] Jesus... wishes to save everyone. But his Father is adamant. He will only save some. Thus the heavenly arches shudder as God the Father and God the Son quarrel over the salvation of sinners... Father and Son contend over the souls of sinners... Whereas Christ wishes to save all, the Father insists on only saving some'.[5] I say nothing of the sort. Ella's approach cannot be called serious debate.

Ella has also stooped to nasty suggestion and assertion. On what authority did he say, for instance, 'Gay tactically leaves out' 'the decreed will of God to adopt for himself [that is, God] an elect people for whom Christ died', 'so that [Gay] might preach as if God never granted an assured and certain salvation for those for whom Christ died'?[6] Where have I ever hinted at such a thing? Has Ella ever heard me preach? Can he produce one witness to back his assertion? And I object to what lies behind the word 'tactically'. I also resent Ella's suggestion that I have a scheme in mind in which I have to 'drop' biblical doctrines to leave myself 'free to preach to persuade men according to their natural abilities to repent and believe on the purely rational grounds that God, if he is God, must desire it'.[7] Nor do I think the 'secret law of God regarding his decrees must fade away before the revealed law of God'.[8]

Leaving aside these personal remarks of abuse, which add

---

[2] Ella: *The Free Offer* p9.

[3] Ella: *The Free Offer* p22.

[4] Ella: *The Free Offer* p19.

[5] Ella: *The Free Offer* p20.

[6] Ella: *The Free Offer* p21.

[7] Ella: *The Free Offer* p22.

[8] Ella: *The Free Offer* p22. In chapter 10 I will answer Ella's criticism of what I said about Spurgeon. Ella is not alone in his misunderstanding (or misrepresentation) of the free offer. John H.Gerstner in his Foreword to Engelsma's book, for instance, was wrong to state that 'the "well-meant offer" is understood... to include the notion that God intends and desires the salvation of reprobates' (Engelsma vii). Whoever 'understands' the free offer like this, misunderstands it! The fact is, God intends the salvation of the elect and the damnation of the reprobate, but desires the salvation of all.

nothing to the discussion but rather cloud it, let me turn to a far more important question: What Scriptures did Ella tackle on the subject? None! But, reader, I have not grabbed my views out of thin air. That I may be mistaken, I freely admit, but I sincerely believe that Scripture teaches what I have tried to set out. I believe God has shown he has various desires, desires which he has expressed in passionate terms, but which desires, obviously, he has not decreed to fulfil. I say, 'obviously', because they are not fulfilled. I am absolutely committed to the doctrine of God's sovereignty. Whatever God has decreed comes to pass; it always comes to pass; it must come to pass. No power in hell or earth can hinder it. Therefore if God expresses any desire which is not fulfilled it can only mean he has not decreed it. But this is precisely what I *do* find in Scripture. Now I confess I cannot understand it. It is a paradox to me. Even so, I accept and teach what (I think) Scripture says. I do not try to explain the facts away. I may be wrong in my views, and if Ella can show me a better way, I shall be grateful to him, but merely to abuse me and my words is not the best way to help me to understand. I would like to see his scriptural arguments.

Scriptural examples of where God has not decreed to satisfy his desire

Make no mistake, reader, the Scriptures do speak of this matter; I will give some examples. I wish I had space to go further and expound these passages properly, but since I am trying to keep this book in bounds, I submit only brief summaries of my conclusions. I make this offer, however: *If Ella cares to set out his views on these verses, I will debate with him.* I refer to such passages as these:

Oh, that they had such a heart in them that they would fear me and always keep all my commandments, that it might be well with them and with their children for ever! (Deut. 5:29)
See, I have set before you today life and good, death and evil... I have set before you life and death, blessing and cursing; therefore choose life... that you may love the LORD your God, that you may obey his voice (Deut. 30:15-20)

Oh, that they were wise, that they understood this, that they would consider their latter end! (Deut. 32:29)[9]

Wrath came upon Judah and Jerusalem because of their trespass. Yet [the LORD God] sent prophets to them, to bring them back to the LORD; and they testified against them, but they would not listen (2 Chron. 24:18-19)

Hear, O my people, and I will admonish you! O Israel, if you will listen to me!... But my people would not heed my voice, and Israel would have none of me... Oh, that my people would listen to me, that Israel would walk in my ways! (Ps. 81:8,11,13)

I have called and you refused, I have stretched out my hand and no one regarded... you disdained all my counsel, and would have none of my rebuke (Prov. 1:24-25)

Oh, that you had heeded my commandments! (Isa. 48:18)

I have stretched out my hands all day long to a rebellious people (Isa. 65:2; Rom. 10:21)

When I called, you did not answer; when I spoke, you did not hear, but did evil before my eyes, and chose that in which I do not delight (Isa. 65:12; see also Isa. 66:4)

I have sent to you all my servants the prophets, rising early and sending them, saying, 'Oh, do not do this abominable thing that I hate!' But they did not listen or incline their ear (Jer. 44:4-5)[10]

---

[9] Even though these are Moses' words, they express God's own desire since they are a part of the song he gave Moses, and which he said was 'a witness for me against the children of Israel' which would 'testify against them as a witness' when they turned away from him (Deut. 31:19-21). 'This song... would be a testimony for God of his goodness to them, of his tender care of them, and concern for them... and a testimony against them for their ingratitude and other sins' (Gill: *Commentary* Vol.1 p811, emphasis mine). Gill, however, seemed to forget this when commenting on Deut. 32:29.

[10] See also 2 Kings 17:13-14; 2 Chron. 36:15-16; Neh. 9:26,29-30; Isa. 5:1-7; Jer. 7:13,23-28; 11:7-8,10; 13:8-11; 19:15; 25:3-7; 26:2-15; 29:19; 32:33; 35:14-17; Ezek. 2:3-7; 3:7; Hos. 7:13 (NASB, NIV); 11:1-2; 11:7 (AV, NASB); Zech. 1:4; 7:7-12; Mal. 1:10 (NASB, NIV); Matt. 5:12; 23:34,37; Luke 7:30; 13:34; Acts 7:51-53. See also Isa. 15:5; 16:9,11,13; Jer. 48:30-38, especially 31,32,36. Above all, the Jews rejected Christ

Here God shows he earnestly desired or wished the Hebrews to listen to him, to fear and obey him from the heart, to choose life and not death, and so on, and he commanded and urged them to do so. But they would not. It is clear, then, God desired something which he did not decree, for if he had decreed it, they would have feared him, they would have got their priorities right, they would have heeded his commands. And as Gill, commenting on Psalm 81:13, expressed it: 'If they had hearkened to him... it would have been well-pleasing to him; for that is what is designed by this wish,[11] which does not express the purposing will of God; for who has resisted that? [The fact is,] if he had so willed, he could have given them ears to hear; but [this wish expresses] his commanding will, and what is his approving one'.[12] This is the paradox in question.[13]

(Matt. 21:33-46; 23:37; Luke 13:34; 19:41-44; John 1:11; 3:11-19; 5:37-43; 8:37-38,40,42-43,47; 10:25-26; 12:44-50; 15:24-25; Acts 2:23; 3:14-15; 4:10-11; 7:52), who spoke 'that you may be saved' (John 5:34), whom God sent (and was sending), as Peter said, 'to bless you, in turning away every one of you from your iniquities' (Acts 3:26); that is, God desired them all to repent and receive his Son, commanding them to do so (Acts 3:19-20), but in general they did not. The apostles met the same refusal (Acts 13:46; 18:5-6; 19:8-9; 28:23-31; 1 Thess. 2:14-16 etc.) If Rom. 11:32; 16:25-27 and Tit. 2:11 express a thought similar to Acts 3:26, extended to all nations, note once again the link between duty faith and God's desire.

[11] That is, God, by this declared wish, intended that Israel should know how they could please him.

[12] Gill: *Commentary* Vol.3 p203.

[13] As for the link between duty repentance/faith and God's desire, take Gill on 'the Pharisees and lawyers [who] rejected the will [counsel] of God for themselves, not having been baptised by' John the Baptist (Luke 7:30): 'By their impenitence and unbelief, and through their rejection of Christ and his forerunner, and the gospel and the ordinances of it, they brought ruin and destruction, both temporal and eternal, upon themselves... that is, they rejected the command of God unto them... for by "the counsel of God" here, is not meant his purpose, intention and design... which... never is frustrated; but the precept of God... the command of God' (Gill: *Commentary* Vol.5 p463). Although Gill went on to speak of 'the ordinance of baptism', the fact is John commanded these hearers to repent and be baptised (Matt. 3:1-11) because God desired them to do it – it was his 'will' or 'counsel' for them – but they refused; they

'Do I have any pleasure at all that the wicked should die?' says the LORD GOD, 'and not that he should turn from his ways and live?... Repent, and turn from all your transgressions, so that iniquity will not be your ruin. Cast away from you all the transgressions which you have committed, and get yourselves a new heart and a new spirit. For why should you die, O house of Israel? For I have no pleasure in the death of one who dies', says the LORD GOD. 'Therefore turn and live!' (Ezek. 18:23,30-32)

Say to them: 'As I live', says the LORD GOD, 'I have no pleasure in the death of the wicked, but that the wicked turn from his way and live' (Ezek. 33:11)

God here tells us he delights in, takes pleasure in – that is, desires – the salvation of sinners; negatively, he does not delight in the death of the wicked. The people of Israel were desperate; they saw no hope, no hope whatsoever; their sins had ruined them. God would damn them. Death stared them in the face. But God, in his great mercy, sent the prophet to offer hope to this sinful people. True, they were sinners. True, their sins would damn them. But if this should happen, God would take no pleasure in their death. He wanted them to return. He wanted them all to return. If only they would turn! If only they would turn from their sins and turn back to him, he would have mercy upon them. He would forgive them. Indeed, he would take pleasure in their return; it would please him. He wanted them to come. But, unless they did return, they would perish. God wanted them to turn, but they must do it. If they perished, it would be their own fault. Turn, therefore, turn. Now did all those who heard the Lord's plea turn? Were they all saved? No! Clearly, therefore, God had not decreed to bring about his expressed desire. This is the paradox in question.[14]

I have cleansed you, and you were not cleansed (Ezek. 24:13)

The Jews, particularly in Jerusalem, had become wicked in the extreme, rebellious (Ezek. 24:3), violent (Ezek. 24:6,9), deceitful

---

would not repent and believe, as Gill observed. See also John 1:7; Acts 19:4.

[14] For Calvin's comments, see chapter 9.

(Ezek. 24:12) and lewd (Ezek. 24:13). So bad had things become, God pictured the city as a filthy cauldron (Ezek. 24:11,13), encrusted with scum (Ezek. 24:6,11,12). God was about to judge her; indeed, Babylon was at the gates even as the prophet was speaking (Ezek. 24:2). Even so, God had brought judgement only as a last resort, having, he said, tried to reform the people and recall them to his ways, but with no success. In the parable, filthy cauldron that she was, a fire had been lit beneath Jerusalem to burn off the scum, but it had failed (Ezek. 24:9-13); that is, God had sent prophets to preach, and had visited the people with judgements to get rid of the sin, but Jerusalem would not be cleansed. 'I have cleansed you', he said; that is, 'I have taken all necessary steps to cleanse you', but 'you were not cleansed', you would not be cleansed (Ezek. 24:13). 'I would have cleansed you, yet you are not clean' (NASB). God had 'made use of means for the purgation [cleansing] of them, by his prophets, and by exhortations and instructions given by them, and by various corrections and chastisements; but all in vain, and to no purpose, they were all without effect'.[15] God, it is clear, had desired their cleansing, and taken steps to procure it, even though he had not decreed it. If he had, they would have been cleansed. This is the paradox in question.

Is this the only time God said such a thing? It is not:

In vain I have chastened your children; they received no correction (Jer. 2:30)
I said, after she had done all these things: 'Return to me'. But she did not return (Jer. 3:7)
You have stricken them, but they have not grieved; you have consumed them, but they have refused to receive correction. They have made their faces harder than a rock; they have refused to return (Jer. 5:3)
She has not obeyed his voice, she has not received correction; she has not trusted in the LORD, she has not drawn near to her God... I said: 'Surely you will fear me, you will receive instruction'... But they rose early and corrupted all their deeds (Zeph. 3:2,7)

---

[15] Gill: *Commentary* Vol.4 p372.

Listen to what Gill said on these verses: 'The rod of chastisement was used in vain; the afflictions that came upon them had no effect on them to amend and reform them; they were never the better for them'. 'The Lord sent to them by the prophets... who... entreated them, saying, "turn unto me"... They were not without admonitions, exhortations and declarations of grace... but remained in idolatry, obstinate and inflexible'. 'The Lord had corrected and chastised them... he had brought his judgements upon them, and had smitten them... and yet it had not brought them to a sense of their sin, and to a godly sorrow for it... [they] remained obstinate and incorrigible, [and] refused to receive any correction or instruction by such providences'. 'This is spoken after the manner of men; as if God should say within himself, and reason in his own mind... "Surely... the Jews will take notice...". This, humanly speaking, might be reasonably thought would be the case... [namely, that] by these judgements, [the Jews] taking warning by them [would] repent, reform, and amend, and thereby escape the like... [God] chastised them in a gentle manner, in order to reform them, but in vain... The goodness of God should have brought them to repentance, yet it did not'.[16] So said Gill. And he was quite right.

In all this, God had been sincere in his use of means for Israel's good, and complained of – was grieved over – their refusal to listen. It is clear, therefore, that although he had desired their return, he had not decreed it. If he had, Israel would not have refused him. This is the paradox in question.

O Jerusalem, Jerusalem, the one who kills the prophets and stones those who are sent to her! How often I wanted to gather your children together, as a hen gathers her chicks under her wings, but you were not willing! (Matt. 23:37; Luke 13:34)

Christ said he 'wanted'; the people were not 'willing'. Both words 'wanted', and 'willing', are translations of θελω, which can mean 'to be resolved, determined, intend, to purpose', or 'to desire, to wish', or 'to take delight in, to have pleasure'. As for Christ, he

---

[16] Gill: *Commentary* Vol.4 pp10,14,25,800. See also Jer. 26:1-3; 36:1-3; Ezek. 12:1-3; Luke 20:13.

could not have meant *intend*. If he had intended to gather the Jews, if he had decreed and purposed their gathering, they would have been gathered. No! Christ *desired* to gather them, he *wanted* to gather them, but they did not *want* to be gathered. He had a heart for them; they had none for him. Jesus wept over them. He desired, yearned, longed for them to yield to his appeals and entreaties, but they were not willing, they had no mind, no desire to turn and be saved. He desired their salvation but he had not decreed it. This is the paradox in question.[17]

Christ taught the same principle in two parables recorded close by the passage in Luke.[18] Let us glance at them.

In the first, 'a certain man had a fig tree... and he came seeking fruit on it and found none' (Luke 13:6). Did the man want fruit? Did he desire it? Of course he did! Did he get it? He did not. In the parable's reference to God, this is the paradox in question.

In the second parable, 'a certain man gave a great supper and invited many, and sent his servant at supper time to say to those who were invited: "Come, for all things are now ready"' (Luke 14:16-17). Was the man sincere? Did he desire those he invited to accept? Most definitely. He made this very clear when he finally instructed his servant to 'go out into the highways and hedges, and compel [urge, persuade, entreat] them to come in, that my house may be filled' (Luke 14:23). The man wanted *all* he had invited to come, but not all came.

The gospel parallel is clear. I cannot understand it, but that is not the point! In coming across this principle in Scripture, do I concentrate on my lack of understanding or on the obvious desire of the Godhead to see sinners saved? God in the gospel has revealed that he desires the salvation of sinners, some whom he has not decreed to save. This is the paradox in question.

Jesus, looking at him, loved him... But he... went away (Mark 10:21-22)

The rich man wanted to know what he had to do to inherit eternal life. Jesus 'loved him' and told him the way, but the man 'was sad

---

[17] See also chapters 9 and 10.
[18] See also Matt. 22:1-10.

at this word, and went away grieved, for he had great possessions'. Jesus drew the lesson: 'How hard it is for those who have riches to enter the kingdom of God'; only God can change a man's heart (Mark 10:17-27). Now, it is possible that the man came to his senses, returned and obeyed Christ, but we are not told that he did, nor is there a shred of evidence to support the conjecture. And that it what it is – conjecture. In other words, as far as we can tell – as far as Scripture makes clear – Christ desired the man's obedience – he loved him – yet, although he had the power to effect it, he did not. This is the paradox in question.[19]

Jesus said: 'Father, forgive them, for they know not what they do' (Luke 23:34)

Jesus was sincere; it is blasphemous to suggest otherwise. Christ desired the forgiveness of his crucifiers, all of them.[20] Did he pray for the forgiveness of only the elect among them? No! He desired and prayed for the forgiveness of them all. It did not matter whether or not they were elect; Christ prayed for them all. But were all of them forgiven? Of course not. Clearly, therefore, he desired something he had not decreed. This is the paradox in question.[21]

Christ, addressing the church of the Laodiceans, said:

---

[19] See also Matt. 9:35-38. As for Gill's comment – Christ was here showing love 'as man, he had a human affection for [the rich man]' (Gill: *Commentary* Vol.5 p371) – see my note, in chapter 9, on Christ speaking in Matt. 23:37 as both God and man. In Scripture, God often speaks as though he is a man (see the next chapter), and as such he expresses desires which, although he could fulfil them, he chooses not to.

[20] See also Luke 24:47 and Acts 1:8. From Luke 24:47, John Bunyan showed how Christ would have his gospel preached first at Jerusalem, the very place where he was crucified, and have it preached to his crucifiers (Bunyan: *Jerusalem Sinner*). See chapter 10 for a further note. As an example of free-offer preaching, I cannot too highly recommend Bunyan's book.

[21] As for reconciling Luke 23:34 and John 17:9, see my *Particular*. But to try to use John 17:9 (and 11:42) to evade Luke 23:34 is wrong. Luke 23:34 stands in Scripture and has to be reckoned with, not explained away.

You are neither cold nor hot. I could wish you were cold or hot. So then, because you are lukewarm, and neither cold nor hot, I will spew you out of my mouth... I counsel you to buy from me gold... Be zealous and repent. Behold, I stand at the door and knock. If anyone hears my voice and opens the door, I will come in to him and dine with him, and he with me (Rev. 3:14-20)

Christ wanted changes in the church at Laodicea, and made large promises to encourage those changes. But the changes were not forthcoming. He wanted the church to be either cold or hot, but it was neither. He went so far as to picture himself as knocking outside a closed door, asking to come in. Did the church open to him? The evidence is against it. Christ was not impotent, of course; he was going to spew the church out of his mouth. But if he had decreed it, the church would have reformed itself and welcomed him. Consequently, he could not have decreed what he desired. This is the paradox in question.

Do you despise the riches of [God's] goodness, forbearance, and longsuffering, not knowing that the goodness of God leads you to repentance? (Rom. 2:4)

Paul asks this question of unbelievers – some of whom at least are reprobate (Rom. 2:5) – addressing them as 'O man, whoever you are' (Rom. 2:1,3). We know they are unbelievers, since they despise or underestimate God's goodness, treating it with contempt. They deliberately and wilfully (2 Pet. 3:5) reject God's goodness, God's kindness to them. They do not understand – or want to understand – why he shows them such kindness. Now what is God's goodness? What is his purpose in showing kindness to sinners? The answer is: God is good to sinners in that he does not merely point them to repentance; rather, he leads or conducts them to it (Rom. 2:4). Sadly, not all sinners do repent. The reprobate never do, but remain hardened in their unbelief, and perish. Indeed, things get worse for them in that they mock the tokens of God's kindness, and despise his goodness, thus adding to their guilt and condemnation under his wrath (Rom. 2:5). This kindness, it goes without saying, does not speak of God's inward, effectual, saving grace which is irresistible. Nevertheless, it is God's goodness. And

God shows this non-saving, resistible goodness to all men, including the reprobate: 'The LORD is good to all, and his tender mercies are over all his works' (Ps. 145:9). God 'is longsuffering', and this 'longsuffering of our Lord is salvation' (2 Pet. 3:9,15). God is sincere. He desires the repentance of all sinners – indeed, he commands them all to repent (Acts 17:30) – but he has not decreed it. This is the paradox in question.

God our Saviour, who desires all men to be saved and to come to the knowledge of the truth (1 Tim. 2:3-4)

The NASB is the same as the NKJV: 'God... who *desires* all men to be saved'; the NIV is virtually the same: 'God... who *wants* all men to be saved'; the AV: 'God... who *will* have all men to be saved'. Should it be 'will' in the sense of 'decree' or 'desire'? θελω can mean either.[22] And what about 'all'? Did Paul mean 'all sorts of men'? If so, Paul was saying either, 'God decrees all sorts of men to be saved',[23] which has no bearing on the issue – all sorts of men will be saved; or, 'God desires all sorts of men to be saved', which leaves the issue as it was – if all sorts of men are not in fact saved, then God desires something he has not decreed, and if all sorts of men *are* saved, then the 'desire' in effect amounts to 'decree'. But if 'all' means either 'all the elect' or 'all without exception', Paul was saying:

'God decrees to save all the elect', which is a truism; or
'God decrees to save all men without exception', which is false; or
'God desires to save all the elect', which is a truism; or
'God desires to save all men without exception'.

---

[22] Please note, reader, three out of the four versions I quote opt for 'desire'; the AV is neutral.

[23] As Gill: *Commentary* Vol.6 pp596-597. But what, precisely, is 'all sorts of men'? Gill thought, 'agreeably to the use of the phrase in verse 1, are here intended, kings and peasants, rich and poor, bond and free, male and female, young and old, greater and lesser sinners'. Now on verse 1, Gill included 'all the inhabitants of the country and city in which men dwell'. Would those who agree with Gill include such in God's decree to save? If the 'all' is in any way restricted, however, the verse, it seems to me, amounts to: 'God does not will to save all men'. See chapter 10 for Spurgeon's comments.

Of these, the last is the only possibility: God desires to save all men, even though he has not decreed it.[24] This is the paradox in question.[25]

The Lord is not slack concerning his promise... but is longsuffering toward us [or, you], not willing that any should perish but that all should come to repentance (2 Pet. 3:9)

There are two points. *First*, βουλομαι means either 'to will deliberately, to have a purpose, to be minded', or 'to desire, to will as an affection'. God is said to be 'not willing that any should perish'; that is, either he does not *decree* any to perish, or he does not *desire* any to perish. Both, from a language point of view, are perfectly proper. Which is it? *Secondly*, there is the 'any' – which is often taken to mean 'any of the elect', but it could mean 'any sinner'. Therefore Peter was saying:

'God has not decreed that any of the elect should perish', which is a truism; or
'God has not decreed that any sinner should perish', which is false; or
'God does not desire any of the elect to perish', which is a truism; or
'God does not desire any sinner to perish'.

This last is the only possibility: God 'is longsuffering' (2 Pet. 3:9), rich in 'goodness, forbearance, and longsuffering' (Rom. 2:4), and this 'longsuffering of our Lord is salvation' (2 Pet. 3:15). So much so, as Peter explained, God does not desire any sinner to perish.

---

[24] While Calvin thought the passage 'relates to classes of men, and not to individual persons', he was very clear: 'God has at heart the salvation of all'. And even if the passage does teach that 'God wishes all men indiscriminately to be saved' – which Calvin did think Scripture teaches elsewhere, though not here – it would not contradict predestination, he said. He argued this from the distinction between God's decree and his revealed will (Calvin: *Commentaries* Vol.21 Part 3 pp54-55). See also *Calvin's Calvinism* pp105-106,166-167,276-279, where Calvin claimed he had set out the 'solution' 'in my writings in a hundred different places'.
[25] Of course, Paul might have been expressing a truism, but it seems most unlikely.

Yet he has not decreed to save all of them. This is the paradox in question.[26]

* * *

Because of one of Ella's recurring criticisms, there is one particular point I wish to emphasise in all this: Whatever I have said about the paradox between God's decree and his desire, it applies equally to the Father and the Son. I have drawn your attention, reader, to passages which show both the Father and the Son expressing desires which are not fulfilled; *both* the Father and the Son, I say.

So I hope I have nailed once and for all Ella's attack upon me for positing a tension or quarrel in the Godhead over the matter.[27] I do no such thing. There is no tension within any person of the Godhead,[28] nor is there any quarrel between the members of the Godhead. None whatsoever. Let me repeat myself, and make it as clear as I can: Whatever I have said about the paradox between God's decree and his desire, it applies equally to the Father and the Son. There is no frustration or tension with the trinity – the very suggestion is blasphemous.

Even so, reader, I have put before you many passages of Scripture which, I submit, show that God is pleased to reveal himself as having desires which are not always satisfied. This is a paradox, of course – the very point I am trying to make.

* * *

Before I move on, let me illustrate how the principle I have set out has ramifications for all believers. 'Imitate me' (1 Cor. 4:16), said Paul, 'imitate me, just as I also imitate Christ' (1 Cor. 11:1), 'be imitators of God' (Eph. 5:1), 'join in following my example' (Phil. 3:17). That these commands are far wider than the principle I am dealing with, I admit at once, but they do include it, and as such

---

[26] As with Paul, Peter might have been expressing a truism, but in the context it seems most unlikely.

[27] See Ella: *The Free Offer* pp9,20. If there is any remaining doubt, see chapter 9.

[28] But see chapter 9 for Gill on Hos. 11:8.

they sharpen the focus of Paul's reply to Agrippa's statement (or outburst): 'You almost persuade me to become a Christian' (Acts 26:28). This is what the apostle called out:

I would to God that not only you, but also all who hear me today, might become both almost and altogether such as I am, except for these chains (Acts 26:29)

Did Paul desire Agrippa's salvation? Did Paul desire the salvation of all his hearers? Of course he did. Was he sincere? Of course he was. His heart longed for it.[29] Gill:

This prayer of the apostle's shows his affection for the souls of men, and his great desire for their conversion... His wish was not that only Agrippa, but that all that were present, were... entirely, in the highest and fullest sense, Christians, as he was; that they knew as much of Christ, and had as much faith in him, and love to him, as he had, and were as ready to serve and obey him... He wished that they were... regenerated by the Spirit of God, new creatures in Christ, called by the grace of God with a holy calling, believers in Christ, lovers of him, pardoned by his blood, justified by his righteousness, sanctified by his grace, children of God, and heirs of eternal life: and all this he wishes for of God... And this wish is expressive of true grace, which desires the good of others... It is an evidence of grace, when the heart is drawn out in desires after the salvation of others... To be made a real Christian... this the apostle wished for, for Agrippa and all that heard him; as does every gospel minister for their [*sic*] hearers.[30]

Were all Paul's hearers elect? Were they sensible sinners? Was Paul's desire satisfied? Almost certainly, not. Was this an isolated

---

[29] I am sure Paul would have added poignancy to his words by stretching out his arms as far and wide as he could, the chains hanging from his wrists. Reader, if you think this far-fetched, see Prov. 1:24; Isa. 65:2; Rom. 10:21. I am certain he did not utter his heartfelt cry with his hands stuffed in his pockets!

[30] Gill: *Commentary* Vol.5 pp999-1000. I heartily agree, of course, with Gill, when he spoke of Paul's 'sense of the power and grace of God, as necessary to it... knowing that the whole of this [which he desired] is not of men, but of God; all grace, and every blessing of it, which make or show a man to be a Christian indeed, are from him... To be made a real Christian is the work of God, and to be ascribed to him'. But this does nothing to detract from the point I am making. The very opposite!

case? It was not:

I tell the truth in Christ, I am not lying, my conscience also bearing me witness in the Holy Spirit, that I have great sorrow and continual grief in my heart. For I could wish that I myself were accursed from Christ for my brethren, my countrymen according to the flesh... My heart's desire and prayer to God for Israel is that they may be saved (Rom. 9:1-3; 10:1)

These are very solemn statements, not to say staggering. So much so, Paul stressed he was speaking as before Christ, and assured his readers he was telling the truth and not exaggerating. He also claimed to have the witness of the Spirit.

Paul was deeply grieved over the unbelief of the Jews, never free of the sadness, night or day. He was tormented by the thought of their unbelief and eternal doom. Even though Paul was hated by the Jews (Acts 9:23,29; 13:45,50; 14:5,19; 18:6,12; 2 Cor. 11:24,26), still he loved them, and was deeply anxious for their salvation. Gill: Paul desired 'that they might be spiritually converted, turned from their evil ways, and brought to believe in Christ... and so be saved in the Lord with an everlasting salvation: this he might desire not only from a natural affection for them, but as a minister of the gospel, who cannot but wish that all that hear him might be converted and saved'.[31]

Now where did Paul get such love? Surely from Christ! Where else? Paul told us so: 'The love of Christ compels us' (2 Cor. 5:14).[32] As he said: 'We are ambassadors for Christ, as though God were pleading through us: we implore [you] on Christ's behalf, be reconciled to God' (2 Cor. 5:20). Christ, as part of his law, told his disciples: 'Love your enemies... and pray for those who spitefully use you and persecute you, that you may be the sons of your Father in heaven... You shall be perfect, just as your Father in heaven is perfect' (Matt. 5:44-48). Believers, therefore, must imitate the apostle (as above, 1 Cor. 4:16; 11:1; Eph. 5:1; Phil. 3:17), and thus imitate their Saviour and his Father, and love all men, including their enemies, desiring their salvation.[33]

---

[31] Gill: *Commentary* Vol.6 p86.

[32] Stephen demonstrated the same (Acts 7:60).

[33] See also Acts 26:15-23. I will return to this vital matter in chapter 9. It

Paul was, of course, persuaded of the doctrine of election;[34] indeed, he more than any taught it! And never more plainly than in this section of Romans, chapters 9 – 11. Yet he opened the passage with this heartfelt desire for the salvation of all Jews, both the elect and reprobate. Paul – who wrote all three chapters! – was not hung up on trying to reconcile Romans 9:1-3; 10:1 with Romans 9:6-29; 11:1-10,25. Nor should we! If all we can see in this passage is the problem of reconciling – or explaining away – the desire for all sinners to be saved, with an unshakeable conviction of God's electing decree, shame on us! What is more, if we do not openly preach both, shame on us!

Listen to Spurgeon addressing preachers on the issue:

I question whether we have preached the whole counsel of God, unless predestination with all its solemnity and sureness be continually declared – unless election be boldly and nakedly taught as being one of the truths revealed of God. It is the minister's duty, beginning with this fountain head, to trace all the other streams... effectual calling... justification by faith... the certain perseverance of the believer, and delighting to proclaim that gracious covenant [or decreed agreement within the Godhead] in which all these things are contained, and which is sure to all the chosen, blood-bought seed...

But beloved, a man might preach all these doctrines to the full, and yet not declare the whole counsel of God. For here comes the labour and the battle; here it is that he who is faithful in these modern days will have to bear the full brunt of war. It is not enough to preach doctrine; we must preach *duty*, we must faithfully and firmly insist upon practice. So long as you will preach nothing but bare doctrine, there is a certain class of men of perverted intellect who will admire you; but once begin to preach responsibility – say outright, once for all, that if the sinner perishes it is his own fault, that if any man sinks to hell, his damnation will lie at his own door – and at once there is a cry of 'Inconsistency! How can these two things stand together?' Even good Christian men are found who cannot endure the whole truth, and who will oppose the servant of the Lord who will not be content with a fragment, but will honestly present the whole gospel of Christ...

I do not see that the whole counsel of God is declared, unless those

---

is, in fact, the climax of what I want to say.

[34] I agree with Gill – Paul prayed and expressed his desire for the Jews, 'in submission to the will of God' (Gill: *Commentary* Vol.6 p86). Even so, he had the desire, expressed it openly, and prayed for its fulfilment.

two apparently contradictory points are brought out and plainly taught. To preach the whole counsel of God it is necessary to declare the promise in all its freeness, sureness and richness. When the promise makes the subject of the text the minister should never be afraid of it. If it is an unconditional promise, he should make its unconditionality one of the most prominent features of his discourse; he should go the whole way with whatever God has promised to his people. Should the command be the subject, the minister must not flinch; he must utter the precept as fully and confidently as he would the promise. He must exhort, rebuke, command with all long suffering. He must ever maintain the fact that the preceptive part of the gospel is as valuable – indeed, as invaluable – as the promissory part. He must stand to it... But let me imagine that I can improve the gospel, that I can make it consistent, that I can dress it up and make it look finer, I shall find that my Master is departed, and that Ichabod is written on the walls of the sanctuary.[35]

* * *

Reader, I acknowledge I may have drawn the wrong inferences from these passages. As I explained, I have put forward only the briefest of summaries of my conclusions, regretting the lack of space to do more. I realise there are honest differences of opinion. I would like to hear them. Would Ella let us have his? Though he attacked my views on the two aspects of God's will, Ella made no attempt to demolish them scripturally in his book on the free offer. Will he do so now?

But, reader, I submit I have set before you plenty of evidence to show that God has expressed desires which he has not decreed to satisfy; in particular, some of the passages teach that God desires the salvation of sinners whom he has not decreed to save. I go further. God's desire to save sinners – whether elect or not – lies behind all his invitations, commands, declarations and calls to sinners to turn, repent, believe, to come to Christ for salvation. It must be so. God is sincere. If he commands sinners to repent, he must want them to do it. If he argues with them to show them the benefits of trusting Christ, he must want them to trust his Son. If he warns them against refusing his offer, he must want them to accept it. Surely it must be so. God's desire is a *real* desire; the 'seeming'

---

[35] Spurgeon: *New* Vol.6 pp26-29, emphasis his.

applies only to the 'seeming' contradiction between his decree and his desire – and that, only as it 'seems' to us. Of course, God does not desire the salvation of sinners in any other way than by their faith and repentance; but desire it, he does. And this not only lies at the heart of the free offer, it is the crux of the debate in which I am engaged in writing this book.

Reader, ponder such scriptures as Psalm 2:10-12; Proverbs 1:20-33; 8:1-11; Isaiah 45:22; 55:1-3,6-9; 65:2; Ezekiel 33:11; Matthew 11:28-30; 22:1-10; 23:37; Luke 14:16-24; John 3:14-19; 6:29; Acts 17:30; Romans 2:4; 10:21; 2 Corinthians 5:18 – 6:2; 1 Timothy 2:3-4; and 2 Peter 3:9. Can you not feel God's desire? If you are an unbeliever, as you read the verses tell yourself that God commands *you* to turn to his Son and be saved. What is more, he desires it! Think about that! Relish it! Let it melt your heart. Does *God want **me** to come?* He does! Oh! Come, reader, come. Come now. God wants you to yield to his entreaties. He desires it. Obey his command. Repent and come to Christ, now!

* * *

As I say, the seeming conflict between God's determination to save only his elect, and his desire to save all, is but one paradox among many. As with all these paradoxes, the seeming contradiction between election and duty faith, between particular redemption and the universal offer, between God's decree and his desire, is only apparent; both parts of the paradox are true at one and the same time. What is more, although we are not able to explain fully any biblical paradox, there are certain things we may rightly deduce from Scripture.

As Fuller said:

Admitting the divine authority of the Holy Scriptures, their harmony ought not to be called in question; yet it must be allowed by every considerate reader that there are *apparent* difficulties. Nor is it unlawful, but laudable, to wish to see those difficulties removed.[36]

In this spirit, then, I will now go as far as the Bible warrants in trying to explore the paradox between God's decree and his desire;

---

[36] Fuller: *Exposition* in *Works* p529, emphasis his.

but no further! I certainly do not resort to the various (philosophical) arguments Ella rejected, and which took up a sizeable portion of his book.[37]

---

[37] Ella: *The Free Offer* pp14-19,24,27,31-37,55-57,59.

7

God Speaks as a Man

How can we get to grips with the biblical paradox between God's decree to save his elect, and his expressed desire to save all?

God speaks as though he has the feelings of a man

God, at times, reveals himself to us by speaking as a man, and this inevitably leads to paradoxes. For instance: Like a man, God is said to repent, to be sorry, to be grieved, to regret, relent or change his mind (Ex. 32:11-14; 1 Sam. 15:11; 2 Sam. 24:16; Ps. 106:45; Jer. 18:7-10 *etc.*),[1] yet he cannot repent since he is not a man (Num. 23:19; 1 Sam. 15:29). Again, although God is a Spirit and does not have a body (John 4:24), he speaks of his ear, nostrils, arm, hand and heart (Ps. 18:6,8,15; 31:2; 44:3; 75:8; Jer. 31:20 *etc.*) Speaking like a man, 'the LORD was sorry that he had made man on the earth, and he was grieved in his heart', and vowed he would destroy 'both man and beast' for, he said, 'I am sorry that I have made them' (Gen. 6:6-7). God sorry, grieved? On another occasion, he went further; because of their sin, he would have destroyed the Hebrews, he explained, for their misrepresentation of his action, 'had I not feared the wrath of the enemy' (Deut. 32:26-27). God afraid? What does it all mean? Why is it that God, as Calvin said, 'figuratively assumes a human feeling... speaking in the character of a man'? Why this 'figurative appropriation of human affections'?[2] Why?

The answer tells us a great deal about God, about his infinite kindness towards us, displayed in the steps he takes to make himself known to us.

---

[1] In addition to the NKJV, see the AV, NASB and NIV.

[2] Calvin: *Commentaries* Vol.2 Part 1 p337; Vol.8 Part 1 p487. I quote Calvin at large in this chapter, but many others, including Gill, have said similar things.

It is for our benefit that God speaks as though he has the feelings of a man

God wills to make himself known to us, but we are men, fallen men at that, and can only understand things expressed in human terms. As a consequence, God, because of his infinite wisdom and unspeakable grace, is willing to accommodate himself, and picture himself as a man, in order to make himself known to us. He does this for our good, taking pity on our ignorance. If he did not, as I have said, we should be unable to grasp anything of the Godhead. Even as it is, our understanding is, at best, feeble: 'We know in part... Now we see in a mirror, dimly' (1 Cor. 13:9,12; see also 1 Cor. 8:2). As Calvin put it: 'But you will say, "How can it be that God, who is ever consistent with himself... should yet will that which is contrary to that which seems to be?" I reply, It is no matter of wonder that God, when speaking with men, should accommodate himself to the limits of their comprehension. Who will affirm that God ever appeared to his servants, even in visions, such as he really is?'[3] Again: 'It is evident that [God] is constrained to borrow comparisons from the common practice of men, because he could not otherwise express what is necessary for us to know'.[4] But, I would add, God is 'constrained' only because in his grace he wills to reveal himself to us; pitying our weakness, he delights to 'constrain' and accommodate himself to our limitations, in order that we might know him. The 'constraint' is entirely his own pleasure, from within himself; it is not 'forced' upon him.

Scripture, said Calvin:

Ascribes human affections to God, because [it] could not otherwise express what was very important to be known... Certainly God is not sorrowful or sad... yet, because it could not otherwise be known how great is God's hatred and detestation of sin, therefore the Spirit accommodates himself to our capacity... God, in order more

---

[3] Calvin: *Calvin's Calvinism* p254; see also pp122-123,127,180,190,193, 253,256,275-277,313.
[4] Calvin: *Commentaries* Vol.15 Part 1 p215; see also p248. The same applies to God's use of human names in order to reveal himself to us. See Berkhof pp47-48.

effectually to pierce our hearts, clothes himself with our affections.[5]

In short, God accommodates himself to our ignorance in order to help us grasp such infinite spiritual mysteries as his hatred of sin, the immensity and importance of his glory, his love for us, his kindness, his willingness to listen to our prayers and his power to answer, and so on.[6] It is a mark of God's compassion to us, of his grace. Nevertheless, as I say, the very process itself inevitably leaves us with paradoxes. In particular, when God declares he desires to save sinners, he speaks as though he has the feelings of a man, and this leaves us with a paradox between his desire and his decree. But it is in this way that God graciously reveals his love for sinners, and makes known his pleasure and delight in their salvation.[7]

As to God's desire, our difficulty arises, in part, because to desire implies the possibility of disappointment. So, it might be argued, God cannot desire or wish, since he can never be said to be disappointed or frustrated. But this well-intentioned thinking misses the point. God does not need us and our puny logic to protect him from his own revelation of himself. As I showed in the previous chapter, speaking as though he has the feelings of a man, God tells us he does have desires (see also Job 14:15; Ps. 40:6; 51:6,16; 132:13-14; Hos. 6:6; 10:10 *etc.*), desires which are not always fulfilled. Our task is to believe what God has said about himself.

Even though God expresses himself in human terms, no human frailty attaches to him

It is essential to remember, of course, that although God accommodates himself to us by speaking in human terms, we must

---

[5] Calvin: *Commentaries* Vol.1 Part 1 pp247,249.

[6] As Gill on Lam. 3:33: 'It is with reluctance the Lord afflicts his people; he is as it were forced to it, speaking after the manner of men; see Hos. 11:8; [in this way he shows] he does not do it with delight and pleasure; he delights in mercy, but judgement is his strange act' (Gill: *Commentary* Vol.4 p258). See chapter 9 for Gill on Hos. 11:8.

[7] And we should, of course, focus on God's expressed desire, not the difficulties of the paradox.

not ascribe any human weakness to him. On the contrary, the weakness is entirely ours. As Dagg put it: When God expresses his pleasure or desire, he is in fact commanding or requiring the sinner to obey him. 'When the person, whose desire or pleasure it is that an action should be performed by another, has authority over that other, the desire expressed assumes the character of precept... The expressed will of a ruler is [a] command. What we know that it is the pleasure of God we should do, it is our duty to do, and his pleasure made known to us becomes a law'.[8] This is right. In the United Kingdom, to be 'detained during the Queen's pleasure' is a euphemism for being imprisoned until the Crown (nominally the Queen, but in effect the Government) determines otherwise. If a subject is told it is her Majesty's pleasure that he should wait upon her, it has all the force of a command; he is expected to be there!

I repeat, although God speaks in human terms, this does not show any weakness in him; rather it shows *our* weakness. Calvin again:

[God] accommodates himself to our ignorance, whenever he puts on a character foreign to himself... God [of course] does not in vain introduce himself as being uncertain... God... does not deliberate as to himself, but with reference to men... God... accommodates himself to us... He speaks not according to his own majesty, but as he sees to be suitable to our capacities and weakness... God... accommodates himself to our ignorance... Whenever... God puts on a character not his own, let us know that it is through our fault...[9]
It is a mode of speaking which often occurs in Scripture, that God repents of evil... but this is said according to the apprehensions of men... God... is... described to us in such a way as we can comprehend, according to the measure of our infirmity. Hence God often puts on the character of men, as though he were like them...[10]
Because our weakness cannot reach his height, any description which we receive of him must be lowered to our capacity in order to be intelligible. And the mode of lowering is to represent him not as he really is, but as we conceive of him... The mode of speech [is]

---

[8] Dagg p100. Once again, here is the connection between the two issues I am tackling – duty faith and the paradox between God's desire and his decree. It will continue to recur throughout the rest of my book.

[9] Calvin: *Commentaries* Vol.13 Part 2 pp401,440-441,464.

[10] Calvin: *Commentaries* Vol.14 Part 1 p61.

accommodated to our sense... He makes no pretence of not willing what he wills, but while in himself the will is one and undivided, to us it appears manifold, because, from the feebleness of our intellect, we cannot comprehend how, though after a different manner, he wills and wills not the very same thing... Since, on account of the dullness of our sense, the wisdom of God seems manifold... are we, therefore, to dream of some variation in God, as if he either changed his counsel, or disagreed with himself? No, when we cannot comprehend how God can will that to be done which he forbids us to do, let us call to mind our imbecility...

Why do they not attend to the many passages in which God clothes himself with human affections, and descends beneath his proper majesty in accommodation to our weakness?[11]

Edward Marbury agreed:

Where it is in Scripture charged upon God that he repents, we say... it is... a word accommodated to our weakness... This, for want of understanding in us to comprehend the ways of God, is called repentance and grief in God.[12]

What is more, although God speaks of himself as having human feelings – and this does not imply any weakness in him – even less does it imply that his feelings are sinfully tainted like those of fallen man. God loves, desires and hates, but not as we do. As Calvin said: 'God is exempt from every passion'.[13]

Edwards put it this way:

Though it be not just the same with our desiring and wishing for that which will never come to pass, yet there is... all in God that is good, and perfect, and excellent in our desires and wishes for the conversion and salvation of wicked men... These things are infinitely more agreeable to his nature than to ours. There is all in God that belongs to our desire [for] the holiness and happiness of unconverted men and reprobates, excepting what implies imperfection... Therefore, there is no reason that his absolute prescience, or his wise determination and ordering of what is future, should hinder his expressing this

---

[11] Calvin: *Institutes* Vol.1 pp195-196,202-203; Vol.2 p257; see also *Commentaries* Vol.10 Part 2 pp108-109; Vol.12 Part 1 pp265-266; Vol.14 Part 1 pp122-123; Part 2 pp115,330,348-349; Vol.15 Part 2 pp32,35.

[12] Marbury p365.

[13] Calvin: *Commentaries* Vol.13 Part 2 p402; see also Vol.13 Part 2 p372; Vol.15 Part 1 p248.

disposition of his nature, in like manner as we are wont to express such a disposition in ourselves, *viz.* by calls and invitations, and the like.[14]

William Greenhill:

Repentance sometimes in Scripture is attributed to God, and then it is spoken after the manner of men; and it must warily be understood, so as God may not be wronged in men's apprehensions thereby. In men's repentance there is grief, change, something falls out as they did not foresee... These things are not in God; he foresees all events, he grieves not, he changes not; therefore in this sense he cannot be said to repent... His repentance is alteration of things and actions, no change of his purpose and will. In human repentance there is the change of the will; in divine repentance there is the willing of a change, and that in the thing, not in the will or counsel of God, which are unchangeable.[15]

As with God's repentance, so with his desire to save sinners. Neither implies the slightest weakness in the Almighty.

But there is a further point.

Even though God assumes the character of a man, the desires he expresses are real desires

That is to say, although God speaks as a man, we must never imagine that this means he 'pretends'. For instance, when God speaks of his ears being open to the cry of his people (Ps. 34:15), his ear not being heavy so that it cannot hear (Isa. 59:1), he is telling us he really will hear his people when they pray, he sincerely wants his people to cry to him. Although God does not have an ear, this does not mean that his willingness to listen to his children is anything but sincere and real. The same goes for his desire to save all sinners. God's desire is expressed in human terms, yes, but the desire is real, true and sincere. God really does desire the salvation of sinners.

* * *

---

[14] Edwards p528. See the previous chapter for my comments on Paul's desire for the salvation of sinners.

[15] Greenhill p577. Gill used very similar words in his comments on Jonah 3:10 (Gill: *Commentary* Vol.4 p709).

God speaks to us as though he is a man. Regarding the salvation of sinners, therefore, it means that God expresses what seems to us to be a twofold will; namely, his decree to save his elect, and his desire to save all sinners. In the next chapter, I will look at this twofold will of God.

8

The Twofold Will of God

As I closed the previous chapter, I said that since God in Scripture speaks as if he is a man, we find in God what we can only call a twofold will. Let me explain by making three points:

1. There are two aspects to the one will of God
2. These two aspects of God's will are completely consistent; they make one will
3. These two aspects of God's will, though completely consistent, do not always seem to be so

1. There are two aspects to the one will of God

When we read in Scripture of the will of God, to what does it refer? To one of two things. On the one hand, there is God's absolute decree; on the other, there is God's good pleasure, his desire, that which pleases him.

Some passages speak of God's absolute decree, his inscrutable will which is certain to be fulfilled (Ps. 33:11; Isa. 14:24-27; Dan. 4:24,34-35; Rom. 9:18-19; Eph. 1:11; Rev. 4:11 *etc.*) Other passages speak of the will of God's pleasure or desire, which might not be fulfilled (Ps. 5:4; 40:6; 51:6; 132:13-14; Prov. 16:7; Eccl. 5:4; Hos. 10:10; John 8:29; Rom. 8:8; 1 Cor. 7:32; 10:5; 2 Thess. 1:11; Heb. 11:5-6 *etc.*)[1] For instance, the following must refer to

---

[1] But what of Job 23:13? 'Whatever [God's] soul desires, that he does'. Although he used the word 'desire', Job was clearly speaking of God's decree. God 'is unique, and who can make him change? And whatever his soul desires, that he does. For he performs what is appointed for me' (Job 23:13-14). It is the same as Ps. 115:3. Gill, in his comments on Job, having already spoken of God's purposes, counsels and unchangeable will, did refer to what God 'desires earnestly and vehemently'. Gill, however, immediately explained his meaning, by referring to God's counsel, the good pleasure of his will, the doing of what he pleases,

God's pleasure, that which would please him, that which he has commanded, not his absolute decree, that which he has purposed: Matthew 6:10 (God's absolute will is certain to be done); Matthew 7:21; 12:50; 1 John 2:17 (God's absolute will is fulfilled in all men); Ephesians 5:17; Colossians 1:9 (no man can know or understand God's secret decree); 1 Thessalonians 4:3; Matthew 5:48 (God has commanded his people to be perfect in daily life; he has not decreed it); John 7:17; Ephesians 6:6; 1 Peter 4:2 (a man must want to please God, not merely carry out the inevitable); and so on.[2]

The majority of Calvinists agree with this twofold distinction in the will of God, even though they might use different terms. Perhaps the most common way of describing the distinction is to speak of God's *secret* will and his *revealed* will; that is, God's decree, purpose, determining counsel, on the one hand, and his declared revelation as found in the Bible, on the other. 'The secret things belong to the LORD our God, but those things which are revealed belong to us' (Deut. 29:29). The secret things are those things which, unknown to us, God has decreed; the revealed things are those things which he has been pleased to tell us about, including those things which he has commanded us to do. Indeed, some Calvinists describe this twofold aspect as God's will of *purpose* and his will of *precept*.[3] Speaking for myself, I prefer the terms *secret* and *revealed*.

Ella will have none of it. Indeed, he showed nothing but contempt for the very idea, and caricatured it in terms of a 'soap opera' in the Godhead. He dismissed my claim of 'a difference

---

illustrating the point by creation, providence and redemption (Gill: *Commentary* Vol.2 p761). God 'does whatever he pleases' (NIV).

[2] There is, of course, a considerable overlap between the two aspects of God's will, and it is not always easy to say into which category a particular passage fits; sometimes it fits both. God's will is too vast for the logic of our puny minds! I will return to this. Nevertheless, in addition to the absolute will of God's decree – which is always fulfilled – the Scriptures do speak of God's will of desire – which is not always fulfilled.

[3] R.B.Kuiper argued for *three* aspects to the will of God: 'His secret or decretive will, his revealed or preceptive will, and what may be termed the will of his desire' (Kuiper p181). To my mind the third is contained in the second.

between the revealed and secret wills of God [and] also between God's desires in Christ and his decrees as the Father'. Indeed, he cited with approval the reviewer who called my words 'blasphemous'.[4] Leaving aside the caricature, I wonder what Ella makes of Deuteronomy 29:29? But there are other questions. Ella claimed he 'first came across this view[5] when reading through an article' written by me.[6] If he was saying he had never met the twofold distinction in the will of God before 1994, I can only say I am very surprised indeed. From his published works, I know Ella is a voracious reader, so I find it staggering to think he did not come across it before. I certainly didn't invent the idea!

To remove all misunderstanding, let me remind him – and you, reader – of what I actually said – which Ella quoted, and which he found so offensive:

There are two aspects to the will of God [I wrote]. First, there is his absolute purpose and eternal decree. This is always fulfilled (Ps. 115:3; 135:6; Isa. 46:10 *etc.*) Secondly, there is God's revealed will, his commands, invitations, the expression of his benevolence. Jesus said that he often desired that which God, clearly, had not decreed. God is perfectly consistent in this even though it is incomprehensible to us.[7]

I stand by my words.

Now let me remind Ella – and you reader – of the weight of material there is which demonstrates how acknowledged Calvinists have clearly set out two aspects to God's will. I have deliberately and ruthlessly limited these examples; the number I could draw on is legion:

Flavel:

As to the will of God, it falls under a twofold consideration of his secret and revealed will. This distinction is found in that Scripture...

---

[4] Ella: *The Free Offer* pp20-21. Please remember, reader, that what I say about the paradox between God's decrees and desires applies equally to the Father and the Son.

[5] 'This view' was a caricature of what I actually said.

[6] Ella: *The Free Offer* p20.

[7] Ella: *The Free Offer* p20, quoted from my 'Preaching'.

Deut. 29:29. The first is the rule of his own actions; the latter of ours.[8]

Owen:

The secret will of God is his eternal, unchangeable purpose concerning all things which he has made, to be brought by certain means to their appointed ends: of this, [he] himself affirms, that 'his counsel shall stand, and he will do all his pleasure' (Isa. 46:10). This [will] some call the absolute, efficacious will of God, the will of his good pleasure, always fulfilled; and indeed this is the only proper, eternal, constant, immutable will of God, whose order can neither be broken nor its law transgressed, so long as with him there is neither change nor shadow of turning.

On the other hand, said Owen, 'the revealed will of God does not contain his purpose and decree, but our duty; not what *he* will do according to his good pleasure, but what *we* should do if we will please him; and this, consisting in his word, his precepts and promises, belongs unto us and our children, that we may do the will of God... This is the rule of our obedience'.[9]

Again: 'The will of God is usually distinguished into his *will intending* and his *will commanding*... [The first is] his purpose, what he will do... [and the second is] his approbation of what we do, with his command thereof'.[10]

Commenting on Matthew 6:10, 'Your will be done', Manton said:

God's will... signifies two things; either his decree concerning future events, or else that which God has revealed concerning our duty; [in other words, either] his intended [will], or [his] commanded will. The first is spoken of, 'Who has resisted his will?' (Rom. 9:19); that is, his decree and his purpose; and the second, his revealed pleasure concerning our duty is spoken of, 'This is the will of God, even your sanctification' (1 Thess. 4:3). [This second will is] the will not of his purpose, but it is his law, his revealed pleasure. Now it is not meant here [Matt. 6:10] of God's decree or secret will. Why [not]? [Because] God's secret will... is not known, therefore how can it be done upon earth? To that [will] all are subject [including] reprobates, devils... Again, we may, without sin, will that which God wills not by his

---

[8] Flavel: *Mystery* p185. See same volume pp185-190.
[9] Owen: *Display* in *Works* Vol.10 p45, emphasis his.
[10] Owen: *Death* in *Works* Vol.10 p344, emphasis his.

secret will, as [for example] the life of a sick parent, which God [actually] purposes to take away. Indeed, a man may fulfil this secret will and yet perish for ever, as Judas... Therefore [God's] secret will is not here meant, but the will of God revealed. Therefore let me here distinguish again: The will of God is revealed in two ways, in his word and in his works: the one to be done by us, the other to be done upon us.[11]

Richard Sibbes: 'The secret will of God can be no rule, because it is secret. That which is a rule must be manifest and open. Therefore the revealed will of God, that every one may see, that is our rule. We may cross God's secret will, and [yet] do well[12]... [On the other hand] a wicked man may do [something] according to God's secret will, and yet sin... (Deut. 29:29). The will of God, as it is revealed, must be the rule of our actions. A rule must be open, or else it is no rule'.[13]

Pink: 'We much prefer to adopt the distinction made by the older Calvinists between God's secret and revealed will; or, to state it another way, his disposing and his preceptive will'.[14]

Coming closer to Ella, Brine also rightly distinguished between these two aspects of God's will: 'God's word and not his secret purpose is the rule of our conduct'.[15]

And, above all, Gill, in his turn, did the very same:

There is but one will in God; but for our better understanding it, it may be distinguished... The distinction [between] the secret and revealed will of God has generally obtained among sound divines... Whatever God has determined... that is his secret will... There is the revealed will of God in the gospel; which respects the kind invitations, and gracious regards of God to men... The most accurate distinction of the will of God, is into that of precept and [that of] purpose; or, [into that of] the commanding [will] and [that of the] decreeing will of God. God's will of precept, or his commanding will, is that which is often

---

[11] Manton: *Practical* p121.

[12] In the case of a child praying for a sick parent, for instance, referred to by Manton.

[13] Sibbes: *Epitaph* in *Works* Vol.6 p499.

[14] Pink pp243-246. There is plenty more; for instance: Dagg pp99-110; Philip Henry in Williams Part 1 p253; Latimer p369; Bavinck pp236-237,241; Marbury pp365-369; and so on and on.

[15] Fuller: *Worthy* in *Works* p170.

spoken of in Scripture, as what should be done by men... This is the rule of men's duty... The decreeing will of God [however] is [the] only [one], properly speaking, [which should be called] his will; the other is [properly speaking] his word.[16]

Again: 'God's will is either secret or revealed, purposing or commanding; the one is the rule of his own actions, the other of his creatures; now it oftentimes is so, that what accords with the secret and purposing will of God, is a disobedience to his revealed and commanding will'. Gill quoted Manton with approval: 'Things that are most against [God's] revealed will, fall under the ordination of his secret will; and, whilst men break commandments, they fulfil decrees: his revealed will shows what should be done, his secret will what will be done'.[17]

So why did Ella write so dismissively against the biblical principle? Ella was scathing against 'free offer enthusiasts who with greater or lesser surgical skills strive to dissect the mind of God into its desires and decrees... revealed will and secret will... special love and universal love; common grace and saving grace'.[18] Gill was no 'free offer enthusiast' but even he agreed with much of what Ella dismissed!

2. These two aspects of God's will are completely consistent; they make one will

Having said what I have about the two aspects of God's will, I do not want to be misunderstood. God's pleasure and his decree do not exist in two watertight compartments; there is considerable overlap; indeed, they are one. The fact that Scripture speaks of the two aspects of God's will, is, in itself, yet another example of God accommodating himself to the smallness of our understanding. But just because God has pitied our feeble limitations, and spoken in this way, we dare not try to reduce or simplify or resolve the will of God into two neat little packages, which we vainly imagine we are big enough to carry in our pocket. God's will is infinite!

---

[16] Gill: *Body* Vol.1, pp102-106.
[17] Gill: *Cause* p74; Manton: *Jude* p126.
[18] Ella: *The Free Offer* pp70-71; *Gill* p289.

And the two aspects of this infinite will make one will: 'My counsel shall stand, and I will do all my pleasure' (Isa. 46:10). 'The good pleasure of his will... according to his good pleasure which he purposed in himself' (Eph. 1:5,9). 'Now may the God of peace... make you complete in every good work to do his will, working in you what is well pleasing in his sight' (Heb. 13:20-21). 'The Spirit... makes intercession according to the will of God' (Rom. 8:27); that is, 'agreeably to the will of God, as it pleases him'. Sometimes God's pleasure is nothing less than his decree (1 Sam. 12:22; Ps. 115:3; 135:6; Isa. 53:10; 55:11; Gal. 1:15; Col. 1:19 *etc.*) God's will is one.

This must not be forgotten. Although it does not always look like it – since the will of God appears to us to be twofold – the truth is, as Calvin said: 'God's will is simple'; that is, it is a unity, it is one.[19] God does not have two contradictory wills; he is not in two minds; he has one consistent will. As Calvin pointed out:

Augustine did... by way of concession and explanation to his adversaries, make mention of a twofold will, or of different wills of God – a secret will, and an open or revealed will – but he so represented that twofold will as to show that they are in such consummate harmony with each other, that the last day will make it most gloriously manifest that there never was, nor is, in this multiform way of God's workings and doings, the least variance, conflict or contradiction, but the most divine and infinite harmony and oneness.[20]

---

[19] Calvin: *Commentaries* Vol.12 Part 1 p247.

[20] Calvin: *Calvin's Calvinism* p307. So what did Calvin mean when he said: 'For as to that distinction commonly held in the schools concerning the twofold will of God, such distinction is by no means admitted by us'? How could he say this when he so clearly held to the twofold will of God? The answer is, Calvin here was rightly dismissing an aberration of the truth, a doctrine taught by 'the sophists of Sorbon' which, though 'plausible and pleasant to the ears of Pighius', was in fact 'a blasphemy deservedly abhorred in its sound to all godly ears'; namely, that one aspect of God's will is 'ordinate' and the other 'absolute'. Calvin deduced that the sophists were saying God's absolute will is 'inordinate' or 'tyrannical'. Taking this to be the case, Calvin was rightly adamant; there is nothing inordinate about God's will; he decrees everything 'with the highest' or 'most righteous reason'; man should not proudly try to censure God for, if he does, he will find God's 'vengeance is gloriously just!' As for the two aspects of the one will of God, Calvin was not rejecting the

This is right; the twofold will of God is one consistent whole. Gill agreed: 'These two wills, though they differ, are not contradictory'.[21]

3. These two aspects of God's will, though completely consistent, do not always seem to be so

As Jerom Zanchius said: 'Although the will of God, considered in itself, is simply one and the same, yet, in condescension to the present capacities of man, the divine will is very properly distinguished into secret and revealed'.[22] This is the point; even though the will of God 'is simply one and the same', we are right to speak of its twofold aspect. More than that, to us there sometimes seems to be a conflict between the two aspects of God's will, and this is what makes our paradox. Calvin again: 'Although, therefore, God's will is simple, yet great variety is involved in it, as far as our senses are concerned'.[23] As Marbury said: 'Now sometimes there seems to be an opposition between these two wills

---

concept itself. Certainly not! As I have shown, he most definitely held the double aspect of God's will. Indeed, in so doing, Calvin claimed he was 'following Augustine and other godly teachers' in this distinction in the 'twofold will of God' (Calvin: *Calvin's Calvinism* pp118-119,197,266-267). Again, Calvin dismissed the 'madness' of 'unlearned men' who 'vainly talk', showing not only 'their ignorance in religion, but [who] are also wholly destitute of commonsense'. What did he have in mind? When they tried to reason that since God 'wills the salvation of all (1 Tim. 2:4), hence there is no election, which makes a distinction between one man and another'. Calvin gave this short shrift: 'For what is more absurd than to conclude that there is a twofold will in God, because he speaks otherwise with us than is consistent with his incomprehensible majesty? God's will then is one and simple, but manifold as to the perceptions of men; for we cannot comprehend his hidden purpose... Hence the Lord accommodates himself to the measure of our capacities' (Calvin: *Commentaries* Vol.15 Part 1 p277). This is the point I am making. As it seems to us, as revealed in Scripture, God has a twofold will, but the fact is God's will is one. We cannot reconcile the twofold will of God – but God has no need to, since he has but one will.

[21] Gill: *Cause* p159.

[22] Zanchius p47.

[23] Calvin: *Commentaries* Vol.12 Part 1 p247.

of God'.[24] I emphasise the *appears* and the *seems* in all this. To God, there is no conflict whatsoever; the conflict is, as Calvin noted, entirely and only 'as far as our senses are concerned'; it is as it *seems* to us.

* * *

This is the paradox we have to live with. And in doing so, we must remember, as Calvin said: 'Though to our apprehension the will of God is manifold, yet he does not in himself will opposites, but, according to his manifold wisdom... [he] transcends our senses, until such time as it shall be given us to know how he mysteriously wills what now seems to be adverse to his will'.[25] Zanchius illustrated the point: 'Thus it was his revealed will that Pharaoh should let the Israelites go, that Abraham should sacrifice his son, and that Peter should not deny Christ; but, as was proved by the event, it was his secret will that Pharaoh should not let Israel go (Exod. 4:21), that Abraham should not sacrifice Isaac (Gen. 22:12), and that Peter should deny his Lord (Matt. 26:34)'.[26] The lesson is clear. While we often have to admit our inability to discern God's purpose in events, and often find a paradox, to God there is no inconsistency whatsoever. Meanwhile we, obeying his revealed will, must wait his time to make all things clear to us.

Herman Bavinck, noting that 'God's preceptive will *seems* to be in conflict with his decretive will', applied the principle to the specific case I am dealing with in this book: 'According to the former he wills the salvation of all men, while according to the latter he does not'. But, as Bavinck rightly said: 'It should be observed, however, that the idea of the two wills in God [being] opposed to each other is erroneous'.[27]

Let me continue with my previous quote from Gill:

---

[24] Marbury p367.

[25] Calvin: *Institutes* Vol.2 p257; see also Vol.1 pp202-203. Calvin's words were paraphrased by Pink: God 'mysteriously wills what now seems contrary to his will' (Pink p198).

[26] Zanchius p47.

[27] Bavinck p238, emphasis mine. See also Taylor pp20-21; Owen: *Display* in *Works* Vol.10 pp46-49; and so on.

These two wills, though they differ, are not contradictory; the purpose of God is from eternity, his command is in time; the one is within himself, the other put forth from himself; the one is always fulfilled, the other seldom; the one cannot be resisted, the other may; the will of command only signifies [that] what is the pleasure of God should be the duty of man, or what he should do, but not what he shall do. Now admitting that it is God's will of command that... all mankind should repent, believe and obey, it does not follow that it is the determining will of God to give grace to all men to repent, believe and obey. Nor does it contradict such a will in God, determining to give grace to some to enable them to repent, believe and obey, and to deny it to others.[28]

Exactly so. Again:

God sometimes wishes that to be done by others which he himself does not think fit to execute... [This desire] is... expressive of what, if done, would be... well-pleasing to him, but not of what is his proper will and determination should be done... God's commanding and approving will is one thing, and his determining will another. In the former sense, God wills what he does not see fit to execute; it is what he commands and approves of, that men should... repent... when he does not see fit to give them the grace to enable them to do these things; but God never wills, that is determines, anything but he sees fit to execute, and does execute, it. Besides, it is one thing for God to will and wish, that is, command, and approve, what is entirely man's duty to do, though he does not see fit to give him grace to execute it.[29]

This is excellent.[30] Sadly, at this point Gill's hyper-Calvinism reared its head, and he drew back. It is altogether 'another thing', he said, 'to will and wish the salvation of all men... which, if he did wish, he would surely see fit to execute'.[31] Why? Why did Gill make this exception? He had just said that there are some things God desires but does not decree. He was right! I gave evidence of it in chapter 6. The salvation of all sinners is a case in point. God

---

[28] Gill: *Cause* p159; see also same volume pp154-155. Note how Gill was here conceding that God commands all mankind to repent, believe and obey the gospel. This takes us back to the first question – duty faith.

[29] Gill: *Cause* pp173-174.

[30] In fact, by it Gill effectively destroyed his hyper-Calvinism.

[31] Gill: *Cause* p174. Note, Gill here defined 'will and wish' as 'command, and approve... man's duty'.

in his revealed will shows that he desires the salvation of all sinners, but it is clear he has not decreed to save them all. It is a particular example of the general truth that God's revealed precept may command or desire a certain thing, while his secret decree is designed to bring about another.

Gouge, speaking of the free offer, hit the nail on the head:

> It may safely be granted that the offer is general, because it is made by [and to] such as know not the secret counsel of God. Though there is no contrariety between God's secret and revealed will, yet there is a difference between the determination of God's counsel and [the] dispensation thereof. Many things are determined which are not revealed... In the manner also of revealing God's will, many things are so ordered, as they do not directly declare what is determined... God often conceals part of his counsel purposely, to effect what he intended. To apply this to the point in hand: though Christ is, by the outward dispensation of God's ordinances, offered to all, yet it may not thence be inferred that Christ actually died for all. The offer is made to all, without exception of any, that, among those all, they for whom Christ was indeed given might believe, and others made inexcusable.[32]

While God has eternally decreed the certain salvation of his elect, he has commanded us to offer the gospel fully and freely to every sinner, to the elect and the reprobate alike.[33] God's secret will and purpose determines the salvation of his elect; his revealed will shows his desire that all men should be saved. In Scripture, God has expressed his yearning desire that all sinners should come to repentance and faith, turn from their wicked ways and live; he takes no pleasure in their continued refusal to listen to him and yield to his entreaties. He commands and urges all to repent and believe. Naturally, this is a great deep. We cannot reconcile God's invitations in the gospel – his revealed will of precept or command to all sinners to believe and repent – with the undeniable fact that God does not effectually call all sinners. It is, as I say, a paradox.

Manley Sr:

> God is perfectly sincere in his counsels and invitations, notwithstanding his divine foreknowledge of the consequences. That a

---

[32] Gouge p668.

[33] In any case, we do not know who is which.

God of omniscience foresees that one person will repent, and that another will not, must be admitted by all. Yet he offers mercy to all. Now, is God sincere, calling on men to repent, when he knows they will not? Oh yes! He is sincere, and earnest, and has no pleasure in the death of him that dies. Now, can these things be consistent? Facts may show.[34]

Edwards: 'The Arminians[35] ridicule the distinction between the secret and [the] revealed will of God... the distinction between the decree and [the] law of God, because we say he may decree one thing, and command another. And so, they argue, we hold a contrariety in God, as if one will of his contradicted another. However, if they will call this a contradiction of wills, we know that there is such a thing;[36] so that it is the greatest absurdity to dispute about it'.[37]

In short, it is perfectly proper to say that God desires the salvation of all men, and yet assert that he has not decreed that all men shall be saved. Adapting Manley's words: Facts do indeed show! This is a paradox to us, but to God it is not.

The question is: What are we to do with this paradox?

---

[34] *Southern Baptist Sermons* p27.

[35] They are not alone. Some hyper-Calvinists do it too!

[36] Edwards was not saying that there is a contradiction in the two wills of God; rather, though these two wills may *seem* to contradict each other, nevertheless there is no contradiction in God.

[37] Edwards illustrated the point from Abraham and Isaac, Pharaoh, Absalom, Jeroboam, the crucifixion of Christ, and so on (Edwards pp526-529).

9

What Should We Do with the Paradox?

I closed the previous chapter by asking what we should do with the paradox between God's decree to save his elect and his desire to save all. Here is my reply.

We must not dismiss the paradox, even though we cannot reconcile it

Speaking first of paradoxes in general: While the Bible tells us all we need to know about any paradox, it never fully explains it, it never unravels the knot; hence we have paradoxes! The Bible simply states both sides of a truth and leaves it there. Of course, to God there are no paradoxes; it is self-evident that he knows all things and is perfectly consistent. It is *we* who cannot understand; paradoxes arise in *our* poor finite minds. But on no account dare we question God: 'O man, who are you to reply against God?' (Rom. 9:20). 'Who can say to him, "What are you doing?"' (Job 9:12). In trying to cope with puzzles the Bible does not solve, we must not go beyond God's revelation (Deut. 29:29). Nor must we be arrogant: 'What shall we say then? Is there unrighteousness with God? Certainly not!' (Rom. 9:14). Rather, we should be humble: 'Can you search out the deep things of God?' (Job 11:7). Of course not! 'Oh, the depth of the riches both of the wisdom and knowledge of God! How unsearchable are his judgements and his ways past finding out!' (Rom. 11:33).

All we can do, all we may do, all we must do, is examine Scripture to discover the revealed mind of God, and, accepting the limitations of our understanding, hold both sides of any paradox we find: 'What God has joined together, let not man separate' (Matt. 19:6). This is the 'tension' I was speaking about, which Ella derided.[1] If I had spoken of a tension in the Godhead, Ella would

---

[1] Ella: *The Free Offer* pp20-22. I hope I have finally dealt with Ella's

have been right to attack me,[2] but since I was speaking of a tension

---

attack upon me over the issue. I do not believe God the Father and God the Son quarrel over the salvation of sinners. Perish the thought! As John Brown said: 'We are never to think of God the Father as indisposed to save man till prevailed on to do it by the labours, and sufferings, and prayers of his incarnate Son. The whole scheme originated in the will of the one God; and the mediatorial economy is nothing more than the means adopted by infinite wisdom to execute the purpose of infinite mercy, in consistency with the claims of infinite justice' (Brown: *Galatians* p33). M'Cheyne: 'When [Christ] wept over Jerusalem... there was much that was human in it. The feet were human that stood upon Mount Olivet. The eyes were human eyes that looked down upon the dazzling city. The tears were human tears that fell upon the ground. But oh, there was the tenderness of God beating beneath that mantle! Look and live, sinners. Look and live. Behold your God! He that has seen a weeping Christ has seen the Father. This is God manifest in the flesh. Some of you fear that the Father does not wish [desire] you to come to Christ and be saved. But see here, God is manifest in flesh. He that has seen Christ has seen the Father. See here the heart of the Father and the heart of the Son laid bare. Oh, why should you doubt? Every one of these tears trickles from the heart of God' (Bonar: *M'Cheyne* p472). Spurgeon made the same point: 'This is not and could not be the language of a mere man. It would be utterly absurd for any man to say that he would have gathered the inhabitants of a city together... Besides, the language implies that, for many centuries, by the sending of the prophets, and by many other warnings, God would often have gathered the children of Jerusalem... Now Christ could not have said that, throughout those ages, he would have gathered those people, if he had been only a man... but as the Son of God, ever loving the sons of men, ever desirous of the good of Israel, he could say that, in sending the prophets, even though they were stoned and killed, he had again and again shown his desire to bless his people till he could truly say, "How often would I have gathered your children together!" Some who have found difficulties in this lament, have said that it was the language of Christ as man [see, for instance, Gill: *Commentary* Vol.5 pp229-230]. I beg to put a very decided negative to that; it is, and it must be, the utterance of the Son of Man, the Son of God, the Christ in his complex person as human and divine' (Spurgeon: *Metropolitan* Vol.40 p469). Spurgeon never tired of the theme: *New* Vol.4 pp65-69; Vol.6 pp125-126; *Metropolitan* Vol.9 pp171-172; Vol.19 pp426-427; Vol.22 pp20-22; Vol.31 pp387-390; Vol.32 pp391-393. See chapter 6.

[2] But what of Gill on God's words in Hos. 11:8? 'How can I give you up, Ephraim? How can I hand you over, Israel?... My heart churns within me;

in the mind of the believer, his derision was sadly misplaced. Does Ella find no tension in his doctrinal understanding? Is everything in Scripture perfectly clear to his mind? Can he reconcile it all?

Edwards criticised those who 'lay it down for a rule, to embrace no doctrine which they by their own reason cannot reconcile with the moral perfections of God'.[3] Edwards rightly dismissed this as 'unreasonable'. He pointed out the obvious: By such a rule, he noted, if something cannot be true because 'our reason cannot see how it can be... it will follow that we must reject the doctrine of the trinity, the incarnation of the Son of God, *etc.* The Scripture itself supposes that there are some things in the Scripture that men may not be able to reconcile with God's moral perfections. See Romans 9:19... The apostle does not answer the

---

my sympathy is stirred'. 'The words are generally understood as a debate in the divine mind, struggling within itself between justice and mercy; justice requiring the delivery of these persons unto it, and mercy being reluctant thereunto, pleading on their behalf; and which at last gets the victory, and rejoices against judgement. There is a truth in all this'. True, Gill did place another construction on the words, saying that God was showing with what severity he might have dealt with Israel, but even so, Gill did admit the truth of the first view. I myself would go only as far as to say that God was once again accommodating himself to his hearers and speaking as a man – *as though* he had a debate in his mind, when in fact, of course, there is no debate within the mind of God. The same goes for his actions. As Gill rightly went on to say, God, without ever changing 'his mind and purposes', 'sometimes does what men do when they repent; he changes his outward conduct and behaviour in the dispensations of his providence, and acts the reverse of what he had done, or seemed to be about to do... So here, though he could, and seemed as if he would, go forth in a way of strict justice, yet [he] changes his course, and steers another way, without any change of his will. The phrase expresses the warmth and ardour of his affections to his people; how his heart burned with love to them; his bowels and inward parts were inflamed with it; from whence proceeded what is called repentance among men' (Gill: *Commentary* Vol.4 pp621-622). And, reader, please remember that although Israel was in some sense 'the people of God', not all Israelites were elect (Rom. 9:6-29; 11:1-10,25). Bearing this in mind, this last quotation from Gill expresses exactly what I have been trying to say; God's heart burns with desiring love to sinners, including the non-elect.

[3] He had Arminians in mind, but his words apply to all, including hyper-Calvinists.

objection by showing us how to reconcile it with the moral perfections of God, but by representing the arrogancy of quarrelling with revealed doctrines under such a pretence, and not considering the infinite distance between God and us'.[4] Now, however difficult we may find this, as Edwards said:

> There is no inconsistency or contrariety between the decretive and [the] preceptive will of God... To conclude this discourse: I wish the reader to consider the unreasonableness of rejecting plain revelations, because they are puzzling to our reason... Though the doctrine of the decrees is mysterious, and attended with difficulties, yet the opposite doctrine is in itself more mysterious, and attended with greater difficulties, and with contradictions to reason more evident, to one who thoroughly considers things... Since the Scripture is so abundant in declaring it, the unreasonableness of rejecting it appears the more glaring.[5]

Dr Withington had it right: When I come across a paradox, he said, 'I must mingle these truths just as they are mingled in the Bible, and I have no right to make the one weaker than the other. I must leave the compound, with all its perplexities and divine contradictions'. Francis Wayland was of the same mind: 'I stand to whatever God has said; what men infer from it is merely human,

---

[4] Edwards, after giving other scriptural examples, said: 'God's commanding a thing to be done, which he certainly knows at the time will not be done, is no evidence of insincerity in God in commanding'. In an earlier statement he had illustrated the point: 'For God to warn men to beware of damnation, though he has absolutely determined that they shall not be damned, is exactly parallel with his exhorting men to seek salvation, though he has actually determined that they shall not be saved'. God, of course, does both. In facing such issues, Edwards warned, 'there is a way of drawing consequences from Scripture, that begs the question'. He admitted, for example, 'there are many more texts plainly against election, than seem to be for it'; he was speaking of 'those texts that represent that general offers of salvation are made, as though it were left to men's choice whether they will be saved or not'. But Edwards dismissed the false deduction from this fact; namely, that man is the arbiter of his salvation. He did so by rightly saying it 'is begging the question. For the question very much consists in... whether an absolute decree be inconsistent with... a general offer of salvation'. And, as Edwards argued, there is no such inconsistency.

[5] Edwards pp534-543.

and weighs with me just nothing'.[6] Quite! There can be no inconsistency in God, so although we cannot explain how the two seemingly contradictory statements of any paradox fit together, we know they do, we hold both and preach both, without trying to reconcile them. William Jay, it has been said, 'never feared to give from the pulpit what he conceived to be the whole counsel of God. If he apparently met with difficulties in the subject he was at the time treating, he would mention the circumstances, and leave them, without an attempt to combine what was, in his opinion, far beyond man's finite powers'.[7]

Bavinck, in his treatise on the doctrine of God, declared:

The idea that the believer would be able to understand and comprehend intellectually the revealed mysteries is... unscriptural... The truth which God has revealed concerning himself in nature and in Scripture far surpasses human conception and comprehension... As soon as we take upon ourselves the task of speaking about God, the question at once arises: How can we? We are men, and he is the Lord our God... There is between him and us a distance as between the infinite and the finite, as between eternity and time... The history of the universe can never be made to fit into a little scheme of logic.[8]

Calvin, commenting on Ezekiel 18:23, spoke of God's desire as revealed in the prophet's words:

God desires nothing more earnestly than that those who were perishing and rushing to destruction should return into the way of safety. And for this reason not only is the gospel spread abroad in the world, but God wished to bear witness through all ages how inclined he is to pity... In the gospel we hear how familiarly he addresses us when he promises us pardon (Luke 1:78). And this is the knowledge of salvation, to embrace his mercy which he offers us in Christ... We hold, then, that God wills not the death of a sinner, since he calls all equally to repentance, and promises himself prepared to receive them if they only seriously repent.

But what now of God's decree? Calvin tackled anyone who objected to the above: If 'God desires nothing more earnestly than

---

[6] Article in *Bibliotheca Sacra*, 1861, quoted in Wayland Vol.1 pp124-126.

[7] Jay p249. He used Judas as a case in point. See also Jay pp170-171.

[8] Bavinck pp13-14,391. Hodge (p380) made the point from 'the unity of [Christ's] person [in] two spirits'.

that those who were perishing and rushing to destruction should return into the way of safety', and consequently he 'calls all equally to repentance', then it means that God's decree has gone out of the window, and 'there is no election of God, by which he has predestinated a fixed number to salvation'! In other words, both cannot be true. We can have either God's desire or his decree, but not both. He either desires all men to be saved, or else he has decreed that his elect and no others shall be saved. We cannot have both. To this, Calvin replied:

The answer is at hand: the prophet does not here speak of God's secret counsel, but only recalls miserable men from despair, that they may apprehend the hope of pardon, and repent and embrace the offered salvation. If anyone again objects – [that] this is making God act with duplicity, the answer is ready, that God always wishes the same thing, though by different ways, and in a manner inscrutable to us. Although, therefore, God's will is simple [that is, it is a unity, it is one], yet a great variety is involved in it, as far as our senses are concerned. Besides, it is not surprising that our eyes should be blinded by intense light, so that we cannot certainly judge how God wishes all to be saved, and yet has devoted all the reprobate to eternal destruction, and wishes[9] them to perish.

This is a difficulty, Calvin admitted. Of course it is! But he did not seek a solution by explaining it away. Indeed, he returned to it: 'God is said "not to wish the death of a sinner". How so? since he wishes all to be converted... [Now] since... repentance... is not in

---

[9] Surely Calvin meant 'will' ('intend') here, not 'desire'; the context clearly proves it. So why did he use 'wish'? But did he, in fact, use 'wish'? Does the confusion arise because the English version I am quoting is a translation 'from the original Latin, and collated with the French version'? As I have explained, in the New Testament, two Greek words can both be translated as 'will' or 'wish'. And in English, *Concise* has the word 'desire' in the definition of 'will'. The context must decide. 'God wishes [that is, desires] all to be saved, and yet has devoted all the reprobate to eternal destruction, and wishes [that is, decrees] them to perish'. This note also applies to the words which follow. I am not saying, of course, that there is any contradiction within God; he decrees and fulfils all his pleasure (Isa. 46:10). But, as I have shown, speaking as a man, God reveals that he desires the salvation of the reprobate even though he has decreed their damnation.

man's power... [but] is... in God's power... it follows that the reprobate are not converted, because God does not wish [that is, decree] their conversion; for if he wished [that is, decreed] it he could do it: and hence it appears that he does not wish [that is, decree] it'.[10]

But this is impossible, cries the objector: If your claim is true, then God *is* in two minds; worse, he deceives sinners; he tells them he desires their salvation but all the time he has never decreed it. Calvin gave this short shrift! 'But again they argue foolishly', he thundered, if they try to make out that 'since God does not wish [as above, decree] all to be converted, he himself is deceptive'. Nothing of the kind! But what of the difficulty? 'This knot is easily untied', said Calvin:

For [God] does not leave us in suspense when he says that he wishes all to be saved... God puts on a twofold character: for here he wishes to be taken at his word. As I have already said, the prophet does not here dispute with subtlety about [God's] incomprehensible plans, but wishes to keep our attention close to God's word. Now, what are the contents of this word? The law, the prophets and the gospel. Now all are called to repentance, and the hope of salvation is promised them when they repent... Meanwhile, this will of God which he sets forth in his word does not prevent him from decreeing before the world was created what he would do with every individual... God invites all who are in danger of perdition with extended arms, and promises them salvation if they heartily return to him.[11]

Calvin offered what he called a 'small word of advice'; namely, 'that the revealed will of God ought to be reverently acquiesced in, [and so] we will receive, without disputation, those mysteries which offend either the proud, or such as would be over-careful to remove the difficulties, in which, according to their view, such mysteries seem to be involved'.[12] Again: 'The chief part of our wisdom lies in confining ourselves soberly within the limits of God's word'.[13] 'I wish it to be received as a general rule, that the

---

[10] See the previous note for the justification for reading the last three uses of 'wish' as 'decree'.

[11] Calvin: *Commentaries* Vol.12 Part 1 pp246-250; see also pp265-267.

[12] Calvin: *Commentaries* Vol.6 Part 1 p194.

[13] Calvin: *Commentaries* Vol.17 Part 1 p153.

secret things of God are not to be scrutinised, and that those [things] which he has revealed are not to be overlooked[14]... Nor let us decline to submit our judgement to the boundless wisdom of God, so far as to confess its insufficiency to comprehend many of his secrets. Ignorance of things which we are not able, or which it is not lawful to know, is learning, while the desire to know them is a species of madness'.[15]

In short, said Calvin, 'the sum of my doctrine is this':

That that will of God, which is set forth in his law [the Scriptures], clearly demonstrates that righteousness is his delight, and that iniquity is his hatred... This, however, by no means prevents God from willing, by his secret and inexplicable counsel, that those things should be done, in a certain sense and manner, which he yet wills [that is, desires – see above] not to be done, and which he forbids to be done. If you will here raise the objection, that I make God inconsistent with himself, I, in return, would ask you whether it belongs to you to prescribe a law or a bound for God, forbidding him to do anything that surpasses your judgement and comprehension?... Will you, therefore, deny God the right of doing anything but that, the reason of which you can fully comprehend and explain?... But as for you, you will not permit God to have any counsel to himself, but that which you can as plainly see as a thing which you behold with your natural eyes.[16]

Earlier, Calvin had quoted Augustine: 'When men ask us... why God did this or that, our answer is to be, "Because it was his will". If they go on to enquire, Why did he so will it? our reply should be, "Now you ask that which is greater and higher than the will of God itself! You ask that which none can find out!" Let human rashness, then, keep itself within bounds. Let it never seek after that which is not, lest it should not find that which is'. Calvin added his endorsement: 'Most truly does Augustine speak in these words, and he has my fullest assent'.[17]

As Calvin admitted: 'If anyone should reply that this is above the capability of his mind to comprehend, I also acknowledge and

---

[14] A very common tendency! 'Oh! how happy were we, if as forward to obey the declarations of God's will, as we are to pry into the hidden counsels of his secret will!' (Burkitt Vol.1 p315).

[15] Calvin: *Institutes* Vol.2 pp206,233.

[16] Calvin: *Calvin's Calvinism* pp308-309.

[17] Calvin: *Calvin's Calvinism* pp122-123. See also Bavinck p33.

confess the same'.[18] In short, he said, 'let us leave to God his own secrets, and exercise ourselves as far as we can in the law [the Scriptures], in which God's will is made plain to us and to our children. Now let us go on'.[19]

Ella was himself of this mind when speaking of the reasons why God adopts certain sinners, and not others: 'These reasons', said Ella, 'are not entirely given us. We would most certainly not understand them. Nevertheless', as Ella explained, 'Paul gives us some inkling... Such reasons ought to satisfy anyone'.[20] Wise counsel! And my position exactly.

J.I.Packer, on how to approach a biblical paradox (or antinomy):

Accept it for what it is, and learn to live with it. Refuse to regard the apparent inconsistency as real; put down the semblance of contradiction to the deficiency of your own understanding; think of the two principles as, not rival alternatives, but, in some way that at present you do not grasp, complementary to each other. Be careful, therefore, not to set them at loggerheads, nor to make deductions from either that would cut across the other (such deductions would, for that very reason, be certainly unsound). Use each within the limits of its own sphere of reference (*i.e.*, the area delimited by the evidence from which the principle has been drawn). Note what connections exist between the two truths and their two frames of reference, and teach yourself to think of reality in a way that provides for their peaceful coexistence, remembering that reality itself has proved actually to contain them both. This is how antinomies must be handled, whether in nature or in Scripture.[21]

John Bunyan was of this opinion. So elementary he thought the principle, he put it into the mouth of a child in *The Pilgrim's Progress*: Prudence catechised Christiana's children to see how she had brought them up, asking Matthew, the eldest, what he thought of the Bible. 'It is the holy word of God'. Did he find some of it beyond his understanding? 'Yes, a great deal', the boy replied. 'What do you do when you meet with places you do not

---

[18] Calvin: *Calvin's Calvinism* p127.
[19] Calvin: *Commentaries* Vol.12 Part 1 p267.
[20] Ella: *The Free Offer* p10.
[21] Packer p21; see also Packer pp21-36.

understand?' 'I think God is wiser than I. I pray also that he may be pleased to let me know all... that he knows will be for my good'.[22]

Thus it is with God's desire to save all sinners even though he has not decreed it. 'How... do you reconcile these things?' asked D.Martyn Lloyd-Jones. He replied: 'The answer is – and here we come up against a great mystery which we shall never solve in this world – there is clearly a difference between what God desires and what God wills and brings to pass'.[23]

In short, we must treat this biblical paradox in exactly the same way as we treat all the others; namely, we must hold both truths, without trying to reconcile them, certainly not playing down one or the other.[24] As I have shown, some dismiss the paradox,[25] whilst others try to explain it away. What we should do is accept it.

In the following chapter, I will quote Spurgeon using the illustration of the parallel lines of the railway track. The rails always stay exactly the same distance apart, of course. But they do meet! A glance along a long straight track will show the parallel rails meeting in the infinite. Thus it is with this paradox. Let us accept it, therefore, and derive all the benefit to be found in travelling on both rails at once, knowing that in eternity all will

---

[22] Bunyan: *Pilgrim's* p97. See also Delves pp48-49; Bates Vol.4 p156; Kevan pp114-115; Cunningham Vol.2 pp346-348; Tyler and Bonar pp200,216-217; Machen: *Galatians* pp67-68; *Christian* pp45,70-71; Parks p99.

[23] Lloyd-Jones: *Romans* p54.

[24] Ella will not do this. While he rightly emphasises God's decree to save his elect, he has nothing but contempt for anything to do with God's desire to save all sinners.

[25] As just one further example, take John Foreman: 'Things that cannot be reconciled are opposed to one another, are against each other, and go to destroy and overturn each other'. In particular, Foreman was thinking of 'universal invitations, which... are really so opposed, that no man can reconcile them with the counsels of God. As we therefore cannot be consistent to hold and preach both, we will endeavour... to abide by the whole counsel of God... opposed to universal invitations; and leave [free-offer preachers] in duty faith, by their universal invitations, which are admitted to be irreconcilable with the counsels of God' (Foreman Vol.1 p42).

become clear.

But even this falls short of what is required. So let me ask the question once more: What are we to do with the paradox between God's decree and his desire to save sinners?

We must not only accept the paradox; we should preach it

Why do I not contend for a mere *acceptance* of the paradox? Just this. If the Bible teaches us that God desires the salvation of sinners, and commands us to preach his gospel to them on that basis, then it is our duty to declare his gospel to all men, and, in our appeals to them, to be as unrestrained as God's word allows – and demands. This is what is meant by the free offer. This is what is meant by preaching the gospel to sinners. This is what so many Calvinists in previous generations have done, and done with outstanding success. May God grant us the same sense of earnestness, the same freedom in preaching, and the same success. I would be delighted if my book made any contribution to this end.

As Fuller said: 'It is the revealed will of Christ that every one who hears the gospel should come to him for life'.[26] And as Zanchius put it: 'The brief of the matter is this: the secret things belong to God, and those that are revealed belong to us; therefore, when we meet with a plain precept, we should simply endeavour to obey it, without tarrying to inquire into God's hidden purpose'.[27] Just so! And a major part of God's revealed will, his precept or command is that we must invite, exhort, encourage, beg, command, call, and plead with all sinners to come to Christ, offering salvation to them all. We must tell them that God has revealed in his word that he desires their salvation, even though we know he has not determined to work effectually in all sinners to bring them to Christ. How this paradox can be reconciled no man comprehends, nor is it our concern to comprehend. As Zanchius declared, we must obey the precept and leave the decree to God. Let us get on with preaching the gospel, not wasting time in idle

---

[26] Fuller: *Exposition* in *Works* p530.
[27] Zanchius p49.

speculation. Idle? It is far worse! It is an abuse of God's twofold will. Both ministers and sinners can be guilty. Ministers, when they stifle the invitation by misusing the decrees; sinners, when they plead God's secret will against his revealed will, in order to excuse their unbelief.[28]

Owen dealt with the first: 'A minister is not to make inquiry after, nor to trouble himself about, those secrets of the eternal mind of God; namely, whom he purposes to save, and whom he has sent Christ to die for in particular. It is enough for them to search his revealed will, and thence take their directions'.[29]

Thomas Shepard answered the second; namely, the sinner who refuses to trust Christ because he does not know God's secret will, trying to excuse himself by saying: 'But I am not elected, nor redeemed; if I knew that, I [would] dare [to] receive the Lord and his love'. Shepard replied: 'What have you to do with God's secret decree of election? It is your duty to look to the gospel, which is the will of God's command... there is a will of God's command, and this you are to look to... Receive this love, and it is certain it is for you'.[30]

---

[28] Arminians stress the revealed will; hyper-Calvinists, the secret. Both should be biblically preached.

[29] Owen: *Death* in *Works* Vol.10 p300.

[30] Shepard p232. Shepard had no doubt about the free offer of the gospel: 'It is offered universally to all wherever it comes, and therefore personally to every man... and not only to them that do belong to Christ, and shall believe; for though it is offered with the power of it effectually to these [only], yet offered it is also unto those that never shall have God... There is not a man here that can exempt himself. And I would make no doubt to go to every man particularly, and say, The Lord entreats you to be reconciled'. But Shepard knew and owned that 'neither does this universal offer infer [*sic*, imply] a universal redemption'. Even so, 'there is not one here present, but the Lord would have you receive his love... It is God's command, and Christ's desire, [that] you should receive it... It is offered really' (Shepard p231). There is much more in the same vein: 'Not one soul that hears me this day but the Lord Jesus is a suitor unto... Whatever the secret purpose of Christ is, I regard not [in this connection]. In this evangelical dispensation of grace, he makes love to all... If there is a gospel in the world, there is this love of Christ yearning toward all... The Lord is real in his desires... If the Lord did not make love to you, he would not be really angry for [your] rejecting of this love; but the Lord is really

Such testimonies could be multiplied. Marbury: In 'our preaching, wherein we persuade [for] repentance, and promise life eternal, [the will of God... revealed to man] serves to direct all that look for salvation in the way of life, and it serves to convince the world of unrighteousness if they obey not... Let us not dispute the will of God, or search beyond that which is revealed; if [since] God has revealed his will to us, that must be our guide'.[31] Pink: 'It is sufficient for us to know that we are bidden to preach the gospel to every creature. It is not for us to reason about the consistency between this and the fact that "few are chosen". It is for us to obey. It is a simple matter to ask questions relating to the ways of God which no finite mind can fully fathom... It is not for us to reason about the gospel; it is our business to preach it'.[32] Septimus Sears: 'The Lord will not own our paring down his exhortations [in order] to preserve ourselves from the appearance of contradiction in our preaching. Who that, when he first reads the word of God with solemn desire to receive it as it is in truth the word of God, but has found great obstacles in the way of harmonising its doctrines and its exhortations? And I am persuaded that the more scriptural our preaching is, the more likely will many hearers be to find the same difficulty in harmonising our preaching'.[33]

So we accept both sides of the paradox, we believe both, we preach both. We do not try to explain the inexplicable, or meddle with that which does not belong to us. God has revealed what he wants us to know. Just as we may open only those letters addressed to us, and have no business to pry into those which are not, let us keep to that which is revealed. I am not saying we should not

---

angry for [your] rejecting it... [His love] is fervent, vehement, earnest love. Sometimes a suitor is real, but he is not earnest. Now, thus the Lord is... The Lord longs for this... pleads for this... thinks long for this... mourns when he has not this... [he is] content to give away anything for it... If you come not at once, he is content to wait that he may be gracious... See [the Lord Jesus] really before you, and see him willing to give himself unto you, even to you in particular' (Shepard pp18,23-25,62-63,166,230-232,237). I have, of course, for lack of space omitted the many scriptural arguments Shepard used in making his pleas.

[31] Marbury pp367,369.

[32] Pink pp210-211.

[33] Sears pp40-43.

preach the decrees;[34] far from it! No! But while we preach God's decree, we must also preach his desire; we must preach both, without trying to reconcile the two.[35]

But even this is not enough! So let me ask the question yet again: What are we to do with the paradox between God's decree and his desire to save sinners?

We must preach God's desire with passion

It all depends on the word 'preach'; if used biblically, then the heading is a tautology. Let me explain. To use Ella's words once more – which, I remind you, reader, he limited to repentance, but I apply to God's desire to see sinners saved: 'Sinners must be called, commanded, even *beseeched*'.[36] In other words, merely to 'present' the gospel, to make an accurate statement of the facts, to pass on information, or deliver a doctrinal lecture, is not enough, not by a long chalk. We must plead with sinners, we must preach God's desire *with passion*.[37] Light in a sermon is important, but warmth is vital. 'Did not our heart burn within us?' (Luke 24:32). As R.B.Kuiper said:

A most striking biblical paradox is that God, who sovereignly chose out of the fallen race of men a fixed number to everlasting life, yet offers to all men without distinction eternal life and, when doing so, assures them that nothing would please him more than their acceptance of his offer. God assures sinners everywhere that he 'will have all men to be saved' (1 Tim. 2:4). That, too, is an expression of the sovereignty of God, and its proclamation is a recognition of that sovereignty. The Calvinist declares it passionately.[38]

---

[34] As Ella insinuated (Ella: *The Free Offer* pp21-22). See Spurgeon: *Soul Winner* pp18-21.

[35] But, as I said in the Introduction and above, God's decrees ought not to be preached in such a way as to stifle the invitation of the gospel.

[36] Ella: *The Free Offer* p71, emphasis mine.

[37] Lloyd-Jones: *Preaching* pp91-99; Murray: *Fight* pp619,693.

[38] Kuiper pp182-183. See also Kuiper pp41-43. This is a subject on it own, even more vital than a mere understanding of the free offer. Preaching the gospel to sinners raises three issues: Who are the *sinners* to whom the gospel is to be preached? What is the *gospel* which is to be preached? What is *preaching*?

The principle is right. 'The Calvinist declares it passionately'. But does he? Many Calvinists are confused about God's desire, and, as a consequence, leave well alone. But what of those who are convinced of it? Do *we* declare it passionately? Reader, do you? Is there any danger that we might be what I call 'incipient' or *de facto* hypers?[39] I fear so. Far from preaching it with passion, too often we soft pedal God's desire, wrongly thinking we must defend God from charges raised by Reformed logicians, fearing the scorn

---

[39] See chapter 3. As in chapter 4, I assure you, reader, I include myself in the above, and what follows; 'physician, heal yourself!' (Luke 4:23) has to be reckoned with, as does Jas. 3:1. I say what I say because I believe it to be right, not because I pretend to have attained to it. In fact, in writing this book, I have come to see how for years I have concentrated too much on the theoretical aspect of this matter, and missed the practical. However, I am encouraged (I hope I use the right word) – but also challenged – by M'Cheyne's letter to his congregation on leaving for his visit to Palestine. He grieved over his hearers who had not been converted. One cause, he said, was in himself. He openly acknowledged his failure – his sin – to be what he should have been, and to do as he should have done (Bonar: *M'Cheyne* pp246-247). Elias: 'I have much to be ashamed of, by reason of preaching in such a dark, carnal, cold, sleepy manner. The greatest loss I feel, is that of the Spirit, and earnestness of secret prayer. It is bad and poor in the study, dark and embarrassing in the sermon owing to this. I want to go there oftener, and be more anxious before preaching' (Morgan p319). Lloyd-Jones: 'The element of pathos... perhaps is what has been most lacking in my own ministry. [It] should arise partly from a love for the people. Richard Cecil... said something which should make us all think. "To love to preach is one thing, to love those to whom we preach quite another". The trouble with some of us is that we love preaching, but we are not always careful to make sure that we love the people to whom we are actually preaching... And if you know nothing of this you should not be in a pulpit... Not only will your love for the people produce this pathos, the matter itself is bound to do this in and of itself. What can possibly be more moving than a realisation of what God in Christ has done for us... It is only when we begin to know something of this melting quality that we shall be real preachers... This element of pathos and of emotion is, to me, a very vital one. It is what has been so seriously lacking in the [twentieth] century, and perhaps *especially among Reformed people*' (Lloyd-Jones: *Preaching* pp92-93, emphasis mine; see also Murray: *Fight* p694). See also the extracts from Spurgeon and M'Cheyne in the main text above.

of those who deny our Calvinistic credentials.[40] Perhaps we are embarrassed at showing emotion in our preaching, and we do not plead with sinners as we ought, shrinking from being reckoned one of the 'fools for Christ's sake' (1 Cor. 4:10). But how wrong this is, for if earnestness is absent from our preaching, we rob it of much of its power. And how trivial is the disapproval of men compared to honouring God and seeking the salvation of sinners in his appointed way!

Spurgeon:

Very earnestly, I would speak to you a little upon the manner in which this [gospel] message is to be delivered... First, it is to be delivered *by beseeching* men, and begging[41] men. 'As though God did beseech you by us we beg you' [2 Cor. 5:20]. Then [this means that] if I should merely tell you, dear hearers, the gospel, though God might bless it, I have not done all my duty. To inform the intellect is not the minister's sole work; we are to proclaim, but we are to do far more – we are to beseech and to beg. We are not merely to convince the intellect, but to beseech the heart. Neither are we alone to warn and threaten; though that has its place, yet it is not to be our main work; we are to beseech. You know how a beggar... implores you when he is starving, that you will give him bread: with like earnestness are we bound to beseech you to be saved. You know how you will beg a fellow-creature to help you when you are in sore distress: in that same way are we to beg you to be reconciled to God. As I ponder this I feel self-condemned. I have besought you, and I have begged you sometimes, but not as I ought to have done. Oh, to be taught how to beseech men, how to beg them! God forbid we should fall into the error of those who think beseeching and begging [sinners] to be unlawful; it is the Christly principle which leads God's ministers so to do; it is the main part of a minister's business, and he who neglects it will have to answer for it before God's great bar...

Oh, how God beseeches men, and he means his ministers to beseech them in the same way, with weeping tenderness and melting pathos, if perhaps the stony heart may be softened, and iron sinew be bowed. Do I hear some strong-doctrine brother say, 'I do not like this'? My dear brother, I am not careful [that is, anxious how] to answer you in this matter. If the Lord appoints it, you ought to approve it, and if you do

---

[40] Scorn? What I have been arguing for has been dismissed as 'blasphemous' (Ella: *The Free Offer* p21).

[41] Where Spurgeon used 'pray' in this extract, I have used 'beg', which better conveys Paul's meaning. The NKJV uses 'implore'.

not, you are wrong, but the Scripture is not. If God beseeches and bids me beseech as he does, I will do it; and, though I be counted vile for it by you, then so must it be. Besides, it is no derogation for God to beseech his creatures. You say we make God beg to his creatures. Assuredly that is how the Lord represents himself.[42]

This is it: Telling sinners, informing sinners, proclaiming to sinners, convincing sinners, warning sinners, is not enough; we must beseech and beg them to be reconciled to God.

Robert Murray M'Cheyne:

Oh, for the bowels of Jesus Christ in every minister, that we might long after [sinners] all!... And here I would observe what appears to me a fault in the preaching of [today].[43] Most ministers are accustomed to set Christ before the people. They lay down the gospel clearly and beautifully, but they do not urge men to enter in. Now God says, 'Exhort' – beseech men – persuade men; not only point to the open door, but compel them to come in. Oh to be more merciful to souls,[44] that we would lay hands on men and draw them in to the Lord Jesus!... [We must do it] with urgency. If a neighbour's house were on fire, would we not cry aloud and use every exertion? If a friend were drowning, would we be ashamed to strain every nerve to save him? But alas! the souls of our neighbours are even now on their way to everlasting burnings – they are ready to be drowned in the depths of perdition. Oh, shall we be less earnest to save their never-dying souls, than we would be to save their bodies? How anxious was the Lord Jesus in this! When he came near and beheld the city, he wept over it. How earnest was Paul! 'Remember that by the space of three years I ceased not to warn every one night and day with tears'.[45] Such was

---

[42] Citing, amongst other verses, Isa. 1:2,18; 55:1-2; 65:2; Jer. 44:4; Ezek. 33:11; Hos. 11:8; Matt. 11:28; 23:37; John 6:37 and Rom. 10:21, Spurgeon rightly argued, as did Paul, that the preacher must beg sinners to be reconciled to God because that is precisely what God himself does through the preacher, and what Christ himself did in his earthly ministry: 'Never such a pleader as Jesus' (Spurgeon: *Metropolitan* Vol.19 pp428-431, emphasis his). Again: 'Lost souls, you doubly lost, you more than ruined, my Master begs you to come' (Spurgeon: *The Pulpit Library* pp192-194). See also *Metropolitan* Vol.33 pp361-372; *Second* pp179-192.
[43] M'Cheyne had, 'of our beloved Scotland', speaking in 1840. What would he say today? and not only of Scotland?
[44] A searching thought; preachers are cruel to sinners if they merely *present* the gospel to them.
[45] See chapter 6.

George Whitfield; that great man scarcely ever preached without being melted into tears. Brethren, there is need of the same urgency now. Hell is as deep and as burning as ever. Unconverted souls are as surely rushing to it. Christ is as free – pardon as sweet as ever! Ah! how we shall be amazed at our coldness when we do get to heaven!

Again:

It is to be feared there is much unfaithful preaching to the unconverted... We do not speak to those who are [Christless] with anything like sufficient plainness, frequency and urgency. Alas! how few ministers are like the angels at Sodom, mercifully bold to lay hands on lingering sinners!... Many of those who deal faithfully, yet do not deal tenderly. We have more of the bitterness of man than of the tenderness of God. We do not *yearn over* men in the bowels of Jesus Christ. Paul wrote of 'the enemies of the cross of Christ' with tears in his eyes! There is little of his weeping among ministers now. 'Knowing the terrors [*sic*] of the Lord', Paul persuaded men. There is little of this persuading spirit among ministers now. How can we wonder that the dry bones are very, very dry – that God is a stranger in the land?... Some set forth Christ plainly and faithfully, but where is Paul's *beseeching* men to be reconciled? We do not invite sinners tenderly; we do not gently woo them to Christ; we do not authoritatively bid them to the marriage; we do not *compel* them to come in; we do not travail in birth till Christ be formed in them the hope of glory. Oh, who can wonder that God is such a stranger in the land?[46]

And this, reader, lies at the very heart of what I am trying to say. I have not locked horns with Ella over a theoretical nicety. The free offer is an important principle or doctrine, yes, but it is not so much a controversy over doctrine which is at stake; *it is the practical consequences of that controversy.* I want to let believers know how far we have fallen away from real gospel preaching. Above all, I pray that preachers who read my book – and I include myself – may be moved to fulfil the task God has laid upon them.

But what, precisely, is this task? What is the great need of the hour in this respect? These questions bring me to the climax of my book. Is the great need to preach the free offer? is it to preach God's desire for the salvation of sinners? is it to preach the universal invitation and duty faith? to preach it even with passion?

---

[46] Bonar: *M'Cheyne* pp402-404,590-591, emphasis his.

I may startle you, reader, by my reply. The answer is, No! This *in itself* is not the need.

So what is the need?

We must preach God's desire with our heart constrained by that desire

Rather than merely accepting the paradox, or preaching it, or preaching it with passion, we must preach God's desire for sinners' salvation *with that desire burning in our heart*; we need to preach the free offer *constrained by the love of Christ*. Let me underline it; we are to show passion in our addresses to sinners, yes, but the passion we are to show must come from our *heart*. We, like God, must love sinners and desire their salvation. With sincerity, we must, like Spurgeon, be able to say: 'Oh! I want to bring you in'.[47] Let me repeat some of my quotation from M'Cheyne a few moments ago: 'Oh, for the bowels of Jesus Christ in every minister, that we might long after [sinners] all!' he cried. 'We do not yearn over men in the bowels of Jesus Christ', he complained. How searching is this thought! May the Holy Spirit fill our hearts with the love of God!

Hyper-Calvinists talk about need of a sinner's fitness to be invited to Christ.[48] They are mistaken; the sinner requires no fitness to be invited, none whatsoever. Even so, there is a fitness which *is* required. Which is? *The preacher needs to be fit – fit to invite the sinner!*[49] Warm lips and a cold heart, orthodox doctrine from a heart unmoved, is a diabolical combination in any believer who would win souls for Christ.[50] How easy it is to be a mere actor

---

[47] Spurgeon: *The Pulpit Library* p39.

[48] As I have shown. I will return to it in Appendix 2.

[49] 'I never was fit to say a word to a sinner, except when I had a broken heart myself; when I was subdued and melted into [repentance], and felt as though I had just received pardon to my own soul, and when my heart was full of tenderness and pity – no anger, no anger' (Payson Vol.1 p415).

[50] See Murray: *Spurgeon* pp93-97,113-114. And this applies not only to preachers: 'Weeping Christians! Weep for [sinners]. Let your tears flow in rivers... What! will you not weep and feel for them? Will your hearts be like stone and steel? And will you be worse than brutes, and let them

in the pulpit! But, my reader, it must not be. Spurgeon: 'The most damnable thing a man can do is to preach the gospel merely as an actor'; 'you must feel it yourself, and speak as a man who feels it; not *as if* you feel it, but *because* you feel it, otherwise you will not make it felt by others'; 'we do not want pranks and performances which are the mere sham of earnestness, but real white-heat earnestness is the want of the times'.[51] Our fervent words must be sincere; our heart must keep in step with our lips; indeed, we should feel more than we can express. Once again, I say: How searching is this thought! May the Holy Spirit help us.

Let Spurgeon explain my meaning:

If you think to do any great good in saving sinners, you must not be half-asleep yourself: you must be troubled even to tears. Perhaps the most difficult thing in winning souls is to get ourselves into a fit state. The dead may bury their dead, but they cannot raise the dead. Until a man's whole soul is moved, he will not move his fellow. He might, possibly, succeed with those who are willing to be impressed; but the careless will be unmoved by any man who is unmoved himself. Tears storm a passage [make a way] for warnings. If Christ's whole self must be stirred before Lazarus is raised, *we* must be thrilled before we can win a soul... We must feel, if others are to feel... Your Lord was all alive, and all sensitive, and you must be the same. How can you expect to see his power exercised on others if you do not feel his emotion in yourselves? You must be quickened into tenderness as he was, or you will not receive his life-giving power. When I am weak, then am I strong. 'Jesus wept' when he raised dead Lazarus.

---

perish without a sigh, without a prayer, without a tear?' (Spurgeon: *The Pulpit Library* pp174-175).

[51] Spurgeon: *Soul Winner* pp74,100,193, emphasis his; see also same volume pp72-74,100-102,178-184. 'A man who tries to produce an effect becomes an actor, and is an abominable impostor' (Lloyd-Jones: *Preaching* p93). Commenting on 2 Cor. 2:4, Calvin said: 'There are many noisy reprovers, who... display a surprising ardour of zeal, while in the mean time they are at ease in their mind, so that it might seem as if they exercised their throats and sides [in crying] by way of sport. It is, however, the part of a pious [preacher], to weep within himself, before he calls upon others to weep; to feel tortured in silent musings, before he shows any token of displeasure; and to keep within his own breast more grief than he causes to others... Paul's tears... show tenderness of heart' (Calvin: *Commentaries* Vol.20 Part 2 pp147-148).

In short: 'Except the spirit of the Lord rests upon you, causing you to agonise for the salvation of men even as Jesus did, you can do nothing'.[52] This is it – we must 'agonise... even as Jesus did'.

Let me drive this home with what I can only call a deliberate understatement by Owen. Speaking of 'the terms of the gospel', Owen, exhorting sinners, said:

It is God himself who proposes these terms; and not only proposes them, but invites, exhorts, and persuades you to accept... them. This the whole Scriptures testify to. It is fully expressed (2 Cor. 5:18-20). He has provided them [the terms], he has proposed them, and makes use only of men, of ministers, to act in his name. *And excuse us if we are a little earnest with you in this matter.*[53] Alas! our utmost that we can, by zeal for his glory or compassion to your souls, raise our thoughts, minds, spirits, words unto, comes infinitely short of his own pressing earnestness herein. See Isa. 55:1-4. Oh, infinite condescension! Oh, blessed grace![54]

What a standard! 'Who is sufficient for these things?' (2 Cor. 2:16). To which question there is only one answer: 'Not that we are sufficient of ourselves to think of anything as being from ourselves, but our sufficiency is from God, who also made us sufficient as ministers of the new covenant' (2 Cor. 3:5-6). May we prove it by experience!

* * *

Working on the principle that an ounce of demonstration is worth a ton of theoretical explanation, I close this chapter with an example of what I am talking about. There is no shortage of excellent material from which to pick, but the sample I have chosen is from a sermon by Clarkson, Owen's successor.

In light of his words, I am bound to ask myself if I have ever

---

[52] Spurgeon: *Metropolitan* Vol.35 p344, emphasis his; Vol.27 p600; *Soul Winner* pp21-22,27,46-47,58-61,74-79,83-87,102-103,110-112,140-141, 156,162-165,180-184,192-193,214-215. See chapter 6 for Paul being constrained by Christ's love.

[53] The 'deliberate understatement'.

[54] Owen: *Psalm 130* in *Works* Vol.6 p517, emphasis mine. See also, for instance, Kelly pp49-51,76-78,83,146,150,153-154,172; Bridges pp318-339; Morgan pp349-355.

preached.[55] I ask my fellow-preachers: Can you honestly say that you have pleaded with sinners like Clarkson? If not, why not? How few sinners today can report they have felt such love and power flowing from the preacher as he addressed them. We must recover this way of preaching, my brothers, we must. The plight of sinners demands it. Our own peace of conscience demands it. Above all, the glory of Christ demands it.

So, then, let Clarkson, though long dead, preach again. May he speak to all who read these words – both believers and unbelievers:

[Take] Luke 14... Though Christ invites them again and again, though he lifts up his voice and cries aloud to them in the ministry of the word... they do not hear Christ; he speaks to stocks and stones, no more are they moved by his invitations... Though Christ weeps... yet they regard not... Though Christ knocks at the door of their hearts, and stands there knocking and knocking... by his word and Spirit... knock he may, and stand knocking till his head be wet with the dew... yet they will not open. Or if his importunity makes them listen, yet usually he gets no other answer, no other return than this, We are not now at leisure, trouble us not now; come another time and we may hear you...

Christ has... cause to complain of every one, You will not come to me... Such an averseness [unwillingness, dislike] is in [you][56] towards Christ, as you will rather die than come to him. Nor fear of death, nor desire of life itself, can make men willing to come to Christ. Christ himself could not prevail with many sinners to make them willing, though he preached several years... and made this the chief scope of his sermons, and spoke so to this purpose as never man spoke, yet all that he could say or do was not effectual with the greatest part of those that heard him. Hence he concludes his sermons sometimes with complaints, sometimes with tears (Luke 13:34; Matt. 23:37). So few

---

[55] Lloyd-Jones quoted James Henry Thornwell, whom he described as 'a very great preacher': 'My own [attempts at preaching]', said Thornwell, 'fill me with disgust. I have never made, much less preached, a sermon in my life, and I am beginning to despair of ever being able to do it'. Lloyd-Jones commented: 'Any man who has had some glimpse of what it is to preach will inevitability feel that he has never preached. But he will go on trying, hoping that by the grace of God one day he may truly preach' (Lloyd-Jones: *Preaching* pp98-99). I seem to recall that Lloyd-Jones said he felt he himself had preached only twice – and on both occasions he was dreaming.

[56] Clarkson had 'them', referring to what he called 'our natures'.

did he prevail with... [Isa. 49:4; 53:1; 65:2; John 12:37-38]...
If you are willing to come to Christ, you are already come, for there is nothing stands between Christ and a sinner but this unwillingness [on your part]; as soon as you are willing, you are with him...
Come to Christ, and you shall be... united to him, one with him. This is Christ's aim in inviting you, this he desires, this he prays for (John 17:20-21). He invites you... all that Christ requires is but your consent; consent but to come, and the match is made, your Redeemer will be your husband (Isa. 54:5)... Are you not willing to come to Christ upon such terms?... Upon condition you will come, you shall have all that Christ can give you...[57] Christ would have you come... Does he require you to come upon any unreasonable terms? Oh no. Even those that must perish for their refusals, as all must that will persist [in] refusing, will be forced to confess that it was the most equal thing in the world that Christ desired, when he bade them leave their sins to come to him...
He waits till you come. The great God stoops so low as to wait upon sinners (Isa. 30:18). He waits as one ardently desiring... the return of sinners to himself, and shall he wait in vain? He stands willing to welcome you... There is a time, indeed, when sinners shall not be admitted... when sinners have worn out his patience, and rejected his offers and entreaties, till there be no remedy; but... he who now resolves to come need not doubt of welcome (John 6:37)... [Christ] never did, he never will, cast out a returning sinner. He will not do it in any way, upon any terms and considerations whatsoever...
And so he waits for your coming, waits industriously, waits patiently. He waits so as he uses all means to draw you to him. He speaks to you by his providence, he woos you by his word, he sends his messengers to invite, to entreat, to beseech you to come, he puts words in their mouths by which he would have them woo you, he suggests arguments to their minds by which he would have them persuade you, he assists them by his Spirit to manage these persuasions, to enforce these arguments, so as they may prevail, or leave you inexcusable...
Though you refuse to hear, and be weary of hearing, yet the Lord is not weary of waiting, not weary of entreating. And when others or yourselves would put away the word, and break off this treaty for reconciliation, yet the Lord maugres [despises, ignores?] all provocations, [and] continues it. Oh the wonderful indulgence of Christ.[58]

---

[57] Clarkson drove on page after page: 'Come, come, come...'

[58] Clarkson: *Men by Nature* in *Works* Vol.1 pp334-355.

Reader, this is but one example out of hundreds which might have been chosen.[59] And the bulk, I assure you, is as good as the sample.

---

[59] I have not seen an unpublished paper by S.Isbel: 'A Bibliography of the Free Offer of the Gospel', but David Silversides called it 'very useful' (Silversides pp83-84). Of the many examples I have come across, I mention Clarkson: *Invitation* in *Works* Vol.2; Flavel: *Christ*; Alleine; Bunyan: *Jerusalem Sinner*; Whitefield; Shepard; Bonar: *M'Cheyne* pp365-371; see also pp583-584; M'Cheyne: *Fragments* pp92-96 (*Sermons* pp148-154); Boston: *Beauties* 1979; *The Sum* pp334-336; Owen: *Meditations* in *Works* Vol.1 pp419-432. For Spurgeon, see chapter 10.

10

Spurgeon and God's Desire to Save Sinners

Why a chapter devoted to Spurgeon? For two reasons. *First*, Spurgeon was a fine example of a free-offer preacher. I have already shown that he preached duty faith; now I will demonstrate that he preached God's desire to save all sinners. *Secondly*, as I have already noted, Ella criticised a small book-review I wrote, in which I expressed my views on the paradox between God's decree to save his elect and his desire to save all sinners. Referring to the review, Ella accused me of having 'the audacity to thrust forward Charles H.Spurgeon, citing him as one who believed that the testimony of Scripture is irreconcilable with itself'.[1]

By answering Ella, I will make it clear that Spurgeon was one who preached God's desire to save all sinners, one who was not hung up on the seeming contradiction this involves. And his example will more-than-adequately illustrate what I have been trying to say throughout the book.

As for Ella's criticism, I would like to set the record straight. In the first place, I did not 'thrust forward' Spurgeon; after all, I was reviewing a book on the good man! And secondly, this is what I said: 'Spurgeon did not try to reconcile the irreconcilable – he preached what the Bible teaches'. I was not saying the truths of God's word cannot be reconciled. Of course they can. Not always by man, of course, but always by God! In fact, he has no need to reconcile them! What I was saying was that Spurgeon was happy to preach what he found in Scripture, even though he sometimes found paradoxes. When confronted with statements he could not reconcile – and which no man can – he did not try to do that for which God had given him no tools; namely, reconcile them. He simply got on and preached what he found in Scripture. In

---

[1] Ella: *The Free Offer* p22.

particular, he preached both the desire of God to save all sinners and his decree to save the elect. That is what I was saying. Here are my words:

Spurgeon argued from the Bible. A consistent Calvinist, he said that gospel invitations are sent to all sinners, that all sinners *may* trust Christ, that all sinners *must* trust Christ, and that God has a desire to see all sinners saved. Spurgeon did not try to reconcile the irreconcilable – he preached what the Bible teaches.

Now let me prove it. First, did Spurgeon find paradoxes in Scripture? And did he preach both aspects of these paradoxes? Indeed, he did! Hear him:

We hold tenaciously that salvation is all of grace, but we also believe with equal firmness that the ruin of man is entirely the result of his own sin. It is the will of God that saves; it is the will of man that damns...
There are great deeps about these... points... The best thing is to take what God reveals to you, and believe that... If you so act, you will be safe; but if you try to be wise above that which is written, and to understand that which even angels do not comprehend, you will certainly befog yourselves.[2]

Again:

The system of truth is not one straight line, but two. No man will ever get a right view of the gospel until he knows how to look at the two lines at once... That God predestines, and that man is responsible, are two things that few can see. They are believed to be inconsistent and contradictory; but they are not. It is just the fault of our weak judgement. Two truths cannot be contradictory to each other... it is my folly that leads me to imagine that two truths can ever contradict each other. These two truths, I do not believe, can ever be welded into one upon any human anvil, but one they shall be in eternity.

After speaking on God's sovereignty, Spurgeon moved on to the other side of the gospel: God stretches out his hand to those who refuse him. 'There now', says the hyper-Calvinist, 'he is going to contradict himself'. Spurgeon replied:

No, my friend, I am not, I am only going to contradict *you*... You ask me to reconcile the two. I answer, they do not want any reconcilement; I never tried to reconcile them to myself, because I could never see a discrepancy. If you begin to put fifty or sixty quibbles to me, I cannot give any answer. Both are true; no two truths can be inconsistent with each other; and what you have to do is to believe them both.[3]

As he said on another occasion:

They say that if we preach the gospel freely we are inconsistent, to which charge we are at no pains whatever to reply. So long as we believe that we are consistent with Scripture, it never enters into our heads to want to be consistent with ourselves. To hold all revealed truth is our desire, but to compress it all into a symmetrical creed is beyond our expectation. We are such poor fallible creatures that if we were once to fabricate a system which should be entirely logical, we should feel sure that we must have admitted portions of theory and masses of mere guess-work into the singular fabric. In theology we live by faith, not by logic... If we will keep simply to what the word of God says, we shall find in it truths apparently in conflict, but always in agreement. On every subject there is a truth which is set over against another truth: the one is as true as the other; the one does not take away from the other, nor raise a question upon the other; but the one ought to be stated as well as the other, and the two set side by side. The two relative truths make up the great road of practical truth, along which our Lord travels to bless the sons of men. Some like to run on one rail. I confess a partiality to the two, and I should not like to make an excursion tomorrow on a railway from which one of the rails had been taken.[4]

In short: 'O that... seeming opposites would be received, because faith knows that they are portions of one harmonious whole'.[5]

So much for Spurgeon on the paradoxes of Scripture.

---

[3] Spurgeon: *New* Vol.4 pp337,341,343, emphasis his.

[4] Spurgeon: *Metropolitan* Vol.30 p473.

[5] Spurgeon: *Metropolitan* Vol.9 vii. Spurgeon returned to this theme repeatedly; see, for instance, *New* Vol.5 pp120,353; Vol.6 p302; *Metropolitan* Vol.9 pp358-359 (but note the omission of the 'not' on the last line of p358); Vol.15 p458; Vol.16 p501; Vol.30 pp49-50; Vol.40 pp529-530; Vol.45 pp325-327; *Early* pp173-174. See also Murray: *Spurgeon* pp81-84.

What about the second point? Did Spurgeon believe God desires the salvation of all sinners? Indeed, he did! Hear him on 1 Timothy 2:3-4:

It is quite certain that when we read that God will have all men to be saved it does not mean that he wills it with the force of a decree or a divine purpose, for, if he did, then all men would be saved. He willed to make the world, and the world was made: he does not so will the salvation of all men, for we know that all men will not be saved...
What then? Shall we try to put another meaning into the text than that which it fairly bears? I think not. You must, most of you, be acquainted with the general method in which our older Calvinistic friends deal with this text. 'All men', say they, 'that is, *some men*': as if the Holy Ghost could not have said 'some men' if he had meant some men. 'All men', say they; 'that is, some of all sorts of men': as if the Lord could not have said 'all sorts of men' if he had meant that. The Holy Ghost by the apostle has written 'all men', and unquestionably he means all men. I know how to get rid of the force of the 'alls' according to that critical method which some time ago was very current, but I do not see how it can be applied here with due regard to truth. I was reading just now the exposition [by] a very able doctor[6] who explains the text so as to explain it away; he applies grammatical gunpowder to it, and explodes it by way of expounding it. I thought when I read his exposition that it would have been a very capital comment upon the text if it had read, 'Who *will not* have all men to be saved, nor come to a knowledge of the truth'. Had such been the inspired language every remark of the learned doctor would have been exactly in keeping, but as it happens to say, 'Who *will* have all men to be saved', his observations are more than a little out of place. My love of consistency with my own doctrinal views is not great enough to allow me knowingly to alter a single text of Scripture. I have great respect for orthodoxy, but my reverence for inspiration is far greater. I would sooner a hundred times over appear to be inconsistent with myself than be inconsistent with the word of God. I never thought it to be any very great crime to seem to be inconsistent with myself, for who am I that I should everlastingly be consistent? But I do think it a great crime to be so inconsistent with the word of God that I should want to lop away a bough or even a twig from so much as a single tree of the forest of Scripture. God forbid that I should cut or shape, even in the least degree, any divine expression. So runs the text, and so we must read it, 'God our Saviour; who will

---

[6] Gill? See chapter 6.

have all men to be saved, and to come unto the knowledge of the truth.'

Does not the text mean that it is the wish of God that men should be saved? The word 'wish' gives as much force to the original as it really requires, and the passage should run thus – 'whose wish it is that all men should be saved and come to a knowledge of the truth.' As it is *my* wish that it should be so, as it is *your* wish that it might be so, so it is God's wish that all men should be saved; for, assuredly, he is not less benevolent than we are.[7] Then comes the question, 'But if he wishes it to be so, why does he not make it so?' Beloved friend, have you never heard that a fool may ask a question which a wise man cannot answer, and, if that be so, I am sure a wise person, like yourself, can ask me a great many questions which, fool as I am, I am yet not foolish enough to try to answer. Your question is only one form of the great debate of all the ages – 'If God be infinitely good and powerful, why does not his power carry out to the full all his beneficence?' It is God's wish that the oppressed should go free, yet there are many oppressed who are not free. It is God's wish that the sick should not suffer. Do you doubt it? Is it not your own wish? And yet the Lord does not work a miracle to heal every sick person. It is God's wish that his creatures should be happy. Do you deny that? He does not interpose by any miraculous agency to make us all happy, and yet it would be wicked to suppose that he does not wish the happiness of all the creatures that he has made. He has an infinite benevolence which, nevertheless, is not in all points worked out by his infinite omnipotence; and if anybody asked me why it is not, I cannot tell. I have never set up to be an explainer of all difficulties, and I have no desire to do so... I cannot tell you why God permits moral evil, neither can the ablest philosopher on earth, nor the highest angel in heaven.

This is one of those things which we do not need to know. Have you never noticed that some people who are ill and are ordered to take pills are foolish enough to chew them? That is a very nauseous thing to do... The right way to take medicine of such a kind is to swallow it at once. In the same way there are some things in the word of God which are undoubtedly true which must be swallowed at once by an effort of faith, and must not be chewed by perpetual questioning. You will soon have I know not what of doubt and difficulty and bitterness upon your soul if you must needs know the unknowable, and have reasons and explanations for the sublime and the mysterious. Let the

---

[7] I refer you, reader, to chapter 6 for my comments on Paul's desire for the salvation of sinners.

difficult doctrines go down whole into your very soul, by a grand exercise of confidence in God.

I thank God for a thousand things I cannot understand... I do not intend meddling with such lofty matters. There stands the text, and I believe that it is my Father's wish that 'all men should be saved, and come to the knowledge of the truth'. But I know, also, that he does not will it, so that he will save any one of them, unless they believe in his dear Son; for he has told us over and over that he will not. He will not save any man except he forsakes his sins, and turns to him with full purpose of heart; that I also know. And I know, also, that he has a people whom he will save, whom by his eternal love he has chosen, and whom by his eternal power he will deliver. I do not know how that squares with this; that is another of the things that I do not know. If I go on telling you of all that I do not know, and of all that I do know, I will warrant you that the things I do not know will be a hundred to one of the things that I do know. And so we will say no more about the matter, but just go on to the more practical part of the text. God's wish about man's salvation is this – that men should be saved and come to the knowledge of the truth...

What truth? It is gospel truth, truth about Christ that they want. Tell it in a loving, earnest, affectionate manner, for God wills that they should be saved... by a knowledge of the truth. He wills that all men should be saved in this way... by bringing the truth before them. That is God's way of saving them.[8]

Again, speaking of God's voice, 'the voice of love':

How wooing are its tones! The Lord in Holy Scripture speaks of mercy and of pardon bought with blood, the blood of his dear Son. O man, he calls you to him, not that he may slay you, but that he may save you. He does not summon you to a prison, but he invites you to a banquet... Do not be cruel to almighty love! Be not ungenerous to eternal pity![9]

Preaching on Isaiah 65:1, Spurgeon said:

We speak of God after the manner of men, for so God speaks of himself. It is true, then, that he is hurt and grieved when he stretches out his hands in vain... When his kindness is rejected God is grieved... As a relief to such a lamentation this verse has in it a true joy, an intensity of satisfaction, because some are coming to peace and love.

---

[8] Spurgeon: *Metropolitan* Vol.26 pp49-60, emphasis his.

[9] Spurgeon: *Metropolitan* Vol.26 p439. How daring a statement this sounds today!

God speaks it with pleasure: 'I am found of them that sought me not'. Do not forget that utterance, 'As I live, says the Lord, I have no pleasure in the death of him that dies, but that he turn unto me and live'. It gives God pleasure to see men turn to him. Infinitely happy as he must be from his own glorious nature, yet there is a joy which he only feels when he is sought after and found by the sons of men... What a delight it must be to God's heart when at last the poor sinner cries, 'Lord, I believe; help my unbelief'!... God rejoices when he is sought and when he is found! Oh do not think that you seek an unwilling God. He comes to meet you; he falls upon your neck and kisses you.[10]

Spurgeon preached a sermon he entitled: 'The Lamentations of Jesus', taking Luke 19:41 as his theme:

This weeping of the Saviour should much encourage men to trust him. Those who desire his salvation may approach him without hesitation, for his tears prove his hearty desires for our good. When a man who is not given to sentimental tears... is seen to weep, we are convinced of his sincerity. When a strong man is passionately convulsed from head to foot, and pours out lamentations, you feel that he is in downright earnest, and if that earnestness be manifested on your behalf you can commit yourself to him. Oh, weeping sinner, fear not to come to a weeping Saviour! If you will not come to Jesus it grieves him; that you have not come long ago has wrung his heart; that you are still away from him is his daily sorrow: come, then, to him without delay. Let his tears banish your fears; indeed, he gives you better encouragement than tears, for he has shed for sinners, not drops from his eyes alone, but from his heart. He died that sinners who believe in him might live... how can you doubt his readiness to receive you?...

Linking this with Matthew 23:37, he went on:

His love had gone so far that even prophet-killers he would have gathered.[11] Is not this wonderful that there should be grace enough in Christ to gather adulterers, thieves, liars, and to forgive and change them, and yet they will not be gathered? That he should be willing even to gather such base ones into a place of salvation, and yet should

---

[10] Spurgeon: *Metropolitan* Vol.32 pp498-499.
[11] As I noted in chapter 6, Bunyan in his *Jerusalem Sinner* made the point even more graphically. Christ would have his gospel preached *first* at Jerusalem, the very place where *he* was crucified, and have it preached to Christ-killers, let alone prophet-killers.

be refused?... See, here, the case stands thus – I would, but you would not. This is a grief to love... The failure of will is in you that perish, not in Christ who cries, 'I would, but *you* would not'. Yes, and he adds, 'How often would I'... Every prophet that had come to them had indicated an opportunity for their being gathered, and every time that Jesus preached there was a door set open for their salvation, but they would not be gathered, and so he foretells their fate in these words... 'gathered', that is what you might have been; 'desolate', that is what you shall be; and Jesus weeps because of it... Desolate! Desolate! Desolate! Because you would not be gathered! Well does the tender Saviour weep over men since they will perversely choose such a doom.[12]

Yet again on Matthew 23:37:

From this utterance of our Lord, I learn that, if any man be not saved, the cause of his non-salvation does not lie in any want of graciousness or want of willingness on the part of God... and so far as it is applicable to the sons of men in general, it declares that God wills not the death of any, but desires that they should turn unto him and live... Now... there is a great doctrinal difficulty; but I do not think you or I need go fishing for it... What Christ would have done for the Jews, but which they would not accept... I am sure he is willing to do... for us now...

Oh, how I wish that this might be the time when Jesus would securely cover you as the hen covers her chicks! Do you really desire this blessing? I know you would not desire it if he did not desire it. If there is a spark of desire towards Christ in your heart, there is a whole flaming furnace of desire in Christ's heart towards you. You never get the start of him... No sinner can ever say that he stopped for Christ, and waited for Jesus. I more willing than Christ? Never! A sinner more anxious for pardon than Christ is willing to pardon him? Never! There was never seen, and there never shall be seen... a soul more hungry after Christ than Christ is hungry after that soul... O poor, guilty sinner, do not doubt your welcome to Jesus! The gate of salvation is flung wide open. The door is taken off the hinges... Your[13]

---

[12] Spurgeon: *Metropolitan* Vol.26 pp661,666,671-672, emphasis mine.

[13] In this section, Spurgeon was addressing those who had a desire towards Christ, who were anxious for pardon, who were hungry after Christ, and so on; that is, those in whom the Spirit was at work. I presume, therefore, in such circumstances Spurgeon felt able to speak of Christ as '*your* Saviour'. I myself would still have preferred '*the* Saviour'. The original, naturally, had 'thy Saviour'. Just because I quote him, it

Saviour waits for you. The Father tarries for you; no, he does more; he comes to meet you. I see him running. Is it true that I see you coming? And what a spectacle is now before me! I see you coming with feeble footsteps, and I see him running faster than the angels fly. I see the father falling on the neck of the prodigal, I see him kiss him, and delight in him... There is joy tonight.[14]

One last word:

And now, you that are outsiders, see what trouble the Saviour takes with you; for what he did for men of his age he does for men of every age: he longs that you should come to him; he puts the truth so that you may see it, and he preaches it persuasively and affectionately. Alas, that men should require such trouble to be taken with them! If anyone were giving away gold and silver he would not need to go down on his knees and entreat men to accept the precious metals; but when we have to preach 'the word', how must we entreat, implore, beseech men to come, or else they will not come at all; nor even when we have implored and besought will they lend a listening ear and a believing heart unless the arm of the Lord be revealed. See you this, you outsiders; let the reflection of this make you ashamed, and cause you to resolve that now henceforth, having ears to hear, you will hear, and when Jesus pleads you will bow to him. May God the Holy Spirit make it so.[15]

---

does not mean I endorse Spurgeon's every turn of phrase, of course. On the point at issue, this passage may not be strictly relevant, since it may be argued that Spurgeon was addressing only sensible sinners. But was he? Not only are his sermons replete with warnings against preparationism, he here used the phrase 'O poor, guilty sinner' not 'O poor, guilty, *sensible* sinner'. Furthermore, I am bound to ask, while hyper-Calvinists *in theory* could address sensible sinners like Spurgeon did, do they? See Appendix 2. In the various extracts above, note Spurgeon's constant use of the most general of terms when addressing sinners, such as 'all men', 'O man', the universal 'you', 'men', 'the sons of men', 'the poor sinner', 'any man', 'you... outsiders', 'men of every age'.

[14] Spurgeon: *Metropolitan* Vol.45 pp325-334.

[15] Spurgeon: *Metropolitan* Vol.28 p391; see also, for instance, *New* Vol.4 pp341-344; Vol.5 pp17-24,77-78,130,323-328,406-407,433-440,487-488; Vol.6 pp126-131,467-468; *New and Metropolitan* Vol.7 pp110-111,126-127,145-152; *Metropolitan* Vol.9 pp65-66,169-180,461-466, 521-528; Vol.15 p688; Vol.19 pp128-129,421-432; Vol.20 pp126-127, 132; Vol.22 pp20-22,154; Vol.26 pp414-420,439; Vol.28 pp653-660; Vol.29 pp199-204,337-348; Vol.31 pp124,236-237,673-684; Vol.32 pp345,393-396,

Reader, I believe the above to be a fair representation of Spurgeon's position, drawn from his own words. I believe it substantiates my claim that he preached God's decree to save his elect, and God's desire to save all sinners, without attempting to reconcile the two, knowing they form one perfect will of God. Just because Spurgeon did this, of course, it does not make it right. But do it, he did.

Conclusion

Reader, now that I have come to the end of my book, do I need to explain the title? I chose *The Gospel Offer is Free*, because that is the truth; the gospel offer *is* free.

That is, God in the gospel offers every sinner everlasting salvation through the work, merit and person of his Son, the Lord Jesus Christ, promising it to all who repent and believe.[1] God makes this offer fully and freely, commanding all to repent and believe, because he desires all to turn and be saved. God attaches no pre-conditions whatsoever to the offer. The preacher does not have to ask if his hearers have had this-or-that experience, or are in such-and-such a state; the hearer, likewise, does not have to try to determine whether or not he is sensible – he is invited, commanded to come to Christ at once, and to come freely. The gospel offer *is* free! That which is said of the National Health Service – free at the point of need – is abundantly true of the gospel. Salvation, of course, was earned by Christ; he paid the price for his people's sin. But it really is free at the point of need; the preacher offers it freely to sinners; every sinner is welcome; and all who come receive the gift of God's mercy. 'Ho! Everyone who thirsts, come to the waters; and you who have no money, come, buy and eat. Yes, come, buy wine and milk without money and without price' (Isa. 55:1).[2]

Reader, if you should be unconverted, let me tell you yet again: God desires you to turn from your sin, desires you to turn to him in repentance, and desires you to trust his Son for salvation. He takes no pleasure in your death. Christ stands open-armed, ready to welcome you, never turning away any sinner who comes (John 6:37) – and that includes you. That which his enemies said in sneering indignation, Christ wears as one of the brightest gems of his crown: 'This man receives sinners' (Luke 15:2). And so he does! Note well the present tense, reader; Jesus receives sinners

---

[1] Just in case it needs repeating yet again: I am not saying that Christ died for all. The offer is to all; the atonement is for the elect.

[2] See Appendix 2.

still (Heb. 13:8). He will receive you, if you come. There is nothing you have to bring, nothing you can bring, nothing you dare bring. Come as you are; come and welcome; come now.

How do I know all this? Because my Master has said it is so. He has told me what to say to you: 'Come, for all things are now ready' (Luke 14:17). Indeed, he has told me to press you to come: 'Compel them to come in', he said (Luke 14:23). But what if you refuse the invitation, and never come? Then you shall never taste the supper (Luke 14:24).

So what shall be my closing word to you? Hebrews 12:25. 'See that you do not refuse him who speaks'. If the Jews did not escape when they refused God who gave them his law, how much worse will it be for you – if you reject God's offer of mercy through his Son?

Appendix 1

Ella's Criticisms of the Free Offer

Ella's book contains many sweeping generalisations and unsubstantiated assertions which are gratuitously offensive, and this does nothing to advance the debate on the free offer. This Appendix lists some examples.

Reader, I am conscious of the personal nature of much of what follows. Since, however, some of Ella's remarks were directed against what I have written, if I am to offer a reply, inevitably it is bound to be personal. And even where this is not the case, I cannot always speak for what every free-offer preacher does or says; I can only speak for myself. *But I do not want to personalise this discussion.* So much so, I have debated – struggled within myself – as to whether or not to include this Appendix. But I have decided to let it stand because some of Ella's comments – which could prove damaging to the biblical practice of preaching the free offer – should not go unchallenged.

* * *

Meney's opening remarks in his Introduction set the mistaken tone of Ella's book. It is not right to say that the free offer is used 'to explain an imagined lack of consistency between the biblical doctrine of sovereign grace and the church's obligation to preach the gospel to every creature'.[1]

Meney again: 'The free offer is works mixed with grace'.[2] Oh?

Meney categorically, but wrongly, stated: 'All free-offer preachers... either... *must* preach a mongrel gospel of works and duty where the sinner is urged to commit to a Saviour who is ill-defined and a way of salvation that is *necessarily* vague – such preachers generally ignore anything to do with God's electing decrees, the divine source of repentance and faith, the purposely

---

[1] Ella: *The Free Offer* p5.
[2] Ella: *The Free Offer* p5.

limited extent of the atonement and the necessity of Holy Spirit regeneration. Or else, they *must* try to establish an alternative doctrinal basis, other than the shed blood of Jesus Christ, upon which to offer salvation to all'.[3]

Why is the following stated as a fact, when not only is it a part of the accusation which has to be proved, but in any case the definition of the free offer precludes it? I refer to: 'The "free offer" describes a method of preaching that undermines sovereign grace and denies that salvation is unconditionally the gift of God'.[4] And since the definition says the opposite, how could Ella state, as a fact, that 'the free offer... has an insufficient view of the gospel which is not based on God's electing grace'?[5]

How could Ella say the free-offer preacher thinks of 'the atonement as merely a providing of salvation and not a procuring and securing of it'?[6]

Which free-offer preacher makes 'man... an agent in

---

[3] Ella: *The Free Offer* p6, emphasis mine. And what did Meney mean by this last? Was he saying free-offer preachers do not hold to substitutionary atonement, or that the extent of the atonement governs the extent of the gospel call, or what? In the definition of the free offer as set out in the Introduction – as near as I can get it to his own – nothing is said about the shed blood of Christ being the basis of the offer. In fact, it is specifically removed from the definition as, indeed, the back cover of Ella's book makes clear: The free-offer preacher 'teaches that God genuinely offers forgiveness of sin and salvation to sinners, irrespective of the eternal decree of election, despite the particular, substitutionary atonement of the Lord Jesus Christ, and regardless of the distinguishing effectual call of the Holy Spirit'.

[4] Ella: *The Free Offer* back cover.

[5] Ella: *The Free Offer* p9.

[6] On this, Ella was inconsistent. On the one hand, he rightly criticised talk of the mere 'provision' of salvation – as I do – yet he could also state: 'Preaching the gospel must take into consideration two major factors: the *provisions* of our holy God and the needs of sinful man. God's gospel *provisions* for sinful man are grounded in the atonement made by Jesus Christ... The big question is, however, what are the Father's exact *provisions* for salvation?' Even so, on the very same page he dismissed 'some preachers' – when they speak of 'Christ's saving work' – 'which they call God's *provisions*'. Yet he himself spoke of 'God's *providing* of salvation' (Ella: *The Free Offer* pp9,13,16,22,52,53, emphasis mine)!

salvation'?[7]

On what grounds did Ella say the free offer 'is based on law-duties and not faith', or that 'it teaches that law-duties beget faith'?[8]

On what basis did Ella have the right to assume the free offer 'is... *designed* to appeal to the natural man'?[9] That the free-offer preacher may be misguided, I admit – to prove it was Ella's self-appointed task – but it was unjustified of Ella to attribute so perverse a motive to such a preacher. Or is it axiomatic that the free-offer preacher *sets out* to please the natural man, and has *designed* a system with this in mind?

Why is the free offer 'a man-centred and philosophical approach to the gospel rather than a Christ-centred and biblical approach'?[10] Does this not beg the very question to be proved?

On what grounds did Ella assert the free offer credits 'the sinner with a natural ability to respond positively'?[11]

How does the free offer undermine 'the eternal purpose of the Father in choosing, the atoning work of the Son in redeeming, and the regenerating work of the Holy Spirit in calling, the elect'?[12]

To say the free offer 'is a gospel to believers only, [and] therefore it has no evangelistic purpose',[13] is downright silly. As is this: 'It does not pay due attention to the saving application of the gospel'.[14] And on what basis did Ella state: 'Nor does it pay attention to the fact that the gospel comes as a judge to some and a saviour to others'?[15]

---

[7] Ella: *The Free Offer* p9. That is, if Ella was speaking of 'a person... that exerts power' (*Concise*), and meant *natural* power. If, however, Ella was saying the sinner plays no part in conversion – the sinner must, I presume, be a mere stone or robot – then I plead guilty. As I showed in chapter 3, the sinner repents and believes; God does not do it for him.

[8] Ella: *The Free Offer* p9.

[9] Ella: *The Free Offer* p9, emphasis mine.

[10] Ella: *The Free Offer* p9.

[11] Ella: *The Free Offer* p9.

[12] Ella: *The Free Offer* p9.

[13] Ella: *The Free Offer* p9.

[14] Ella: *The Free Offer* p9.

[15] Ella: *The Free Offer* p9. I have used Ella's words, even though the gospel is not a saviour.

If the section in Ella's book entitled 'Evangelical Arminianism'[16] was meant to be a fair representation of preaching the free offer, it missed the mark by a long way; it is, in fact, an offensive caricature. But Ella certainly included the Reformed in his strictures.[17] It is, therefore, distasteful to see such preachers accused of believing that Christ has died 'to make salvation possible for all', and that they tell sinners, 'Christ desires and wants you so much that he has died for you'.[18] Where is the proof of this practice? It is excluded by the definition of the free offer.

Must a free-offer preacher travel the philosophical route mapped out by Ella under 'Moderate Calvinism'?[19]

Which free-offer preacher has ever said, 'God the Father and God the Son *quarrel* over the salvation of sinners', that they '*contend* over the souls of sinners', that 'there is an eternal tension in the Godhead concerning who should be saved'?[20] Which free-offer preacher speaks of 'a God who is at logger-heads with himself'?[21]

As for my review of Iain Murray's book on Spurgeon and hyper-Calvinism, to which Ella referred, where did I say there are two gospels? Did I 'thrust forward... Spurgeon'? Here is my review:

In this little book, Iain Murray tackles the vital subject of hyper-Calvinism. He does it through the life of Spurgeon.
In a sense, it doesn't matter what Spurgeon thought – what does Scripture say? But, as Murray explains, Spurgeon argued from the Bible. A consistent Calvinist, he said that gospel invitations are sent to all sinners, that all sinners *may* trust Christ, that all sinners *must* trust Christ, and that God has a desire to see all sinners saved. Spurgeon did not try to reconcile the irreconcilable – he preached what the Bible teaches. He faced stern opposition. It has not gone away!
This book is easy to read, is well documented and copiously illustrated from the works of others. There is plenty to choose from. Spurgeon claimed he had almost all the Puritans with him – not all, as Murray

---

[16] Ella: *The Free Offer* pp13-16.

[17] Ella: *The Free Offer* p16.

[18] Ella: *The Free Offer* p16.

[19] Ella: *The Free Offer* pp16-19; see also same volume pp55-56.

[20] Ella: *The Free Offer* p20, emphasis mine.

[21] Ella: *The Free Offer* p9.

said (p50). This didn't make Spurgeon right, but hypers ought to know it. See Owen: *Works* Vol. 10 p141.

One risk with Murray's approach is that some readers will think hyper-Calvinism is a matter of history. It isn't. I disagree with him (xiv); hyperism *is* gaining ground today. And virtual hyperism smothers our preaching. We must break free of it, otherwise we face extinction. Sinners need real preaching, now! I do!

Snap this bargain up. It's a good introduction to the subject. Read it. Pray for a return of proper gospel preaching. And do all you can to support and encourage it where you find it.[22]

I object to Ella's foisting upon me the unwarranted and offensive statement: 'Gay... drops the scriptural passages which refer to Christ's particular atonement. This leaves him free to preach to persuade men according to their natural abilities to repent and believe'.[23] I do no such thing.

Where have I ever said anything which gives Ella the right to allege I 'would throw out of the Parliament of the Saints' – whatever that may mean – men such as Gill, Huntingdon, Hawker and Gadsby?[24]

Why does the free offer imply 'a universal atonement'?[25]

Does the free-offer preacher have to delve into extra-scriptural matters such as the benefits of the atonement for unbelievers?[26]

Does the free offer mean 'Christ's work is not at least part of the contents of the gospel offered'?[27]

Is it a part of the free offer to 'offer repentance'? Which free-offer preacher does it? The suggestion is silly. No free-offer preacher I know offers faith.[28] Who are these men of straw? The free-offer preacher demands faith and repentance, but offers salvation in Christ who gives repentance and faith (Acts 5:31; Eph. 2:8).

Why must the free-offer preacher preach a gospel 'that is void

[22] Ella: *The Free Offer* p22. For more on Spurgeon, see chapter 10.
[23] Ella: *The Free Offer* p22.
[24] Ella: *The Free Offer* p23.
[25] Ella: *The Free Offer* p23.
[26] Ella: *The Free Offer* p24.
[27] Ella: *The Free Offer* p25.
[28] Ella: *The Free Offer* pp58,62.

of content and avoids controversial points'?[29] Indeed, if he makes
the gospel '*void* of content' how can he at the same time 'appear
[merely] to *limit* its contents'?[30] Perhaps Ella would care to tell me
what 'controversial points' I avoid in my preaching. The
suggestion is offensive.

How does Ella know I think 'predestination and election is [*sic*]
for believers only [to hear about] and thus not to be placed in the
"free offer"'?[31]

Why did Ella assume I do not 'provide a solution to the
problem of law, sin and the righteousness necessary to fulfil the
law'?[32] Of course *I* cannot provide the solution, but God in Christ
has accomplished it (Rom. 10:4; Gal. 4:4-5; 1 John 1:7-9), and I
preach it to sinners.

Where have I ever taken 'man's gaze from the atonement... and
place[d] it on a moral or natural law'?[33]

Is it true that I do 'not deal with sin as sin... and [do] not even
begin to answer the question of how a man may get right with an
angry God'?[34]

Do I 'depict God as being narrowly but lovingly benevolent to
the point of exhibiting blindness to justice and mercy'?[35]

Do I 'deny that it was at Calvary that the ransom was paid once
and for all time'?[36] I find Ella's assertion odious.

Is it fair to say Errol Hulse is 'so dogmatic in matters he finds
unclear' and pays only 'lip-service to election'?[37]

I agree with Ella, 'orthodox men' do believe Ephesians 2:8,[38]
but I reject his innuendo that free-offer preachers do not. I do. All
free-offer preachers (as I have defined them) do. But as to the
question of 'orthodoxy' over the free offer – as defined by

---

[29] Ella: *The Free Offer* p28.
[30] Ella: *The Free Offer* p66, emphasis mine.
[31] Ella: *The Free Offer* p66. But, of course, God's decrees have to be preached with care, especially in the presence of unbelievers.
[32] Ella: *The Free Offer* p39.
[33] Ella: *The Free Offer* p39.
[34] Ella: *The Free Offer* p39.
[35] Ella: *The Free Offer* p39.
[36] Ella: *The Free Offer* p39.
[37] Ella: *The Free Offer* p53.
[38] Ella: *The Free Offer* p62.

Scripture – this is the question in hand!

'Fuller believes that pardon comes when faith is exercised'.[39] So do I. Who does not? Does Ella not believe it? Or does he think unbelievers are pardoned?

Ella dismissed free-offer preachers out of hand: 'In the opinion of this author [Ella]... such people do not perform the work of a gospel evangelist, and their opinions and definitions of the "free offer" are thus of little importance'.[40] Was this his premise or conclusion? If it was his conclusion, had he proved it or merely asserted it?

How does Ella know I am 'embarrassed as to what [I] should include in the offer and to whom it should be free'?[41] I am clear on both.

How could Ella say that the free-offer preacher 'preaches to believers only', and imply he does not 'preach to win lost sinners for Christ'?[42]

* * *

Reader, it is because of such unsupported – and often totally unjustified – accusations and innuendoes, to say nothing of unwarranted assumptions, that I think it is fair to say Ella's book is not a serious effort at reaching a biblical position on the free offer. When Ella complained of a certain writer who, Ella claimed, 'says quite untrue and unjust things about' Gill,[43] a certain plank and eye spring to mind. Ella would have done better, in my opinion, if he had kept to the spirit of this good advice:

We have noticed in recent months a willingness by some Christians to lob allegations and employ intemperate language when it comes to theological differences with their brethren. This is unfortunate. Most reasonable Christians accept they are not perfect; even that they have a few things still to learn. Yet that does not restrict the bounds of some people's rudeness when a brother has the temerity to raise a question that challenges their pet interpretation of a doctrine... Common

---

[39] Ella: *The Free Offer* p64.
[40] Ella: *The Free Offer* p66.
[41] Ella: *The Free Offer* p70.
[42] Ella: *The Free Offer* p62.
[43] Ella: *The Free Offer* p52.

courtesy requires that critics criticise *what is said, not what they think is said. It is easy to dress your opponent in black then damn him.* But this is the tactic of those who fear open examination and prefer to censor alternative interpretations of doctrine rather than hold them up to the light of honest investigation. Hurling epithets in public... is conduct unbecoming professors of the gospel of Jesus Christ.[44]

Excellent words.

But, no, reader, I didn't coin them. Nor did any free-offer preacher. It was Meney, Ella's publisher, and the writer of the Introduction to his book, who did.[45] A pity, therefore, Meney did not temper Ella's words before he published his work.

---

[44] Emphasis mine.
[45] At least it appeared under 'Comment' in *New Focus*, Go Publications, Eggleston, October/November 1999, Vol.4 number 3, p2.

Appendix 2

Are Gospel Invitations to All?

Although, as I have explained, I do not wish to explore preparationism in this book, it is necessary to glance at a closely-connected issue: Are gospel invitations[1] universal – that is, indiscriminate to *all* sinners? or are they restricted to *sensible* sinners? The latter, says the hyper-Calvinist.[2] Reader, I remind you of Meney's words: 'The "free offer preacher" presumes to invite all sinners to believe on the Lord Jesus Christ, promising them salvation if they do'. The implication is clear – universal invitations are wrong. But we do not have to rely on implication. Ella was unequivocal: 'Does the Bible invite all men indiscriminately and everywhere to believe...? No, says the Bible'.[3]

Ella is not alone in this, of course:

We believe that the invitations of the gospel... are intended[4] only for those who have been made by the blessed Spirit to feel their lost state as sinners and their need of Christ as their Saviour, and to repent of and forsake their sins... We reject the doctrine that men in a state of nature should be exhorted to believe in or turn to God... While we believe that the gospel is to be preached or proclaimed to all the world, as in Mark 16:15, we deny offers of grace; that is to say, that the gospel is to be offered indiscriminately to all... Therefore... [it is

---

[1] What follows applies not only to gospel 'invitations', but also to 'commands' and 'exhortations'. 'Come', for example, can be an invitation, a command or an exhortation.

[2] 'Sensible' sinners are elect individuals who are regenerate, and, conscious of their sin and need of salvation, repent, and desire Christ. By a 'hyper-Calvinist', I mean one who does not hold with the free offer, who does not hold with duty faith. See chapter 3 for my note on the word 'hyper'.

[3] Ella: *The Free Offer* pp5,61. Even though, as Ella said, God commands all to repent (Ella: *The Free Offer* pp58,71). See chapter 1.

[4] God *intends* the salvation only of the elect, yes, but the question is whether the *invitation* should be to all, or to the 'sensible' elect only. As is clear, these Articles restrict the invitation to the latter.

wrong] for ministers in the present day to address unconverted persons, or indiscriminately all in a mixed congregation, calling upon them savingly to repent, believe, and receive Christ...[5]

Is this right?

Certainly not! Some gospel invitations or commands are obviously unlimited;[6] Isaiah 45:22 and Acts 17:30, for example. This of itself puts the issue beyond doubt. God commands all sinners to look to him and be saved; he commands all sinners to repent, not just 'sensible' sinners.[7]

Besides, if the gospel invitation is to be issued only to those who are 'sensible', then every invited sinner will come – since the 'sensible', by definition, are elect. But we know that God in the gospel invites many sinners who refuse his invitations, and never do come (Prov. 1:24-33; Isa. 65:2; Luke 14:17-24; Rom. 10:21).[8]

---

[5] Articles 24,26,29,33 of Articles of Faith of the Gospel Standard Aid and Poor Relief Societies, The Gospel Standard Societies, Harpenden. These same Articles also 'deny duty faith and duty repentance – these terms signifying that it is every man's duty spiritually and savingly to repent and believe'.

[6] Spurgeon repeatedly dealt with the issue: 'Don't believe that the invitations of the gospel are given only to characters; they are, some of them, unlimited invitations' (Spurgeon: *New* Vol.6 p107).

[7] Indeed, this command is superfluous for sensible sinners – who are, by definition, repentant.

[8] Gill vainly tried to limit this call (in Proverbs) 'to the natural duties of religion, and to an attendance on the means of grace', and (in Luke) to 'outward ordinances', 'to the house of God, and church of Christ; to come and hear the word... and attend the word and worship of God', but it will not do. As he said on Isa. 65:2, 'Israel... believed not in Christ, obeyed not his gospel'; on Luke 14:17, 'John the Baptist... exhorted the people to believe in Christ... [and] Christ himself [was]... sent... to call sinners to repentance... [and] the apostles... were... sent... to preach the gospel'; and on Rom. 10:21, it speaks of 'the ministry of the prophets... the preaching of John the Baptist, of Christ, and his apostles'. Quite! Preaching the gospel does not mean calling sinners to attend a place of worship! As Gill said on Matt. 11:28: 'Christ... kindly invites and encourages souls to come unto him... by which is meant, not a local coming, or a coming to hear him preach; for so his hearers... were come already... nor is it a bare coming under the ordinances of Christ... but it is to be understood of believing in Christ, the going of the soul to him, in the exercise of grace

This means, therefore, that gospel invitations cannot be restricted to 'sensible' sinners.[9]

But what of invitations such as Isaiah 55:1-7 and Matthew 11:28? Are *they* universal? or are they given only to those who show the characteristics (and these spiritual) stated in the invitations? If the latter, and this is said to govern all gospel invitations, then this is where hyper-Calvinism joins forces with preparationism; that is, gospel commands or invitations are given

---

on him, of desire after him, love to him, faith and hope in him: believing in Christ, and coming to him, are terms synonymous (John 6:35)' (Gill: *Commentary* Vol.3 pp430,1035; Vol.5 pp101,507-508; Vol.6 p93).

[9] Gill, commenting on the command 'to bring in... the poor and the maimed and the lame and the blind' (Luke 14:21), said 'the poor' are 'such as have no spiritual food to eat... nor any spiritual clothing, no righteousness... nor money to buy either... of which spiritual poverty some are sensible, and others are not'. As for 'the blind', Gill ruled out the possibility of their being sensible since they are 'blind... as to any saving knowledge of God in Christ; of Christ, and the way of righteousness, life, and salvation by him; of the plague of their own hearts, the exceeding sinfulness of sin, and the need of a Saviour; of the work of the Spirit of God upon their souls, and the necessity of it; and of the truths of the gospel, in a spiritual and experimental way. In short, under these characters are represented natural and unconverted men'. The gospel invitation is to such, but Gill, as above, tried to limit it to an invitation to attend preaching, to read the Bible, and so on, or a command 'to a natural faith' or 'natural repentance' (Gill: *Commentary* Vol.5 pp507-508; *Body* Vol.2 pp282-286. See also above, chapters 1-4). Spurgeon tackled this kind of evasion head-on: 'Certain persons have been obliged to admit that the apostles commanded, and exhorted, and besought men to believe, but they tell us that the kind of believing which the apostles bade men exercise was not a saving faith'. He called this 'an assertion so monstrous. Can we imagine for a moment apostles with burning zeal and ardour, inspired by the Spirit of God within them, going about the world exhorting men to exercise a faith which after all would not save them?... When our Lord bade his disciples go into all the world and preach the gospel to every creature... the faith which was to be preached was evidently none other than a saving faith, and it is frivolous to say otherwise... It is, I repeat, a mere frivolity or worse, to say that the faith enjoined by the apostles was a mere human faith which does not save... That cause must be desperate which calls for such a defence' (Spurgeon: *Metropolitan* Vol.17 pp135-136).

only to those who have had certain experiences which qualify them to be so invited – hyper-Calvinism – and only those who are 'prepared' by these various experiences are 'fit' to come to Christ – preparationism. As I said in chapter 1, this opens a Pandora's box, and starts the preacher on an impossible course of probing to see if the sinner really is 'sensible' and qualified to be *invited* to come to Christ, and the sinner on what might well turn out to be an endless round of self-questioning as to whether or not he is sufficiently *prepared* to come to Christ. It puts the cart before the horse – an undertaking, not only futile, but the cause of much harm. Spurgeon:

At the present time there are large numbers of Calvinistic ministers who are afraid to give a free invitation to sinners; they always garble Christ's invitation thus: 'If you are a sensible sinner you may come'; just as if stupid sinners might not come... I do believe there are hundreds and thousands who remain in doubt and darkness, and go down to despair, because there is a description given and a preparation for Christ demanded, to which they cannot attain – a description indeed which is not true, because it is a description of what they feel after they have found Christ, and not what they must feel before they come to him.

About a year before, Spurgeon, speaking of 'how wide is this [gospel] invitation', challenged those 'ministers who are afraid to invite sinners'; 'then why are they ministers!' he thundered. But he had a confession to make. Very early in my ministry, he admitted:

I somewhat faltered when about to give a free invitation. My doctrinal sentiments did at that time somewhat hamper me. I boldly avow that I am unchanged as to the doctrines I have preached; I preach Calvinism as high, as stern, as sound as ever; but I do feel, and always did feel an anxiety to invite sinners to Christ. And I do feel also, that not only is such a course consistent with the soundest doctrines, but that the other course is after all the unsound one, and has no title whatever to plead Scripture on its behalf. There has grown up... an idea that none are to be called to Christ but what they call *sensible* sinners. I sometimes rebut that by remarking that I call *stupid* sinners to Christ as well as sensible sinners, and that stupid sinners make by far the greatest proportion of the ungodly. But I glory in the avowal that I preach Christ even to *insensible* sinners.

And again:

166

Some of my brethren are greatly scandalised by the general invitations which I am in the habit of giving to sinners, as sinners. Some of them go to the length of asserting that there are no universal invitations in the word of God... [But] we have one here [Isa. 1:18]. Here is most plainly an invitation addressed to sinners who had not even the qualification of sensibility. They did not feel their need of a Saviour... A more accurate description of careless, worthless, ungodly, abandoned souls, never was given anywhere... In the first verse [of the chapter] you will perceive that the text was addressed to *senseless* sinners – so senseless that God himself would not address them in expostulation, but called upon the heavens and the earth to hear his complaints... What a fine poetical setting forth of the thought, that God appealed from man to dead inanimate creatures, for man had become more brutish than the stones of the field; and yet to such is the invitation given, 'Come now, let us reason together, says the Lord'.

And one more word from Spurgeon on this topic:

The gospel comes to all who hear it... [and] it is the same gospel which comes to the unregenerate as to the regenerate... Some of our brethren who are very anxious to carry out the decrees of God, instead of believing that God can carry them out himself, always try to make distinctions in their preachings,[10] giving one gospel to one set of sinners, and another to a different class. They are very unlike the old sowers, who, when they went out to sow, sowed among thorns, and on stony places, and by the way-side; but these brethren, with profounder wisdom, endeavour to find out which is the good ground, and they will insist upon it that not so much as a single handful of invitations must be cast anywhere but on prepared soil. They are much too wise to preach the gospel in Ezekiel's fashion to the dry bones in the valley while they are yet dead; they withhold any word of gospel till there is a little quivering of life among the bones, and then they commence operations. They do not think it to be their duty to go into the highways and hedges and bid all, as many as they find, to come to the supper. Oh, no! They are too orthodox to obey the Master's will; they desire to understand first who are appointed to come to the supper,

---

[10] Spurgeon was not saying that a preacher must be 'inclusive', treating all his hearers as believers (a fault, sad to say, all too common). 'We must divide our congregation before we send you away' (Spurgeon: *The Pulpit Library* p95; see also same volume pp96-97,174; *Metropolitan* Vol.17 p529). A preacher must discriminate between believers and unbelievers, but he must preach the same gospel to both, leaving the distinction to the Spirit – the only one who can make it. See also Morgan pp317-318,352.

and then they will invite them; that it to say, they will do what there is no necessity to do.[11] They have not faith enough, or enough subjugation of will to the supreme commands of the great Master, to do that which only faith dare do; namely, tell the dry bones to live, bid the man with the withered hand stretch out his arm, and speak to him that is sick of the palsy, and tell him to take up his bed and walk. It strikes me, that refusing to set forth Jesus to all men, of every character, and refraining from inviting them to come to him, is a great mistake... [David, the prophets, the apostles] delivered the gospel, the same gospel to the dead as to the living, the same gospel to the non-elect as to the elect. The point of distinction is not in the gospel, but in its being applied by the Holy Spirit, or left to be rejected of man.[12]

* * *

By considering Isaiah 55:1-7, I wish to probe this a little. This passage is particularly relevant since Ella raised it in response to Fuller, and, as he said, because it 'is used time and time again for free offer purposes'.[13] Here is the passage:

Ho! Everyone who thirsts, come to the waters; and you who have no money, come, buy and eat. Yes, come, buy wine and milk without money and without price. Why do you spend money for what is not bread, and your wages for what does not satisfy? Listen diligently to me, and eat what is good, and let your soul delight itself in abundance. Incline your ear, and come to me. Hear, and your soul shall live; and I will make an everlasting covenant with you – the sure mercies of David... Seek the LORD while he may be found, call upon him while he is near. Let the wicked forsake his way, and the unrighteous man his thoughts; let him return to the LORD, and he will have mercy on him; and to our God, for he will abundantly pardon.

---

[11] That is, invite those who are in effect already converted. Spurgeon was here dealing with the second round of invitations spoken of in the parable, and did not contradict the point I made earlier in this Appendix; namely, that since the servants were sent first to those already invited, and they refused, it proves that the gospel invitation includes those who will never come.

[12] Spurgeon: *New* Vol.6 pp397-398; Vol.5 p436; *New and Metropolitan* Vol.7 pp145-146; *Metropolitan* Vol.11 pp494-495, emphasis his; see also, for instance, *New* Vol.5 p130; Vol.6 p302; *Metropolitan* Vol.29 pp337-348; *'Only'* pp301-305; Murray: *Forgotten* pp52-59.

[13] Ella: *The Free Offer* pp49-54.

The picture is very clear. God, *speaking as a man*, pictures himself as a market trader or hawker who, desiring takers for his wares, lifts his voice and calls out to the passing crowd to come and accept his offer. Earnestly pressing his invitation, he commands, and seeks to persuade and encourage, all passers-by to step right up and buy, promising delight and full satisfaction to all who, feeling their need of his goods, do come and take. Observing the people spending their money on rubbish, he argues with them, trying to convince them of their stupidity, urging them to come to him to get what they really need. He appeals to them, pleading the superiority of his goods over the shoddy stuff they are at present wasting their money on, in hope of convincing them to turn to his stall and buy.

What is he offering? Salvation for sinners through Christ. What is his asking price? Nothing to the sinner; it is free.

Does it need to be said? He would be a very odd market-trader, indeed, who put the slightest limit on whom he invites to come and buy. The trader of Isaiah 55:1-7 certainly does not. Rather, he does all he can to arouse an interest in his wares; so much so, he hopes that by spreading his goods before the crowd, raising his voice, appealing to his hearers' thirst, and spelling out the richness of what he is offering, he might in some way or another make the people want his merchandise. He realises, of course, unless they have an appetite for what he carries, and see that his wares *are* superior, he will get no takers – *but that does not stop him inviting.* Indeed, eager for a sale, he presses them all the more! No trader would dream of first asking the people if they like his merchandise, checking to see if they feel their need of it, and intend to purchase, *before* inviting them to buy! Of course not! This trader doesn't! Spreading his wares and extolling their value, he urges the crowd to walk right up and buy, assuring the penniless that their empty pockets will be no bar, pointing to the price-tickets which carry only zeros. Open-armed he stands, looking for takers.

This is how it should be with the preachers of the gospel. This is what God is saying in Isaiah 55:1-7.

Hyper-Calvinists, however, will not have it. 'The text', Ella claimed, 'has to do with Christ and the people he chooses and not the masses... The passage can only be understood as God's providing of salvation for a specific people whom he has chosen for that purpose'.[14] Nothing here, apparently, about a free invitation to all to come to Christ; it is all to do with the elect, and only the elect. Since Ella quoted Gill with approval, let us hear what he thought of the passage:

These words are no call, invitation, or offer of grace to dead sinners, since they are spoken to such who were thirsty; that is, who, in a spiritual sense, were thirsting after pardon of sin, a justifying righteousness, and salvation by Christ, after a greater[15] knowledge of him, communion with him, conformity to him, and enjoyment of him in his ordinances; which supposes them to be spiritually alive; for such who are dead in sin, thirst not after the grace of God, but the lusts of the flesh; they mind and savour the things of the flesh, and not the things of the Spirit; only new-born babes, or such who are born again, are quickened and made alive, [and] desire Christ... Besides, the persons called unto are represented as having no money; which, though true of unconverted persons, who have nothing to pay off their debts... yet they fancy themselves to be rich... whereas the persons here encouraged are such, who not only have no money, but know they have none; who are poor in spirit, and sensible of their spiritual poverty; which sense arises from the quickening influences of the Spirit of God upon their souls... [the words] are not directed to [unconverted persons]... Neither Christ, nor the grace of Christ, are designed by 'the waters', but the ordinances... Now where should hungry and thirsty souls, and such that have no money, attend, but on the ordinances, the means of grace?... [The words, 'Seek the LORD...'] are an exhortation to public worship... These words ['Let the wicked forsake his way'] are [wrongly] represented as a promise of pardon, on condition of forsaking sinful ways and thoughts and turning to the Lord... [when, in fact, they are] declarations of pardoning grace and mercy... made... to encourage souls sensible of the wickedness of their ways... [They] contain no promise to dead men, but [are] a declaration of pardoning grace to sensible sinners... This passage of Scripture... is no promise of pardon to the non-elect.[16]

---

[14] Ella: *The Free Offer* pp51,53.

[15] Note the gloss – 'greater' – which fundamentally alters the meaning of the passage. Gill spoke of the desire for '*more* knowledge of him, *more* communion with him, and *more* conformity to [Christ]' (Gill: *Commentary* Vol.3 p989, emphasis mine). See below for how Gill contradicted himself on this point.

[16] Ella: *The Free Offer* pp51-52; Gill: *Cause* pp19-21; see also Gill: *Commentary* Vol.3 pp989-992.

Not only are there some big assumptions here, it is confused. On the one hand, Gill thought sensible sinners are here invited to Christ for salvation; yet on the other, he thought believers are invited to come to Christ for more grace. But the main thrust is clear: According to Gill, the characteristics listed – thirsty, penniless, wasters, unsatisfied – are qualifications which define and limit those who are invited; and they are spiritual qualifications. The invitation is not universal, therefore; it is limited to the sensible; that is, to the regenerate, the converted, believers; in short, the elect. Indeed, the passage, whilst it may be thought of as a call to sensible sinners, in reality is not a call to sinners at all – sensible or otherwise – but to saints; it is a call, not for justification, but for sanctification; believers are invited to come to the Lord for more grace that they may grow in the knowledge of Christ. Indeed, playing really safe, the invitation is, after all, an invitation to attend preaching services![17]

This misses the meaning of the passage by a mile. Isaiah 55:1-7 is a call to sinners to come to Christ for salvation, with a promise of mercy for those who come; it is not an invitation to believers. *First,* believers are regenerate; they are already living; but here God promises those he invites, 'Your soul shall live'.[18] *Secondly,*

---

[17] When Christ told the woman at the well: 'Whoever drinks of the water that I shall give him will never thirst' (John 4:14), and when he said: 'He who comes to me shall never hunger, and he who believes in me shall never thirst' (John 6:35), was he speaking about attendance at preaching services? Certainly not! He was talking about the gospel, salvation and everlasting satisfaction found by faith in himself.

[18] Hypers disagree: 'Some say that [this] proclamation is made to sinners dead in sin; and, as a proof of it, they say that it runs, "Hear, and your soul shall live". But it would be very strange for a corpse to be invited to come to the [sovereign's] palace in order to be banqueted. It would want something to move it; and if it was dead how could it "come"? The fact is, they are living souls who are here spoken of; but they are famishing, they are starving, they are wanting food; and when God the Spirit brings them to Christ, then they live, and live well too'. 'Who is it that he is speaking to?... Some say... dead sinners. But can the dead do any work?... No indeed. Then they must belong to the people of God, those whom the Holy Spirit has quickened, who are poor, sensible, needy sinners, drawn by his power to the dear Redeemer, to all those who have spiritual faith given to them, and who are led to Christ for life and salvation; these shall

believers are already in an everlasting covenant with Christ, yet God here promises those he invites that he will make such a covenant with them. *Thirdly*, believers are not 'the wicked',[19] nor are they 'unrighteous'. The whole tenor of the passage shows it is addressed to sinners not saints. I do not say that a backslider may not find great encouragement from the invitation – encouragement to return to God, and so on – but that is not its thrust. The passage is an invitation to sinners to come to God to find salvation in Christ.

But what sinners? *All* sinners, or *sensible* sinners? And do the characteristics listed qualify the invitation or the coming? In any case, are the thirst and poverty spiritual characteristics? Gill was sure they are, but is it certain it is so?

Let me take the last issue first. Might the thirst, the hunger, the waste of money on that which does not satisfy, describe the general dissatisfaction and misery and ruin which all sinners know, and not a specific spiritual experience wrought in the sinner by the Spirit? Are not all unconverted sinners thirsting, hungering, dissatisfied, and wasting their resources? Are they not all on a treadmill of

---

hear the voice of mercy, and their souls shall live, and live well too' (Gadsby pp126,144; see also pp347-348). In other words, Gadsby argued, since only the regenerate can come, only the regenerate may be invited; only the believing may be invited to believe. As I have shown throughout my book, there are two points about commanding dead sinners. *First*, this is exactly what we must do. Dead sinners are to be exhorted to look and live; dead sinners are to be commanded to repent. Christ's miracles illustrate it; he often commanded men to do what they could not do. *Secondly*, the Bible frequently leaves us with a paradox, a paradox which we must hold and proclaim in both its parts. It may be 'very strange', but human logic has to give way to biblical logic. In any case, as Gill said: 'Though man by sin has lost his power to comply with the will of God, by an obedience to it, God has not lost his power, right, and authority, to command'. The gospel command does not speak of man's ability but his duty. This is why, as Gill immediately added, 'when... the gospel call [is] rejected, it is most righteously resented by the Lord; and such [as do reject it] are justly punished with everlasting destruction by him (1 Pet. 4:17; 2 Thess. 1:8-9)' (Gill: *Body* Vol.2 p286).

[19] As Gill admitted: 'The word for "wicked" signifies... ungodly, and is expressive of the pollution and guilt of sin all are under' (Gill: *Commentary* Vol.3 p991).

slavery? Are not all unconverted sinners in desperate need, whether or not they realise it? Isaiah 55:1-7 certainly bears this out.[20] God reasons with those he invites, and expressly asks them why they are spending their money for what is not bread, their wages for what does not satisfy. In other words, by no stretch of the imagination can they be said to be looking for Christ! Their desires, far from spiritual, are carnal and futile. They want happiness and fulfilment, certainly, but they are not thinking about everlasting salvation and peace with God. Not at all! And the sort of satisfaction they are looking for, they seek from the world. In other words, they are far from being sensible, awakened, regenerate sinners who know the value of Christ and long for him! Of an awareness of their sin and need of Christ, they show not a trace.[21] In short, are we not talking about natural men with natural desires?[22] Of course we are! And yet these are the ones invited to Christ.

True, only those who spiritually thirst and realise they are spiritually penniless will come to Christ. Yes, a sinner must be regenerated before he can or will believe; he must know he is a sinner, yes, and want salvation from Christ. To borrow the language of the hyper-Calvinist, only sensible sinners will seek salvation. Yes, this is true. In fact, from a Calvinistic point of view – from a biblical point of view – it is a truism. *But we must not confuse the invitation with its acceptance.*[23] Are only the elect –

---

[20] As do a score of other passages; Prov. 27:20; Eccles. 1:8; 4:8; Rom. 6:17,19-20; Heb. 2:15, for instance.

[21] They 'lavish away time, opportunities, and strength, in reading and hearing false doctrine, which is not bread, but chaff... labouring to seek for happiness in worldly things' (Gill: *Commentary* Vol.3 p989). In saying this, Gill contradicted his claim that these were sensible sinners who were thirsting after more knowledge of Christ (see note above).

[22] Ella vehemently criticised this talk of 'natural desire' (Ella: *The Free Offer* pp49-50).

[23] Above all, we must get the right emphasis. Hyper-Calvinists concentrate on the sinner's fitness to be invited, and preparationists on the sinner's fitness to accept. But the gospel invitation focuses on Christ. There is a great deep here, of course. The way the Spirit regenerates, convicts and converts a sinner, is his sovereign prerogative, and known to him alone (John 3:8). Human logic, though it might try to analyse the

indeed, the elect who have been made sensible – to be invited because only they will come? or, is the invitation general even though its acceptance is – like Christ's atonement – particular? This is the issue.

Calvin, commenting on Isaiah 55, far from thinking the hearers were spiritually awakened, drew attention to the opening word, 'Ho!', noting:

So great is the sluggishness of men that it is difficult to arouse them. They do not feel their wants, though they are hungry; nor do they desire food, which they greatly need; and therefore that indifference must be shaken off by loud and incessant cries... Besides, the invitation is general; for there is no man who is not in want of those 'waters', and to whom Christ is not necessary; and therefore he invites all indiscriminately, without any respect of persons.

Not a sensible sinner in sight! Awakened? They were sleep walking! Calvin was clear, however, there is a 'true preparation for receiving this grace' – *for receiving this grace*,[24] please note, *but not for receiving the invitation*. Before sinners will receive this grace, said Calvin, they must be spiritually 'thirsty'; those who are not, 'will not receive Christ'. Why not? 'Because', said Calvin:

They have no relish for spiritual grace... It is therefore necessary that we have 'thirst', that is, an ardent desire, in order that it may be possible for us to receive so great blessings... [The prophet] complains of the ingratitude and madness of men, in rejecting or disdaining the kindness of God who offers all things freely... Men... choose rather to... vex themselves in vain, than to rely on the grace which God offers to them... The prophet... exclaimed against all men, to whatever age they might belong; for all the posterity of Adam... in seeking the road to a heavenly life, they altogether go astray, and follow their own vain opinions rather than the voice of God.[25]

This is clear enough. According to Calvin, Isaiah was addressing all men, 'the invitation is general', 'he invites all indiscriminately',

---

process, and sort out its order in precise detail, is probing where it ought not.

[24] 'These passages [including Isa. 55] declare that none are admitted to enjoy the blessings of God save those who are pining under a sense of their own poverty' (Calvin: *Institutes* Vol.1 p232).

[25] Calvin: *Commentaries* Vol.8 Part 2 pp156-158.

but only those prepared of God will receive the promised grace.[26]

The Sum of Saving Knowledge: 'Here... the Lord... makes open offer of Christ and his grace, by proclamation of a free and gracious market of righteousness and salvation, to be had through Christ to every soul, without exception, that truly desires to be saved from sin and wrath... He invites all sinners, that for any reason stand at a distance from God, to come and take from him riches of grace'.[27] This too is clear. The offer is 'open', God 'invites all sinners' whatever their condition, but only he who 'truly desires to be saved' will obtain that salvation.

Tobias Crisp:

Life now is reached out to such a person, that is a dead person... I am not fit for Christ... What is this to come without money, and without price? It is nothing but to take the offer of Christ, these waters of life, to take them merely and simply as a gift brought, and this is a sure mercy indeed...

The Father expects nothing in the world of men; no one qualification or spiritual disposition, before, or upon the communicating of his Son Christ to men... Consider... Isaiah 55:1; it is plain there... that God

---

[26] Calvin, however, contradicted himself when he went on to say the prophet does not speak of those who 'take no concern about the spiritual life of the soul' – and 'there are many such persons'. Either the prophet addresses all men, or he does not. But whatever the explanation of that contradiction, Calvin lends no support to the hyper-Calvinistic interpretation of the passage. The prophet was not addressing sensible sinners, but 'those who desire life, and yet do not understand the method or way of obtaining it', using 'methods which men contrive, in opposition to the word of God, for obtaining salvation... [using] all the industry, study, or labour which belongs to man... our idle attempts to worship [God]... labours foolishly undertaken [yet which] are reckoned valuable by the judgement of the flesh'. This does *not* describe sensible sinners – since they *are* seeking Christ, and, being taught by the Spirit, are seeking him in his appointed way. As for the 'desire [for] life' and the 'obtaining [of] salvation', does this not describe the overwhelming majority of men? Don't most unbelievers cherish a vain hope that somehow all will be well with them in the end? Indeed, to judge by the confident pronouncements made at many an unbeliever's funeral, they regard it as a certainty! But just because an unbeliever vaguely hopes, or presumes, he is going to heaven, it does not mean he is sensible!

[27] *The Sum* p332.

looks for nothing in the world of men; be they what they will, be they in the worst condition, no matter what it is, they are the men to whom Christ offers himself... that is, everyone that has but a mind to come to him, everyone that would take him, may have him... But what does God require here in the covenant? No money, no price... nor anything at all.[28]

Matthew Henry dealt first of all with those invited:

We are all invited to come and take the benefit of that provision which the grace of God has made for poor souls in the new covenant... Who are invited: 'Ho, every one'... the poor and the maimed, the halt and

---

[28] Crisp: *Christ Alone* Vol.1 pp37-38,100-101; *Sermons* Issue 1 pp41-42; Issue 2 pp42-43. Surprisingly, Gill made no comment on these extracts. He did, however, elsewhere try to limit – to sensible sinners – Crisp's offer of Christ (Crisp: *Christ Alone* Vol.2 p27), as did the Christian Bookshop, Ossett (Crisp: *Sermons* Issue I p48). But this is wrong. In addition to the above, Crisp was clear: 'The secrets of the Lord are with himself; only the names of particular persons are written in the book of life; but they are not written in the word... but... it is as sufficient for the satisfaction of a man, [that] the general tender of free grace and pardon of sin to all sinners... [is] as if his name in particular were set down in that tender' (Crisp: *Christ Alone* Vol.3 p40). See also *Christ Alone* Vol.1 pp47,114-115; *Sermons* Issue 1 pp50-51; Issue 2 pp54-55. Gill, even though he admitted Crisp made 'this general tender, or offer of Christ to all', nevertheless stated that 'the universal offer cannot be supported without supposing universal redemption' (Crisp: *Christ Alone* Vol.1 p114; *Sermons* Issue 2 pp58-59). In this last, he was mistaken; the extent of the atonement has no bearing on the extent of the offer. Owen: 'Christ died... only for the elect... Some then tell us we cannot invite all men promiscuously to believe. But why so? We invite... all men as sinners; and we know that Christ died for sinners' (Owen: *Psalm 130* in *Works* Vol.6 p523). See also my note in Appendix 1. As for Crisp, he preached both the *universal* offer and *particular* redemption (Crisp: *Christ Alone* Vol.2 pp81-82), as Gill recognised (Crisp: *Christ Alone* Vol.1 p10; *Sermons* Issue 1 n5 (not n9) p19; Issue 2 p59). See also Rippon p71; Murray: *Spurgeon* p132. With regard to the offer not specifying persons by name, Spurgeon made a telling point; namely, that if Scripture did put names to the promise, it would provide far less encouragement to doubting sinners. As he said, speaking for himself, he would wonder if there was another Charles Haddon Spurgeon! 'How much worse would it be for the Smiths and the Browns!' he declared (Spurgeon: *Metropolitan* Vol.32 pp645-646; see also Vol.11 pp705-706).

the blind, are called to this marriage supper, whoever can be picked up out of the highways and the hedges. It intimates that... ministers are to make a general offer of life and salvation to all... and that the gospel covenant excludes none that do not exclude themselves. The invitation is published with an 'Oyez – Ho', take notice of it.

The invitation is to all. But 'what is the qualification required in those that shall be welcome'? This:

They must thirst. All shall be welcome to gospel grace upon those terms only that gospel grace be welcome to them. Those that are satisfied with the world and its enjoyments for a portion, and seek not for a happiness in the favour of God – those that depend upon the merit of their own works for a righteousness, and see no need they have of Christ and his righteousness – these do not thirst; they have no sense of their need, and are in no pain or uneasiness about their souls, and therefore will not condescend so far as to be beholden to Christ. But those that thirst are invited to the waters, as those that labour, and are heavy laden, are invited to Christ for rest. Note, where God gives grace he first gives a thirsting after it; and where he has given a thirsting after it, he will give it (Ps. 81:10).

And, finally, 'Whither they are invited':

'Come you to the waters'... Come to Christ...[29] The gifts offered us are invaluable and such as no price can be set upon... He who offers them has no need of us, nor of any returns we can make him. He makes us these proposals, not because he has occasion to sell, but because he has a disposition to give... The things offered are already bought and paid for. Christ purchased them at the full value, with price, not with money, but with 'his own blood' (1 Pet. 1:19)... We shall be welcome to the benefits of the promise, though we are utterly unworthy of them, and cannot make a tender of anything... We are earnestly pressed and persuaded (and O that we would be prevailed with!) to accept this invitation, and make this good bargain for ourselves... That which we are persuaded to is to hearken to God and to his proposals... [to] accept God's offers.

Edwards, citing Isaiah 55:1 with other passages, declared: 'Pardon is as much offered and promised to the greatest sinners as any, if they will come aright to God for mercy. The invitations of the

---

[29] Matthew Henry included 'ordinances' in the invitation, but majored on Christ himself.

gospel are always in universal terms'.[30] Once again, pardon is offered to all, but received only by those who come in faith.

Young: 'Redemption has been accomplished... and now the invitation is extended to all that are in need to come and to partake of the salvation the Lord offers... This [passage] is equivalent to the divine imperative of the gospel message, whereby men who are lost are commanded to come to Christ and in him to find the blessings that they so desperately need and that he alone can give... The invitation is universal, addressed to all who are wicked and men of iniquity'.[31]

Fuller: 'This is the language of invitation... The thirst which [those who are invited] are supposed to possess does not mean a holy desire after spiritual blessings, but the natural desire of happiness which God has implanted in every bosom, and which, in wicked men, is directed not to "the sure mercies of David", but to that which "is not bread", or which has no solid satisfaction in it'.[32]

Boston:

That gospel offer (Isa. 55:1) is the most solemn one to be found in all the Old Testament; and that recorded [in] Rev. 22:17 is the parting offer made to sinners by Jesus Christ at the closing of the canon of the Scripture, and manifestly looks to the former; in the which I can see no ground to think that the thirsting therein mentioned does [in] any way restrict the offer; or that the thirsty there invited are convinced, sensible sinners who are thirsting after Christ and his righteousness; the which would leave outside the scope of this solemn invitation... the far greater part of mankind... The context seems decisive [on] this point; for the thirsting ones invited are such as are 'spending money for that which is not bread, and their labour for that which satisfies not' (Isa. 55:1-2); but convinced, sensible sinners who are thirsting after Christ and his righteousness, are not spending their labour and money at that rate; but, on the contrary, [they are spending it] for that which is bread and satisfies; namely, for Christ. Wherefore the thirsting there mentioned must be more extensive, comprehending, indeed, and principally aiming at that thirst after happiness and satisfaction which, being natural, is common to all mankind. Men pained with this thirst or hunger are naturally running, for quenching

---

[30] Edwards p112.
[31] Young pp374-380.
[32] Fuller: *Worthy* in *Works* p157.

thereof, to the empty creation, and their fulsome lusts; so 'spending money for that which is not bread, and their labour for that which satisfies not', their hungry souls find no food, but what is meagre and lean, bad and unwholesome, and cannot satisfy their appetite. Compare Luke 15:16. In this wretched case, Adam left all mankind, and [this is where] Christ finds them. Whereupon the gospel proclamation is issued forth, inviting them [that is, all mankind] to come away from the broken cisterns, filthy puddles, to the waters of life, even to Jesus Christ, where they may have bread, fatness, what is good, and will satisfy... their painful thirst (John 4:14; 6:35).[33]

And as Boston said on Matthew 11:28: 'I cannot agree with those that restrain these expressions to those that are sensible of their sins and misery, without Christ, and are longing to be rid of the same; but I think it includes all that are out of Christ, sensible or insensible'.[34]

Spurgeon:

I am sorry that some of my brethren entertain the idea that the gospel is to be preached only to certain characters. They dare not preach the gospel to everybody;[35] they try to preach it to the elect; surely, if the Lord had meant them to make the selection he would have set a mark upon his chosen. As I do not know the elect, and have no command to confine my preaching to them, but am bidden to preach the gospel to every creature, I am thankful that the gospel is put in such a way that no creature can be too poor, too wicked, or too vile to receive it, for it is 'without money and without price'... If before I preach the gospel I have to look for a measure of fitness in a man, then I cannot preach the gospel to any but those whom I believe to have the fitness; but if the gospel is to be preached freely, with no conditions or demands for preparations or prerequisites... then I may go to the most degraded [pagans]... and tell them the good news; we may speak of mercy to harlots and thieves... we may penetrate the jungles of crime, and still with the same entreaty from heaven – 'Let the wicked forsake his

---

[33] Boston: *Marrow* p143.

[34] Boston: *Beauties* p261. Boston did not leave it there, but gave his reasons.

[35] Hypers, I acknowledge, claim they do preach the gospel to all, but Spurgeon was referring to the fact that they limit the gospel *invitation* to the sensible. Giving the invitation to *all*, however, is an essential part of preaching the gospel to every creature; without it, the gospel is not being preached as it should be.

way, and the unrighteous man his thoughts, and let him turn unto the Lord, for he will have mercy upon him, and to our God, for he will abundantly pardon'. The fact that the mercy of God is 'without money and without price' enables us to preach it to every man, woman, and child of woman born.

Spurgeon on Matthew 11:28:

Labourers and loaded ones constitute the great mass of mankind, and the Lord Jesus invites them all without exception... Some have ventured to say that this describes a certain *spiritual* character, but I fail to see any word to mark the spirituality of the person; certainly I see not a syllable to limit the text to that sense. Brethren and sisters, it is not our wont either to add to or to take from the word of God knowingly, and as there is no indication here that these words are to be limited in their meaning, we shall not dare to invent a limit. Where God puts no bolt or bar, woe unto those who shall set up barriers of their own. We shall read our text in the broadest conceivable sense, for it is most like the spirit of the gospel to do so. It says – '*all* you that labour', and if you labour, it includes you. It says – '*all* you that are heavy laden', and if you are heavy laden, it includes you, and God forbid that we should shut you out.

And as he had explained in a sermon preached fifteen years before: 'While the invitation is given to the weary and heavy laden, you will perceive that the promise is not made to them *as* weary and heavy laden, but it is made to them *as* coming to Christ'.

Again:

In order that you may come to Jesus, no preparation is required. You may come just as you are, and come at once: only confess that you need him, desire to have him, and then take him by trusting him. He is like wine and milk, supplying delight and satisfaction, and you are to take him as men would take a drink. How could the invitation be put more broadly than it is? How could it be uttered more earnestly? It has a 'Ho!' to give it tongue. Tradesmen in certain parts of London stand outside of their shops and cry 'Buy, buy!' or call out 'Ho!' to the passers-by because they are anxious to sell their wares. Jesus is yet more eager to distribute his rich grace, for he longs to see men saved... There are many such invitations in the Scriptures, and if not all expressed by the same metaphor, they are all equally as free and as clear... Jesus entreats men to look to him and live: he bids them come to him and find rest unto their souls.[36]

Let me bring this to a conclusion: Reading the characteristics set out in some gospel invitations as qualifications which sinners must meet before they are invited, not only turns those invitations upside down, it demands the impossible, since no preacher, nor any sinner, can ever be sure the qualifications have been met in any particular case. The upshot is, whereas the characteristics spelled out in the invitations are intended to encourage – not hinder – sinners in coming to Christ, hyper-Calvinists turn them into barriers – impossibly high barriers – for both ministers and sinners. Ministers have to be sure sinners have surmounted the barriers before they can invite them; sinners have to be sure they have climbed over the barriers before they can be invited, let alone come to Christ. An influence more deadening on the gospel invitation it would be hard to imagine, the consequences of which are serious in the extreme.

I wish John Brown's wise and biblical counsel, based on the words of Christ in John 7:37-38, were known, remembered and acted upon. Rightly depicting those words as the gospel's 'unlimited invitation to participate in the blessings of salvation' – that is, stressing 'the unlimited extent of the invitation' – Brown declared:

The free and unrestricted nature of the invitation [to Christ]... deserves notice. Not only is the descriptive character of those invited, 'those who thirst', common to all human beings, but the invitation is so fashioned, that no human being can find the shadow of a reason for thinking himself excluded... It is not, 'If any man be deeply sensible of his guilt, depravity, and wretchedness, let him come to me and drink'. Such are invited; but if that were all, as some have taught, thus, however unintentionally, clogging with conditions the unhampered offer of a free salvation, men might think that till they had brought themselves, or were in some way or other brought, into a state of deep contrition, and earnest seeking after pardon, and holiness, and salvation, it would be presumption in them to come to Christ, or even look towards the Saviour for salvation. But the invitation is,

---

[36] Spurgeon: *Metropolitan* Vol.20 pp140-141; Vol.22 pp614-615; *New and Metropolitan* Vol.7 p109; *Metropolitan* Vol.26 pp415-416, emphasis his; see also *New* Vol.4 p342; Murray: *Spurgeon* pp69-71.

'Whosoever wishes to be happy, let him come to me, sinful and miserable as he is, and in me he shall find salvation. If you are not a brute, if you are not a devil – however like the one in sensuality, or the other in malignity – you are invited. If you are on earth, not in hell, you are invited'.

As Brown had said: 'A more comprehensive description of human beings, I believe, could not be conceived. "If any man thirst", is just equal to, "Whosoever wishes to be happy". If a man can be found who is perfectly happy, or who has no wish to be happy, that man is not invited. Till such a person is found, we must hold that the invitation has no limits'.[37]

* * *

Forgive me, reader, but I cannot leave such a glorious subject there. Permit me to quote just one more free-offer preacher actually going about his business. Observe how Edward Payson makes the gospel invitation general, *but not generalised*; that is, he invites all his hearers, but makes sure that everyone in particular knows he is personally invited. Whilst the invitation is all-embracing, there is nothing vague about it.

First, let Payson state the facts:

My friends, God offers you the water of life, without money and without price. Everyone may come and take it if he will...
[Christ] was... pleased to express his invitations in the most general and encouraging terms which language could afford... He intended that no man, who heard the gospel, should have any cause to pretend that he was not invited to share in its benefits. He therefore made his invitations as general and comprehensive as possible, so as to exclude none who did not exclude themselves.

Now let us hear Payson preach it:

Permit me then to apply the subject by pressing everyone present, who has not already embraced the Saviour, to come to him without delay. As the mouth of God, and in my Master's name, I invite everyone of you to do this. Our Creator, our God has made a great feast, a

---

[37] Brown: *Discourses* Vol.2 v, pp1,5-10. Note that Brown cited Bunyan's *Jerusalem Sinner*, and linked John 7:37-38 to other gospel invitations including Isa. 55:1-3 and Matt. 11:28.

marriage feast for his Son; a feast for the [reception] of sinners... To this feast you are now invited. No tickets of admission are necessary. The Master of the feast stands at the door to receive you, declaring that not one, who comes, shall be cast out; and as his servant, sent forth for this very purpose, sent especially to you, I now invite you to come. I invite you, children; for there is a place for you. Leave your toys and follies then, and come to Christ. I invite you who are young; for your presence is especially desired. Leave your sinful amusements and companions then, and come to the Saviour. I invite you who are [middle-aged]. To you, O men, I call, and my voice is to the sons of men. Particularly do I invite you, who are parents, to come... to the Saviour's feast. I invite you, who are aged, to come and receive from Christ a crown of glory, which your grey hairs will be, if you are found in the way of righteousness. I invite you to come, you poor, and Christ will make you rich in faith and heirs of his kingdom. I invite you to come who are rich... I invite you, who are ignorant, to come and Christ will impart to you his treasures of wisdom and knowledge. I invite you who possess human learning... I invite you who are afflicted to come, for my God is the God of all consolation, and my Master can be touched with the feeling of your infirmities. I invite you, who feel yourselves to be the greatest of sinners, to come... I invite you, who have long despised, and who still despise this invitation, to come; for Christ's language is, Hearken to me, you stout-hearted, and far from righteousness. And if there be any one in this assembly, who thinks himself overlooked; if there be one who has not yet felt that this invitation is addressed to him, I now present it to that person, particularly, and invite him to come.

Then the warning:

And now, my friends, I have done. My directions were to invite to the Saviour's marriage feast as many as I should find. I have accordingly invited all and each of you. I take you to record, as witnesses against each other, that you have all received the invitation. I take each of your consciences to record, as witnesses against yourselves, that you have been invited, and as a witness for me, that I have discharged my commission. If then any of you do not come, you cannot ascribe it to the want of an invitation. If any of you perish, it will be, not because Christ did not offer to save you; nor because you did not hear the offer, but solely because you would not accept it. You are, therefore, left without excuse. I am aware, however, that you will fancy you have an excuse. You will pretend that you wish to come, but are unable. My friends, I know nothing of that. I am not directed to answer such objections. I have nothing to do with them. My business is simply to preach to you the gospel; to proclaim to you the glad tidings; to invite you to Christ, and to assure you, in his name, that, if you come, you shall most certainly be received. If you say that you cannot come; if you can make God believe it; if you dare go to the judgement seat with this excuse, and venture your eternal interests on its being accepted as sufficient, it is well. But if you determine on this course, permit me to remind you, that God's sentiments, as revealed in his word, differ very widely from yours, with respect to this excuse. He evidently considers your unwillingness, or inability, or whatever you choose to call it, to come to Christ, as your greatest sin. He, once and again, denounces upon you the most dreadful punishments for this very thing. He declares, not only that all who do not believe in Christ shall be condemned, but that they are condemned already. What you consider as your best excuse, he considers as your greatest sin. Beware then, my friends, how you make this excuse...

Instead, therefore, of seeking for excuses, which will only prove your destruction, let me persuade you rather to comply with Christ's invitations.

Payson returns to mercy:

The blessings which [Christ] offers and dispenses... cost him their full value. They cost thirty-three years' labour... No! more, they cost him his life. He paid the dreadful price in tears and groans and blood, in agonies unutterable. There is not a single blessing he offers you, O sinner, which did not cost him a pang. He purchased the privilege of offering you those very blessings which you have a thousand times rejected... Now he offers you, without money and without price, all that cost him so dear. He even beseeches you as a favour to accept it, and will consider the joy arising from your acceptance and salvation as a sufficient recompense for all that he suffered in procuring it.

To conclude:

Man is happy and free... if he... embraces the Saviour and the salvation thus freely offered; otherwise, [he is] lost, more fatally, hopelessly lost, than ever.[38]

Are gospel invitations universal? They are, praise God, they are. Thank God it is so, for it means that God invites me – and, reader, it means that God invites YOU.

---

[38] Payson Vol.1 p474; Vol.2 pp484,490-495; Vol.3 p156.

Source List

Alford, Henry: *The New Testament for English Readers...*, Vol.1 Part 2, Rivingtons, London, 1863.

Alleine, Joseph: *An Alarm to the Unconverted*, The Banner of Truth Trust, London, 1964.

Arndt, William F. and Gingrich, F.Wilbur: *A Greek-English Lexicon of the New Testament and Other Early Christian Literature*, The University of Chicago Press, Chicago... and The Syndics of the Cambridge University Press, London, 1957.

Articles of Faith of the Gospel Standard Aid and Poor Relief Societies, The Gospel Standard Societies, Harpenden.

Baldwin, R.J.: *Is Saving Faith a Duty?*, being the paper read at The Strict and Particular Baptist Minister's Fellowship Conference, London, on April 18th, 1961.

Bates, William: *The Whole Works of... William Bates...*, Sprinkle Publications, Harrisonburg, 1990.

Bavinck, Herman: *The Doctrine of God*, The Banner of Truth Trust, Edinburgh.

Berkhof, L.: *Systematic Theology*, The Banner of Truth Trust, London, 1959.

Berridge, John: *Observations on Passages of Scripture* in *The Works of... John Berridge...*, edited by... Richard Whittingham, Old Paths Gospel Press, Choteau.

Bonar, Andrew A.: *Memoir and Remains of... Robert Murray M'Cheyne...*, Oliphant Anderson & Ferrier, Edinburgh & London, 1892.

Boston, Thomas, notes in Edward Fisher: *The Marrow of Modern Divinity...*, Still Waters Revival Books, Edmonton, reprint edition 1991.

Boston, Thomas: *The Beauties of Thomas Boston...*, edited by Samuel M'Millan, Christian Focus Publications, Inverness, 1979.

Bridges, Charles: *The Christian Ministry...*, The Banner of Truth Trust, London, 1961.

Brown, John: *An Exposition of The Epistle of Paul the Apostle to the Galatians*, The Sovereign Grace Book Club, Evansville, 1957.

Brown, John: *Discourses and Sayings of Our Lord Jesus Christ,*

Vol.2, The Banner of Truth Trust, Edinburgh, 1990.

Bunyan, John: *The Pilgrim's Progress* in *The Works of John Bunyan*, Vol.2, edited by Henry Stebbing, John Hirst, London, 1862.

Bunyan, John: *The Jerusalem Sinner Saved; or, Good News for the Vilest of Men...* in *The Works of John Bunyan*, Vol.2, edited by Henry Stebbing, John Hirst, London, 1862.

Burkitt, William: *Expository Notes with Practical Observations upon the New Testament...*, Henry Mozley and Sons, Derby, 1833.

Calvin, John: *Institutes of the Christian Religion*, A new translation by Henry Beveridge, James Clarke & Co., Limited, London, 1957.

Calvin, John: *Calvin's Commentaries*, Baker Book House, Grand Rapids, 1979.

Calvin, John: *Calvin's Calvinism: Treatises on the Eternal Predestination of God & the Secret Providence of God*, translated by Henry Cole, Reformed Free Publishing Association, Grand Rapids.

Candlish, Robert S.: *A Commentary on 1 John,* The Banner of Truth Trust, London, 1973.

Clarkson, David: *Of Faith* in *The Works of David Clarkson*, Vol.1, The Banner of Truth Trust, Edinburgh, 1988.

Clarkson, David: *Men by Nature Unwilling to Come to Christ* in *The Works of David Clarkson*, Vol.1, The Banner of Truth Trust, Edinburgh, 1988.

Clarkson, David: *Christ's Gracious Invitation to Sinners* in *The Works of David Clarkson*, Vol.2, The Banner of Truth Trust, Edinburgh, 1988.

Colquhoun, John: *Repentance*, The Banner of Truth Trust, London, 1965.

Crisp, Tobias: *Christ Alone Exalted...*, edited by John Gill, Old Paths Gospel Press, Choteau.

Crisp, Tobias: *The Sermons of Tobias Crisp... with John Gill's Notes*, Christian Bookshop, Ossett, 1995.

Cunningham, William: *Historical Theology: A Review of the Principal Doctrinal Discussions in the Christian Church since the Apostolic Age*, The Banner of Truth Trust, Edinburgh, 1994.

Dagg, J.L.: *A Manual of Theology*, Gano Books, Harrisonburg, 1990.

Delves, Stanley: *Forest Fold Pulpit*, The Stanley Delves Trust, 1980.

Durham, James: *Christ Crucified: or, The Marrow of the Gospel...*,

Edinburgh, 1726.

Edwards, Jonathan: *Miscellaneous Remarks Concerning the Divine Decrees...* in *The Works of Jonathan Edwards, Revised and Corrected by Edward Hickman*, Vol.2, The Banner of Truth Trust, Edinburgh, 1974.

Ella, George M.: *John Gill and the Cause of God and Truth*, Go Publications, Eggleston, 1995.

Ella, George M.: *The Free Offer and The Call of the Gospel*, Go Publications, Eggleston, 2001.

Engelsma, David J.: *Hyper-Calvinism & The Call of the Gospel: An Examination of the 'Well-Meant Offer' of the Gospel*, Revised Edition, Reformed Free Publishing Association, Grand Rapids, 1994.

Fisher, Edward: *The Marrow of Modern Divinity...*, with notes by Thomas Boston, Still Waters Revival Books, Edmonton, reprint edition 1991.

Flavel, John: *The Mystery of Providence*, The Banner of Truth Trust, London, 1963.

Flavel, John: *Christ Knocking at the Door of Sinners' Hearts; or, A Solemn Entreaty to Receive the Saviour and his Gospel in this the Day of Mercy*, Evangelical Press, Welwyn, 1978.

Foreman, John: *Remarks on Duty Faith*, Christian Bookshop, Ossett, 1995.

Fuller, Andrew: *The Gospel Worthy of All Acceptation, or the Duty of Sinners to Believe in Jesus Christ...* in *The Complete Works of... Andrew Fuller...*, Henry G.Bohn, London, 1866.

Fuller, Andrew: *A Defence of a Treatise entitled The Gospel Worthy of All Acceptation...* in *The Complete Works of... Andrew Fuller...*, Henry G.Bohn, London, 1866.

Fuller, Andrew: *Exposition of Passages Apparently Contradictory* in *The Complete Works of... Andrew Fuller...*, Henry G.Bohn, London, 1866.

Gadsby, William: *Sermons by William Gadsby...*, Gospel Standard Trust Publications, Harpenden, 1991.

Gay, David H.J.: 'Preaching the Gospel to Sinners', an address at the Banner of Truth Ministers' Conference 1993, a summary of which was published in *The Banner of Truth*, July & August/September 1994.

Gill, John: *Gill's Commentary*, Baker Book House, Grand Rapids, 1980.

Gill, John: *The Cause of God and Truth*, W.H.Collingridge, London, 1855.

Gill, John: *Sermons and Tracts*, Old Paths Gospel Press, Choteau.

Gill, John: *A Complete Body of Doctrinal and Practical Divinity; or, A System of Evangelical Truths, Deduced from the Sacred Scriptures*, W.Winterbotham, London, 1796.

Goodwin, Thomas: *Of the Object and Acts of Justifying Faith* in *The Works of Thomas Goodwin*, Vol.8, The Banner of Truth Trust, Edinburgh, 1985.

Gosden, J.H.: *What Gospel Standard Baptists Believe: A Commentary on the Gospel Standard Articles of Faith*, Gospel Standard Societies, Chippenham, 1993.

Gouge, William: *Commentary on Hebrews*, Kregel Publications, Grand Rapids, 1980.

Greenhill, William: *An Exposition of Ezekiel*, The Banner of Truth Trust, Edinburgh, 1994.

Gurnall, William: *Christian in Complete Armour*, The Banner of Truth Trust.

Guthrie, William: *The Christian's Great Interest*, The Publications Committee of the Free Presbyterian Church of Scotland, 1952.

Henry, Matthew: *An Exposition of the Old and New Testament...*, James Nisbet & Co., Limited, London.

Hodge, A.A.: *Outlines of Theology*, The Banner of Truth Trust, London, 1972.

Hulse, Errol: *Adding To The Church – The Puritan Approach To Persuading Souls*, being a paper given at The Westminster Conference, 1973: *Adding to the Church*, The Westminster Conference.

Jay, William: *The Autobiography of... William Jay...*, Hamilton, Adams, & Co., London, 1855.

Kelly, Douglas F.: *Preachers With Power...*, The Banner of Truth Trust, Edinburgh, 1992.

Kevan, Ernest: *Salvation*, Evangelical Press, London, 1973.

Kuiper, R.B.: *God-Centred Evangelism: A Presentation of the Scriptural Theology of Evangelism*, The Banner of Truth Trust, London, 1966.

Source List

Latimer, Hugh: *Sermons by Hugh Latimer*, Vol.1, Cambridge University Press, Cambridge, 1844.

Lloyd-Jones, D.Martyn: *Preaching and Preachers*, Hodder and Stoughton, London, 1971.

Lloyd-Jones, D.Martyn: *Romans: An Exposition of Chapters 2:1 – 3:20. The Righteous Judgement of God*, The Banner of Truth Trust, Edinburgh, 1989.

Machen, J.Gresham: *The Christian View of Man*, The Banner of Truth Trust, London, 1965.

Machen, J.Gresham: *Machen's Notes on Galatians...*, John H.Skilton (ed), Presbyterian and Reformed Publishing Co., New Jersey, 1977.

Macleod, John: *Scottish Theology in Relation to Church History since the Reformation*, The Banner of Truth Trust, Edinburgh, 1974.

Manton, Thomas: *A Practical Exposition of the Lord's Prayer* in *The Works of Thomas Manton*, Vol.1, The Banner of Truth Trust, Edinburgh, 1993.

Manton, Thomas: *The Complete Works of Thomas Manton*, Vol.21, Maranatha Publications, Worthington.

Manton, Thomas: *An Exposition on the Epistle of Jude*, The Banner of Truth Trust, London, 1962.

Marbury, Edward: *Obadiah and Habakkuk*, Klock & Klock, Minneapolis, 1979.

M'Cheyne, Robert Murray: *Sermons of Robert Murray M'Cheyne*, The Banner of Truth Trust, London, 1961.

M'Cheyne, Robert Murray: *A Basket of Fragments*, Christian Focus Publications, Inverness, 1975.

Morgan, Edward: *John Elias: Life, Letters and Essays*, The Banner of Truth Trust, Edinburgh, 1973.

Murray, Iain H.: *The Forgotten Spurgeon*, The Banner of Truth Trust, London, 1966.

Murray, Iain H.: *Arthur W.Pink: His Life and Thought*, The Banner of Truth Trust, Edinburgh, 1981.

Murray, Iain H.: *D.Martyn Lloyd-Jones: The Fight of Faith 1939-1981*, The Banner of Truth Trust, Edinburgh, 1990.

Murray, Iain H.: *Spurgeon v. Hyper-Calvinism: The Battle for Gospel Preaching*, The Banner of Truth Trust, Edinburgh, 1995.

Naylor, Peter: *Picking up a Pin for the Lord: English Particular*

Baptists from 1688 to the Early Nineteenth Century, Grace Publications, London, 1992.

New Focus, Go Publications, Eggleston, October/November 1999, Vol.4 number 3.

Owen, John: *An Exposition of Hebrews*, 7 Volumes in 4, Sovereign Grace Publishers, Evansville, 1960.

Owen, John: *A Declaration of the Glorious Mystery of the Person of Christ...* in *The Works of John Owen*, Vol.1, edited by William H.Goold, The Banner of Truth Trust, London, 1965.

Owen, John: *Meditations and Discourses Concerning the Glory of Christ; Applied unto Unconverted Sinners...* in *The Works of John Owen*, Vol.1, edited by William H.Goold, The Banner of Truth Trust, London, 1965.

Owen, John: *A Discourse Concerning the Holy Spirit...* in *The Works of John Owen*, Vol.3, edited by William H.Goold, The Banner of Truth Trust, London, 1966.

Owen, John: *The Doctrine of Justification by Faith...* in *The Works of John Owen*, Vol.5, edited by William H.Goold, The Banner of Truth Trust, London, 1967.

Owen, John: *An Exposition upon Psalm 130* in *The Works of John Owen*, Vol.6, edited by William H.Goold, The Banner of Truth Trust, London, 1966.

Owen, John: *A Display of Arminianism...* in *The Works of John Owen*, Vol.10, edited by William H.Goold, The Banner of Truth Trust, London, 1967.

Owen, John: *The Death of Death in the Death of Christ...* in *The Works of John Owen*, Vol.10, edited by William H.Goold, The Banner of Truth Trust, London, 1967.

Owen, John: *A Vindication of The Animadversions on 'Fiat Lux'...* in *The Works of John Owen*, Vol.14, edited by William H.Goold, The Banner of Truth Trust, London, 1967.

Packer, J.I.: *Evangelism and the Sovereignty of God*, Inter-Varsity Press, 1976.

Parks, William: *Sermons on the Five Points of Calvinism...*, C.J.Farncombe & Sons, Ltd., London, 1915 (?).

Paul, S.F.: *Memorial of John Hervey Gosden*, 1965.

Payson, Edward: *The Complete Works...*, Sprinkle Publications, Harrisonburg, 1987/8.

Philpot, J.C.: *Ears From Harvested Sheaves*, C.J.Farncombe & Sons, Ltd., Croydon.

Pink, Arthur W.: *The Sovereignty of God*, Baker Book House, Grand Rapids, 1984.

Poole, Matthew: *A Commentary on the Holy Bible*, Vol.3, The Banner of Truth Trust, Edinburgh, reprinted 1975.

Ramsbottom, B.A.: 'Review' of Gay, David H.J.: *The Gospel Offer is Free* in the *Gospel Standard*, Luton, March 2005.

Rippon, John: *A Brief Memoir of the Life and Writings of... John Gill*, Gano Books, Harrisonburg, 1992.

Sears, Septimus: *Gospel Precepts. A letter to the late valued editor of the 'Gospel Standard' by the editor of the 'Sower'*, published by Sears in the 'Sower', Feb. 1st 1871.

Shepard, Thomas: *The Ten Virgins*, Tyndale Bible Society, Florida.

Sibbes, Richard: *A Heavenly Conference* in *Works of Richard Sibbes*, Vol.6, The Banner of Truth Trust, Edinburgh, 1983.

Sibbes, Richard: *King David's Epitaph* in *Works of Richard Sibbes*, Vol.6, The Banner of Truth Trust, Edinburgh, 1983.

Silversides, David: *The Doctrine of Conversion in the Westminster Standards: With special reference to the theology of Herman Hoeksema*, Reformed Theological Journal, Vol.9, November 1993.

Southern Baptist Sermons on Sovereignty and Responsibility, Gano Books, Sprinkle Publications, Harrisonburg, 1984.

Sprague, William B.: *Lectures on Revival of Religion*, The Banner of Truth Trust, London, 1959.

Spurgeon, C.H.: *The Pulpit Library...*, Vol.2, Alabaster & Passmore, London, 1858.

Spurgeon, C.H.: *The New Park Street Pulpit... 1858*, Vol.4, The Banner of Truth Trust, London, 1964.

Spurgeon, C.H.: *The New Park Street Pulpit... 1859*, Vol.5, The Banner of Truth Trust, London, 1964.

Spurgeon, C.H.: *The New Park Street Pulpit... 1860*, Vol.6, The Banner of Truth Trust, London, 1964.

Spurgeon, C.H.: *The New Park Street and Metropolitan Tabernacle Pulpit... 1861*, Vol.7, Passmore and Alabaster, London, 1862.

Spurgeon, C.H.: *The Metropolitan Tabernacle Pulpit... 1863*, Vol.9, Passmore and Alabaster, London, 1864.

Spurgeon, C.H.: *The Metropolitan Tabernacle Pulpit... 1865*, Vol.11,

Passmore and Alabaster, London, 1866.

Spurgeon, C.H.: *The Metropolitan Tabernacle Pulpit... 1867*, Vol.13, Passmore and Alabaster, London, 1868.

Spurgeon, C.H.: *The Metropolitan Tabernacle Pulpit... 1869*, Vol.15, Passmore and Alabaster, London, 1870.

Spurgeon, C.H.: *The Metropolitan Tabernacle Pulpit... 1870*, Vol.16, Passmore and Alabaster, London, 1871.

Spurgeon, C.H.: *The Metropolitan Tabernacle Pulpit... 1871*, Vol.17, Passmore and Alabaster, London, 1872.

Spurgeon, C.H.: *The Metropolitan Tabernacle Pulpit... 1873*, Vol.19, Passmore and Alabaster, London, 1874.

Spurgeon, C.H.: *The Metropolitan Tabernacle Pulpit... 1874*, Vol.20, Passmore and Alabaster, London, 1875.

Spurgeon, C.H.: *The Metropolitan Tabernacle Pulpit... 1876*, Vol.22, Passmore and Alabaster, London, 1877.

Spurgeon, C.H.: *The Metropolitan Tabernacle Pulpit... 1880*, Vol.26, Passmore and Alabaster, London, 1881.

Spurgeon, C.H.: *The Metropolitan Tabernacle Pulpit... 1881*, Vol.27, Passmore and Alabaster, London, 1882.

Spurgeon, C.H.: *The Metropolitan Tabernacle Pulpit... 1882*, Vol.28, The Banner of Truth Trust, London, 1971.

Spurgeon, C.H.: *The Metropolitan Tabernacle Pulpit... 1883*, Vol.29, The Banner of Truth Trust, London, 1971.

Spurgeon, C.H.: *The Metropolitan Tabernacle Pulpit... 1884*, Vol.30, The Banner of Truth Trust, London, 1971.

Spurgeon, C.H.: *The Metropolitan Tabernacle Pulpit... 1885*, Vol.31, The Banner of Truth Trust, London, 1971.

Spurgeon, C.H.: *The Metropolitan Tabernacle Pulpit... 1886*, Vol.32, The Banner of Truth Trust, London, 1969.

Spurgeon, C.H.: *The Metropolitan Tabernacle Pulpit... 1887*, Vol.33, The Banner of Truth Trust, London, 1969.

Spurgeon, C.H.: *The Metropolitan Tabernacle Pulpit... 1889*, Vol.35, The Banner of Truth Trust, London, 1970.

Spurgeon, C.H.: *The Metropolitan Tabernacle Pulpit... 1894*, Vol.40, Passmore and Alabaster, London, 1895.

Spurgeon, C.H.: *The Metropolitan Tabernacle Pulpit... 1899*, Vol.45, Passmore and Alabaster, London, 1900.

Spurgeon, C.H.: *Second Series of Lectures to my Students...*, Passmore and Alabaster, London, 1885.

Spurgeon, C.H.: *The Early Years 1834-1859*, The Banner of Truth Trust, London, 1967.

Spurgeon, C.H.: *'Only A Prayer Meeting!'*, Pilgrim Publications, Pasadena, 1976.

Spurgeon, C.H.: *The Soul Winner, or, How to Lead Sinners to the Saviour*, Pilgrim Publications, Pasadena, 1978.

Taylor, Thomas: *An Exposition of Titus*, Christian Classics, Grand Rapids.

Thayer, Joseph Henry: *A Greek-English Lexicon of the New Testament*, Baker Book House, Grand Rapids, Ninth Printing 1991.

The Concise Oxford Dictionary of Current English, Eighth Edition, BCA, London, 1991.

The Sum of Saving Knowledge... in *The Confession of Faith, The Larger and Shorter Catechisms...*, The Publications Committee of the Free Presbyterian Church of Scotland, 1967.

Tyler, Bennet and Bonar, Andrew: *Nettleton and his Labours*, The Banner of Truth Trust, Edinburgh, 1975.

Vincent, M.R.: *Word Studies in the New Testament*, Macdonald Publishing Company, Florida.

Wayland, Francis and Wayland, H.L.: *A Memoir of the Life and Labours of Francis Wayland*, Sheldon and Co., New York, 1867.

White, Frank: *Should an anxious Enquirer be exhorted 'to pray'?...*, being an article in: *The Sword and the Trowel...*, edited by C.H.Spurgeon, Passmore and Alabaster, London, 1867.

Whitefield, George: *Sermons on Important Subjects by... George Whitefield*, Thomas Tegg, & Son, London, 1838.

Williams, J.B.: *The Lives of Philip and Matthew Henry*, The Banner of Truth Trust, Edinburgh, 1974.

Young, Edward J.: *The Book of Isaiah*, Vol.3, William B.Eerdmans Publishing Company, Grand Rapids, 1972.

Zanchius, Jerom: *The Doctrine of Absolute Predestination Stated and Asserted...*, translated by Augustus Montague Toplady, The Sovereign Grace Union, London, 1930.